GADAMER AND HERMENEUTICS

D1605642

CONTINENTAL PHILOSOPHY IV

GADAMER AND HERMENEUTICS

Edited with an introduction
by Hugh J. Silverman

SCIENCE
CULTURE
LITERATURE

Plato
Heidegger
Barthes
Ricoeur
Habermas
Derrida

ROUTLEDGE: New York and London

Published in 1991 by

BD
241
.G34
1991

Routledge
An imprint of Routledge, Chapman and Hall, Inc.
29 West 35th Street
New York, NY 10001

Published in Great Britain by

Routledge
11 New Fetter Lane
London EC4P 4EE

Copyright © 1991 by Routledge, Chapman and Hall, Inc.

Printed in the United States of America

All rights reserved. No part of this book may be reprinted or reproduced or
utilized in any form or by any electronic, mechanical or other means, now
known or hereafter invented, including photocopying and recording, or in
any information storage or retrieval system, without permission in writing
from the publishers.

Library of Congress Cataloging in Publication Data

Gadamer and hermeneutics / edited by Hugh J. Silverman.
    p.   cm.—(Continental philosophy: 4)
    Festschrift to honor Hans Georg Gadamer.
    Includes bibliographical references.
    ISBN 0-415-90373-4;   ISBN 0-415-90374-2 (pbk.)
    1. Hermeneutics.   2. Gadamer, Hans George, 1900-
3. Philosophy, Modern—20th century.   I. Gadamer, Hans Georg, 1900-
    II. Silverman, Hugh J.   III. Series.
    BD241.G34   1991
    121'.68—dc20   90-25404
                                                                                          CIP

British Library Cataloguing in Publication Data

Gadamer and hermeneutics.—(Continental philosophy, 4).
    1. Hermeneutics. Theories of Gadamer, Hans-George, 1900-
    I. Silverman, Hugh J.   II. Series
    121.68092

    ISBN 0-415-90373-4
    ISBN 0-415-90374-2 pbk

CONTENTS

CONTENTS

CONTENTS

Abbreviations

DD	*Dialogue and Dialectics*
GW	*Gesammelte Werke*
HD	*Hegel's Dialectic*
IGPAP	*The Idea of the Good in Platonic-Aristotelian Philosophy*
PH	*Philosophical Hermeneutics*
RAS	*Reason in the Age of Science*
TI	*Text and Interpretation*
TM	*Truth and Method*
WM	*Wahrheit und Methode*

INTRODUCTION

Hugh J. Silverman

Hans-Georg Gadamer published *Truth and Method* at the age of sixty. Born at the turn of the century, Gadamer inaugurated a whole new phase in the development of continental philosophy. While Gadamer was carrying on the tradition of hermeneutics set forth by Schleiermacher (in biblical studies), by Dilthey (in historical studies), and by Heidegger (in ontological studies), his contribution to philosophical hermeneutics was ground-breaking. Like Paul Ricoeur, his somewhat younger counterpart in France, Gadamer gave hermeneutics the task of interpreting philosophical tradition. While Ricoeur stressed the interpretation of competing contemporary philosophies, Gadamer moved in the direction of examining the whole Western development of aesthetic and intellectual thought since the Renaissance (with frequent excursions back to Plato). Gadamer took it upon himself to enter into dialogue with philosophical tradition, to interpret it and to understand it. He sought to articulate the very question of truth as it emerges in the experience of art from humanist conceptions to Kant's subjectivation of aesthetics and the romantic ideals that followed. He showed how these aesthetic formulations of truth lead to the question of "understanding" in the human sciences. And out of the theory of hermeneutical experience, he formulated his own account of language as "the horizon of a hermeneutic ontology."

Gadamer was a crucial figure in reorienting continental philosophy as it was practiced in the postwar Germany of the 1960s and 1970s. The prevalence of Husserl's phenomenology in the early decades of the century was eclipsed by the ontological hermeneutics of Martin Heidegger. And from the publication of *Being and Time* (1927), hermeneutics as the interpretation of Dasein, of the ontico-ontological difference, and subsequently of

1

Ereignis as event, appropriation, and happening (from the *Beiträge* in the 1930s through the 1940s and 1950s) held a certain power over those fascinated by his special brand of existential phenomenology. Though Gadamer was loyal to Heidegger and even edited the celebrated "Origin of the Work of Art" in 1960 (the same year he himself published *Truth and Method*), he also made it possible to think not only time and the history of Being but also the history of philosophical and aesthetic thought.

As the dominant movement of the 1960s in France, structuralism began to replace the existential phenomenology that had prevailed in intellectual circles since the outbreak of the Second World War. Lévi-Strauss' structural anthropology, Lacan's structural psychoanalysis, and Barthes' cultural criticism arose out of the earlier Saussurian semiology and established themselves as the principal formulations of this new orientation. Correspondingly in Germany, Gadamer's hermeneutics broke with the transcendental and even existential phenomenologies that had characterized this tradition since Husserl. Gadamer thereby offered a new way of understanding Western philosophical thinking. Having schooled himself in various languages including French, Italian, and English, Gadamer found that he was able to discourse knowledgeably about these different modes of thought and culture and to incorporate this knowledge into a grand account that sets up his own theory of language. In this way, German hermeneutics went far beyond its nineteenth and early twentieth century foundations set by Schleiermacher, Dilthey, and Heidegger.

In the thirty years since the publication of *Truth and Method* (1960), hermeneutics has come to be regarded as an international and interdisciplinary movement. Philosophical, literary, theological and cultural writers have benefited from the lessons of Gadamerian hermeneutics. They have entered into conversation with it and transformed it. Several generations of Gadamer's students have come to take their rightful places in German, American, Canadian, Italian, and even French universities. Each in turn has learned how to rethink Western thought along hermeneutical lines, to enter into dialogue with its proponents, and to seek understanding of its meaning(s). At the same time Gadamer's hermeneutics has permeated not only philosophy, literary study, and theology, but also legal studies, sociology, intellectual history, art history, and cultural studies. The task of this volume is to appeal to a wide range of students, scholars, and general readers interested in the problem of interpretation and understanding as well as the study of ideas, texts, traditions, and cultures.

In the summer of 1989, a conference was held at the *Wissenschaftsforum* of the University of Heidelberg where Gadamer taught philosophy for many decades and where he is still identified with the Philosophical Seminar. This conference with an international group of scholars—sponsored by his former students and colleagues now holding university positions of their own—rendered hommage to Gadamer's thought. They were rewarded by his generous presence, his constructive comments on their papers, and his helpful answers to their questions. Two memorable sessions of several hours each were devoted to questions posed to Gadamer. He undertook to answer these questions in an elaborate and penetrating way. He discoursed freely on the differences between hermeneutics and deconstruction demonstrating how hermeneutics as dialogue incorporates a whole tradition while deconstruction tends, in his view, to reduce that tradition to its texts. He talked about his theory of *Überlieferung* (transmission of tradition), of *Geschehen* (event or happening), and of the contemporary status of Western thinking, its achievements and its perils. What impressed many of those present was the idea that here was a figure who had lived through two world wars, who had brought continental philosophy to new levels of understanding, and who at the age of ninety was still actively engaged in meaningful discussion—even to the extent of inviting the conference participants to his home in the hills overlooking what he calls the valley of the whole German Romantic tradition. One could not help being struck by the humanity and the learning of this major figure in twentieth century philosophy.

We offer this volume of *Continental Philosophy* both in honor of Hans-Georg Gadamer's ninetieth birthday and in celebration of Gadamerian hermeneutics. We have attempted to produce a unique reading of Gadamer and hermeneutics by taking him at his word. Dialogue and discourse—key elements of his method—have been incorporated into the structure of the volume. For each section, we have asked two philosophers to enter

3

into dialogue with each other concerning either Gadamer's relation to other contemporary philosophers such as Heidegger, Barthes, Ricoeur, Habermas, and Derrida or the current role of hermeneutics in scientific, cultural, or literary studies. Each of the seven dialogical sets offers a well developed position and a direct critical reply to the essay with which it is paired.

The volume begins with a recent interview, published in the *Frankfurter Allgemeine* (October 1989), in which Gadamer talks most extensively about his early studies of Plato and the Socratic outlook. He also recounts how, during the period after his first meeting with Heidegger in the summer of 1923, he went on to study the Aristotelian conception of ethics as the true fulfillment of the Socratic challenge. Gadamer published his first work in this area in a study entitled *Plato's Dialectical Ethics* with the subtitle, "phenomenological interpretations of the *Philebus.*" The role of the Kiekegaardian critique of Hegel was pervasive. Phenomenology, following from Husserl and then Scheler, was the aegis under which the renewal of the Kierkegaardian critique could be carried out. But it was Heidegger's philosophy that offered a truly radical break from the prevalence of neoKantianism in Germany at the time. Phenomenological investigations became the means of describing the phenomena themselves— something that Gadamer also found in Plato's thought. And there he sought to recover the true meaning of Socratic dialogue. This also allowed Gadamer to bring Plato and Aristotle closer together on the question of ethics and the good, for he found that theoretical and practical philosophy could be reunited through hermeneutics. In Gadamer's view, language gains its authentic life only in conversation, for there Platonic dialogue reanimates discussion even now as it did in Plato's time.

Christopher Smith, the well-known translator of several of Gadamer's post-*Truth and Method* books, takes up Gadamer's reading of Plato. As Smith points out, speech as dialogue is both an "impulse" (with its questioning, its openness, and its event-like character) and an "obstacle" (a "sign" of objective, divine, and non-event-like meaning). He repeats Gadamer's claim that language as speech (*Sprache*) is the medium of hermeneutical experience. Exploring further the status of words, Smith indicates that words are not tools to get something done. Words name things, we do not. He points out that Plato is true to the original notion of speech, that speech is a center *between* speeches. And this is Gadamer's conception of dialogue. The impulse and the obstacle, for Smith, is to get clear about the dialogical, active and passive notion of understanding something and interpreting it. Nicholas Davey offers a valuable response to Smith's essay. Davey responds that this view could not have been articulated except *through* Heidegger—and he shows how. He goes back to Heidegger's claim that "language is the house of Being" and that "discourse is the existential-foundation of language." Davey shows that Gadamer's account of discourse and language is itself founded on a conception that was fully articulated in *Being and Time.* He claims that Gadamer is simply extending the Heideggerian notions rather than offering a radical break from them, thereby initiating a debate that will be taken up on a number of occasions throughout this volume.

The juxtaposition of Gadamer and Ricoeur is crucial to the understanding of contemporary interpretation theory. Gary Aylesworth addresses the question of method, showing that Gadamer's dialogical model diverges from Heidegger's ontological hermeneutics. By contrast, Ricoeur sees speech as the key to understanding. Ricoeur's text replaces the relation between interlocutors. For Gadamer, meaning and event are not distinct while for Ricoeur appropriation acknowledges a meaning already produced. Leonard Lawlor responds stressing "presentation" as basic to the hermeneutic experience in both Gadamer and Ricoeur. According to Lawlor, mere events can reverse understanding. Presentation is the perfectibility of the word leading ultimately to improved understanding.

The link with Barthes shows how divergent two readers of texts can be. As James Risser puts it, the "good will" to understand one another in dialogue focuses on the text which, in his view, is situated between two interlocutors. The link between Gadamer's text and the poststructuralist text demonstrates how the lines of rupture interrupt the smooth path of dialogue. For Risser, the poststructuralist intertextuality that is already at work between the reader and the text animates the Gadamerian concept of play as it brings about a communicative situation. Deborah Cook's response carries the conversation further—and includes not only Gadamer and Barthes but also the Derridean notion of the reader's inscription in the relation governed by the trace.

Gary Madison is concerned about the "metaphysics of presence." He wants to show not only that Derrida marginalizes this concept but also that Gadamer offers a post-epistemological and a post-metaphysical reading of philosophy in general. Madison develops what he takes to be Gadamer's three fundamental theses: (1) to understand is in fact to interpret, (2) all understanding is essentially bound up with language, and (3) the understanding of the meaning of a text is inseparable from its applications. The play that is at work in the Gadamerian model is a metaphor for the understanding process itself. Derrida, by contrast, as Wayne Froman points out, is concerned with the indecidability of writing, of *l'écriture*. But writing is not an arbitrary play of signifiers. Writing affirms play and makes the indecidability of writing the play itself. The metaphysics of presence is disrupted in favor of an opening up of discourse.

According to Graeme Nicholson, while the confrontation between contemporary philosophical hermeneutics and neo-marxist critical theory goes back to the 1920s, the specific debate between Gadamer and Habermas dates from the 1960s. Here the struggle between hermeneutic thinking and the methods of the social sciences is highlighted as an epistemological problem based on the role of language and the role of instituted frames of reference within knowledge. With Gadamer, the institutional theory is quickly turned in the direction of a general ontological theory, treating art and history through the study of language. Habermas will recognize Gadamer's more historically-minded philosophy of language as accounting for cross-cultural understanding and translation. But where Habermas turns in the direction of "rationality," Gadamer wants to stress "tradition." Rhetoric as a model for the humanities is a crucial counterpoint to the Habermasian notion of the speech situation. Nicholson points out that in the end, hermeneutics hopes to be an emancipatory discipline just as much as Habermas' critical theory. And in response, Dieter Misgeld, a former Heidelberg student of Gadamer, shows that both Gadamer and Habermas affirm reason as revealed in order to address the relation between research and social practice. Habermas claims that Gadamer understands the power of critical reflection but that, along with a theory of communicative action a "comprehensive" idea of social reason is also required for social action. Here the idea of progress in knowledge confronts claims based on tradition and understanding of the historical.

The dialogue between Patrick Heelan and Joseph Kockelmans extends a discussion that they have been carrying on for many years about the role of hermeneutics in the philosophy of science. While Heelan's account is largely based on a Husserlian view of continental philosophy, Kockelmans proposes to appeal more strongly to Heidegger and Gadamer. What results is a fascinating debate about the status of objectivity and truth, world and meaning, text and interpretation. Heelan points to a certain reciprocity between text and meaning and between the perceptual "score" and its "performance." This he names quite simply "the hermeneutical circle." As Heelan puts it, "spoken words and sentences belonging to the home language of a human community enrich the common experience by linking present agents and speakers immersed in their current worldly involvements with exemplary epochs, spaces, personalities, and transactions adumbrated in the oral narrative resources of a culture." He juxtaposes this role of speech with that of written language and its historical aspects linking past communities with those of the present. Experimental phenomena are then incorporated into a hermeneutical interest with implications that are not just computational or derivational, but also historical, social, artistic, and hermeneutical. While Kockelmans is sympathetic with Heelan's project for the philosophy of science, he also wants to show that his own interests are more ontologically based. For Kockelmans, reality is the totality of "meaning" in relation to the totality of all ontic entities known to us and not just the "life world" *per se.* Kockelmans shows that one can move between both realism and idealism, but goes beyond both in an orientation toward the world. In short, what is evident from this dialogue is that hermeneutics plays a very important role in the ongoing discussion about the contemporary status of thinking about science and scientific activity.

Curiously consistent with the debate about a hermeneutic phenomenology of science is Joel Weinsheimer's insistence on the fundamental metaphoricity of language and the basic metaphoricity of understanding. If it is right that understanding is fundamentally metaphorical, as Weinsheimer forcefully argues, then literal readings of natural or scientific phenomena will also have to be imbued with metaphoricity. This metaphoricity contributes to a *Bildung* in which there is a kind of hermeneutic call for one to "become what one is." Weinsheimer asserts that "perception understands, and understanding involves the construal of something *as* something." Hence, art that attempts to be nonrepresentational is effectively abstract, and such art, like all art, is already interpretation. Whether it be the language of science or of art, language is metaphorical and interpretational. However, if language is indeed "metaphorical" and "interpretational," it is important to understand its full ramifications. As Robin Schott shows in her response to Weinsheimer, a male view of the world interprets it metaphorically often manifesting strong attitudes even imbued sometimes with sexual aggression. In other words, she states, one cannot be "at home" in a language if the language appears hostile at almost every turn. This means that a writer, such as Weinsheimer, will have to recognize that even his own language is biased as well as metaphorical, that it incorporates certain male-oriented prejudices throughout its very practice. So Robin Schott will agree that language—and even understanding—are metaphorical, but that it also includes the concrete (gendered) existence of the interpreter. And such an implication will require an account of power, domination and subordination, inclusion and exclusion.

The final dialogical set takes up the hermeneutic text. Vincent Descombes offers an account of the "interpretative text": what it is and how it differs from a simple text and a simple interpretation. He develops a theory of the interpretive text which builds upon both the hermeneutics of Gadamer and the semiology of Barthes and also parallels the deconstructive moves of Jacques Derrida. He shows that the "obsolete and archaic" term *interpretative* means "that which is subject to interpretation" as opposed to a *gloss* which is an interpretation of a text. Hence the "interpretative text" is a text which calls for or requires interpretation. Such a text is therefore interpretable, but it also has a "right to interpretation," according to Descombes. This could either mean that it results from a "particularity of human existence" or an "obligation to interpret." In any case, the interpretability of a text involves this right to interpretation, which implies showing that it does not belong to a canon or preset determination. The response to Descombes' essay attempts to sort out this theory and to show its content and implications for an understanding of the textuality of interpretation itself. The response divides the discussion into (1) the interpretable, (2) the interpretative text, (3) the interpretation, and (4) the interpreting text. These divisions help to sort out the role of the interpretive process as inseparable from the text of the interpretive situation. Here the interpreting text is exchanged for the interpretative text, which is drawn from the field of interpretables in the act of interpretation. What this process shows is that the dynamics of the interpretative text are such that the text need not be understood as one thing and the interpretation as something entirely other. The text, the reader, and the canon are all interwoven and interrelated. Descombes' essay and its response constitute a frame for rethinking the whole status of texts and their interpretability. This final dialogical set in effect reinterprets the whole enterprise of interpretation itself and offers a further development beyond Gadamerian hermeneutics.

Together the last three dialogues display how the question of interpretation today can be understood in the diverse areas of science, language, and the interpretative text. As throughout this volume, each of these essays is met with a reading that either develops or criticizes the position of its counterpart. They provide the reader with a sense of where Gadamerian hermeneutics might go were it to reach beyond the account which Gadamer himself offers.

Gadamer and Hermeneutics, the fourth volume in the *Continental Philosophy* series, contributes to the growing interest in hermeneutics as a field of inquiry and reaches a broad range of theoretical and practical concerns from philosophy and literature to science, religion and politics. To enhance the wide range of essays on Gadamer and his contemporaries, the volume contains a complete bibliography of Gadamer's writings in English (with a listing of corresponding books published in German) and a full bibliography of writings in English on Gadamer and hermeneutics.

As in the past, the work of *Continental Philosophy* would not be what it is without the extensive contribution of the Assistant Editors. Lajla Lund proofed the bibliography and edited a number of the essays. In addition to helping shape the volume, James Clarke kept the scheduling and growing number of files in good order. James Hatley expertly rendered the notes in consistent shape. Brian Seitz helped maintain focus and enthusiasm at a high level. Jeffrey Gaines worked tirelessly through the summer of 1989 preparing the volume in its preliminary stages. And Nina Belmonte provided useful editorial assistance early in the development of *CP-IV*. The invaluable contribution of those colleagues in the field who refereed papers and offered suggestions for revision is also greatly appreciated. And to the contributors themselves we are especially cognizant, among them Professor Hans-Georg Gadamer who graciously permitted the translation and publication of the 1989 interview.

We are also pleased to acknowledge the thoughtful assistance of Harriet Sheridan who served as Administrative Assistant in the Department of Philosophy during much of the preparatory years of this volume. We are also grateful to Sandy Petrey for allocating computer equipment during his term as Acting Dean of Humanities and Fine Arts and to Lee Miller, Acting Chair of the Philosophy Department at SUNY/Stony Brook in 1988–89, for his willingness to support our work. To Maureen MacGrogan of Routledge we continue to be indebted for her quality professional judgment and enduring interest in this series.

PART I
GADAMER/GADAMER

Chapter 1

GADAMER ON GADAMER

Hans-Georg Gadamer

Translated by Birgit Schaaf and Gary E. Aylesworth

In my view my studies in Greek philosophy are the most independent part of my philosophical work. Although the disserta-
tion of the twenty-two year-old student was based upon an
independent study of Plato's complete works, it still followed
the path of my teacher at that time, Paul Natorp, whose ideas
on the theme of *hedone* (pleasure) I wanted to work out. Later I
began to see the significance of Greek philosophy, especially in
light of Aristotelian ethics. I had come to be familiar with it
through Nicolai Hartmann, who at that time found in Aristotle
a kind of phenomenological help-mate in his break with Neokantianism (inspired by Max Scheler). But my real introduction
to the understanding of Aristotle, and his significance for our
understanding of the world, I owe to my encounter with Martin
Heidegger in the summer of 1923.

At that time, it dawned upon me that one has to conceive of
Aristotelian ethics as a true fulfillment of the Socratic challenge,
which Plato had placed at the center of his dialogues as the
Socratic question of the good. When, in 1927, I finished my
philological studies with the "*Staatsexamen*," I took up once again
the larger project concerning the Socratic question of the good
in Platonic-Aristotelian philosophy. But circumstances com-
pelled me to great haste, for Heidegger let me know that he
would probably leave Marburg and return to Freiburg. So it
happened that only the first part of the project was carried out.
It was published in 1931 under the title *Plato's Dialectical Ethics:
Phenomenological Interpretations of the Philebus (Plato's dialektische
Ethik: Phaenomenologische Interpretationen zum Philebos).*[1] This

book, therefore, was my first contribution to Plato scholarship, and it was to take me fifty years until I published, as a kind of provisional conclusion, a treatise in the *Heidelberger Akademie der Wissenschaften* called *The Idea of the Good in Platonic-Aristotelian Philosophy* (English trans. 1986).

Today perhaps a brief explanation is necessary as to what the subtitle *Phenomenological Interpretations* was supposed to mean at the time. One must imagine the philosophical situation in Germany after World War I. This was the end of an age: the age of liberalism, the unlimited belief in progress, and the unquestioned leadership of science within cultural life. All of this perished in the War's battles of materiel. The young generation returning to the universities after the war could no longer be convinced of these values. This also became apparent in philosophy. The Neokantian philosophy, which was oriented upon the fact of science and dominated the German rostrum, had lost its credibility for us youth.

The Marburg school of Neokantian philosophy, in which I had been brought up, was also in the process of dissolving. My teacher, Paul Natorp, was trying to catch the primordial-concrete with the development of his *General Logic*. Another of my teachers, Nicolai Hartmann, was on the verge of a complete break with transcendental idealism. But more important were the effects produced by Dostoevsky and the German Diederichs-edition of Søren Kierkegaard's writings. To a critical youth, Kierkegaard imparted the concept of existence in the emphatic sense as a clarion call. In his critique of Hegel's ideal of absolute knowledge, Kierkegaard asserts that "the absolute professor in Berlin has forgotten about existing." This critique began to be levelled against Neokantianism and was combined with the general mood of cultural criticism that prevailed throughout an impoverished Germany. It was thus that the phenomenology founded by Husserl and effectively represented by Max Scheler became a critical and revolutionary rallying cry.

If today one wants to describe from a distance what the catchphrase "to the things themselves," formulated by Husserl, meant, it was a program against the subtle argumentation of epistemology which sought to justify science in terms of transcendental philosophy. Against this sort of epistemology, Husserl set the description of phenomena, rejecting all psychological constructions and argumentations that were not intuitively demonstrable. He used to say in his seminar: "No large bills, gentlemen, small change." That was new, indeed, but not exactly a battle-cry. In contrast, the appearance in Marburg of the young *Privatdozent* and young professor Heidegger was something like a revolution. Here, Husserl's phenomenology, which understood itself as transcendental philosophy, was taken with enormous energy back to its basic questions—questions that moved us. This was what Heidegger had in mind when once, in the margin of a book by Husserl in which the catchphrase "to the things themselves" was repeatedly used, he wrote "We want to take Husserl at his word."

"The things themselves": This meant more than just farewell to the traditional conceptual language of transcendental philosophy and its fundamental orientation towards the fact of science rather than phenomena. Husserl himself had paved the way for this turn, and had given it to this day an ever more articulate expression in the new word *"Lebenswelt."* The rejection of the scientifically limited concept of knowledge and truth sent the young Heidegger, driven by religious doubts and questions of existence, into the broad fields of historical thinking that Wilhelm Dilthey had opposed to transcendental philosophy. What is more, he there encountered Kierkegaard, who, in his vehement critique of the lukewarm Christianity of his native Denmark, demanded a halt to understanding "from a distance." What had been a Christian thinker's critical stance against the Church became for Heidegger, and for us, a critical turn against academic philosophy: the history of problems in Neokantianism and Husserl's transcendental phenomenology. This explains the title and subtitle of my first book. In reality, it was a thoroughly academic *Habilitationschrift* that dealt with the Platonic dialectic and its special development in Plato's *Philebus*. However, the formula "dialectical ethics" indicates an intention that remains throughout all of my later work.

When one found oneself exposed to the radicality of Heidegger's energetic questioning, one could not help but remember the ancient task of ethics, the practical philosophy that in theory and practice constitutes a unity that is hardly graspable. This was the first effect of Heidegger in Marburg. And this intention, inspired by Kierkegaard, was later strengthened in *Being and*

Time. In addition, there was the factor of Protestant theology, for whom discourse about God had become a problem. Moreover, the authenticity of *Dasein* was for the most part understood in a moralistic sense. The question I asked myself was how one could speak of an ethics in Plato's adoption of the Socratic question and Socratic dialectic. I attempted to clarify this through phenomenological methods. That meant, at first, going back to the original sense of dialectic as Plato used the word. There, dialectic means the art of leading a conversation. The Socratic dialogue and the Socratic question of the good was the life-worldly background from which Plato could call philosophy "dialectic" in the first place. I tried to make this life-worldly background speak anew in the Germany of the 1920s.

In this Germany of the 1920s the Socratic question had to reveal, with an inner necessity, the weakness and powerlessness of our own national consciousness. Thus in those years, in classical studies as well as in philosophy, there developed an interest in the "political" Plato, in his political attitude and the political intentions of his philosophy. This certainly also stands in the background of my own first book. It was meant to be a proper journeyman's work, seeking to win back the original sense of philosophy, even if in an academic guise, in Plato himself. That allowed me to completely subordinate my philological-historical research to my interests in the subject-matter, and also to set aside the problematic of what was then known as "value-ethics." It allowed me, where possible, to go back to the subject matter, to the phenomena as they showed themselves undogmatically, in an undisguised way, to the questioning gaze of philosophy. *Phenomenological Interpretations* thus means a description of the phenomena themselves, which seeks on this basis the conceptual expression that the phenomena have found in Platonic thought.

I then found myself confronted with a problem that would later lead me to a fundamental problem of hermeneutics—the linguisticality of understanding. How is it possible, I asked myself at the time, to make a Greek text like Plato's *Philebus,* a text which asks about the good in human life, speak anew from the fundamental experiences of our own life-world? It was necessary to make the concepts used by the Greeks speak again. If we were simply to translate and repeat the Greek concepts, we would not discover ourselves in them. That seemed to me to be the limit

16

for Werner Jaeger's school of classical philology. If, for example, we say "pleasure" for the Greek word *hedonē*, we really fail to understand that life must choose whether to take pleasure or knowledge as the highest. To choose pleasure or knowledge— what do we understand here? Everything which is connected with the sweetness of life and which constitutes its joys seems to be included in the Greek *hedonē*. It is a truly expansive world-field that extends into the incomprehensibility of well-being and non-well-being. Here we already stand in the midst of the problematic of the Socratic dialogue. We see that it is necessary to make distinctions within the manifold of pleasure and happiness.

Furthermore, we must distinguish between the forms of knowledge. In Greek it is called *episteme, techne, phronesis, sophia,* and *nous,* which we can render as knowledge, know-how, discretion, sense and understanding, reason and rationality. These words indicate a more or less common feature which has been summarized by the Greeks in the notion of *logos* and which we might rather call intelligence (*Geistigkeit*), but certainly not science. In this respect we immediately understand the problematic of the Platonic dialogue as a tension between impulse (*Drang*) and mind (*Geist*), and no historicism will succeed in estranging this understanding.

In addition, there is the special hermeneutical problem as to what the written retrieval and repeated awakening of the figure of Socrates means in Plato's writing, years and decades after Socrates' death. This is a philosophical way of speaking that operates with manifold shifts of perspective, and which cannot be translated into the later conceptual language of Aristotle without damage. What was imparted to me by Heidegger's introduction to Aristotle's thought in ethics, rhetoric, physics, and metaphysics had to be put to a special kind of test in the Platonic dialogue. For here the language of concepts does not predominate. If anything distinguishes the form of Plato's philosophical expression, it is the obvious and wonderful agreement between *logos* and *ergon,* between discourse and being, comprehension and action.

It was thus that I first pursued the inner links between the Socratic dialogue as it occurs in Plato and the dialectic that Plato puts into Socrates' mouth, with which he at the same time surpasses the persona of Socrates. My first book on Plato therefore dealt with the connection between dialectic and dialogue in Plato's collected works. It also dealt with the special form in which the *Philebus* sought to bring to word, in its true expression, the problem of the relation between *hedone* and *episteme*, between the urge of life and the life guided by consciousness. My later works have illuminated the extraordinary, many-faceted wealth of this difficult dialogue from Plato's latest and richest period through many separate contributions. They have developed the historical background just as much as the direct orientation toward the subject-matter.

It is a question of primary importance as to what the Socratic turn meant for the classical philosophy of Athens, and in which sense Socratic questioning dominates this turn. If one naively follows the dominant opinion, the matter looks very curious. According to this opinion, Socrates taught that virtue is knowledge. Also, in the course of his dialectical ascent, Plato described the idea of the good (in mysterious allusions to something lying behind the manifold of moral phenomena) as the ultimate and highest idea, which is supposedly the highest principle of being for the universe, the state, and the human soul. Against this, Aristotle opposed a decisive critique under the famous formula "Plato is my friend, but the truth is my friend even more." He denied that one could consider the idea of the good as a universal principle of being, which is supposed to hold in the same way for theoretical knowledge as for practical knowledge and human activity. But what is the meaning of this radical critique that Aristotle has levelled in his ethics, and also against the idea of the good and the Platonic doctrine of ideas in general?

To answer that what concerns Aristotle in the fundamental question of human activity is different from what concerns Plato is hardly satisfactory. It is certainly correct that Aristotle grounds the independence of practical philosophy on the fact that human existence, in all its limitations, conditions and finitude, is still guided in all its doings by the question of the good—as indicated in the first sentence of the *Ethics*. However, Plato himself made the question of the good for human existence explicitly thematic in the *Philebus*. Ever since Socrates, it has been unavoidable to ask this question, and even more unavoidable to know that all men must ask it. What human life is not obligated to put the question of the *Philebus* to itself: whether its exalted moments are the fulfillment of human desires and urges, or rather the different enchantment of an open vista upon what is, and is as good as it is beautiful?

Considering the evidence of these similarities, the traditional opposition between Plato and Aristotle could be less and less confirmed. For both are ruled by the enduring urgency of the Socratic question of the good. Thus I would certainly adhere to the guiding thesis, as in my first book, that the Platonic dialogues can be depicted in their content on the conceptual level of Aristotelian teachings. Nevertheless I would admit that the real involvement in a Socratic dialogue, composed for us by Plato, moves us closer to the subject-matter than any conceptual fixation ever could. Today I would see the unique contemporaneity (*Aktualität*) of the Platonic dialogues precisely in the fact that they transcend all ages almost in the same way as great masterpieces of art. The indissoluble entanglement of theoretical and practical-political orientations of life, of theoretical and practical knowledge, testifies to the continuity of the Socratic question that binds Plato and Aristotle to one another, and both to every human present (*Gegenwart*). We, too, should not be on the lookout for abstract alternatives when we ask ourselves whether, in the age of science, we can still pursue metaphysics or whether we must overcome it. As practical metaphysics, both of our tasks will remain: to follow the path of knowledge and to think beyond what science has to say. This is what I vaguely had in mind when I gave my first book about Plato's *Philebus* the title *Plato's Dialectical Ethics*.

If language has its authentic life only in conversation, then the Platonic dialogue will awaken a living discussion now as before, and will achieve the fertile fusion of all horizons in which, questioning and searching, we must find our way in our own world.

PART II
PLATO/HEIDEGGER/GADAMER

Chapter 2

PLATO AS IMPULSE AND OBSTACLE IN GADAMER'S DEVELOPMENT OF A HERMENEUTICAL THEORY

P. Christopher Smith

Kein Ding sei wo das Wort gebricht.
(Where the word breaks off, there is no thing.)
—Stefan George

It would be only consistent to approach Gadamer's hermeneutical theory, whose key concept is "historically effected consciousness," by showing the strands of the philosophical tradition woven into it. Though Hegel's dialectic and Heidegger's destruction of metaphysics are certainly very important, I will assume here that the "effect" of Plato's dialogues on Gadamer's thought is more distinctive than any other. This "effect," however, is both an impulse and an obstacle for Gadamer's endeavors, and I will probe both sides of this ambivalence, focusing chiefly on *Truth and Method.*[1]

Why, let us first ask, is Plato an obstacle? The answer has to do with the role of *Sprache,* language and speech, in Gadamer's hermeneutics. In the third and final part of *Truth and Method,* Gadamer turns to *Sprache* in seeking the underpinnings for his investigations. *Sprache,* he maintains, is the "medium of the hermeneutical experience," "the middle and center [*Mitte*] where partners [in a discussion] reach an understanding and agreement about a subject" (*WM,* 361). *Sprache,* that is to say, is between two or more people, in between them, and as such *it* is the locus of the process of coming to understand something and interpreting it, not they. By *Sprache* Gadamer certainly means what we would normally call language. But etymologically *Sprache* is closer to the English "speech," and like "speech" it belongs together with "speaking" and what is "spoken." Gadamer clearly has these dimensions of *Sprache* uppermost on his mind. Hence the translation of *Sprache* as language, with its now almost wholly obscured reference to the *lingua* or tongue with which we speak, leads us to relapse into just that way of thinking which Gadamer wishes to get behind and for which the written sign takes priority over the spoken word. Now whatever reservations Plato himself might have expressed about writing (*Phaedrus*, 274b ff.), and however far he himself might have remained from ever seeking a univocal sign language with which to replace ordinary speech, the origins of such a sign language, Gadamer finds, and the reduction of *Sprache* to it are to be traced to him.

To be precise, they are to be traced to his encounter with sophism and the steps he takes to rid us of its insidious consequences. Sophism's danger is this: by playing upon the equivocation inherent in the spoken word it can make a thing appear in speech first one way and then the opposite way. For instance, love can be made to look bad or look good, as it is respectively in each of Socrates' two speeches in the *Phaedrus*.[2] Or, what is worse, something can be made to look just or unjust in the law courts, or good or bad in political assemblies (*Phaedrus*, 261c–d). For sophists there is no truth of the matter but only contrary appearances, any one of which the sophist's art can get us to believe. This is the background of the *Cratylus*, to which Gadamer turns in his attempt to come to grips with Plato's theory of language and circumvent it.

Gadamer grants that sophism does call an essential presupposition of his own endeavor into question: "the inmost unity of word and thing" (*WM*, 383). Until sophism's arrival a naive faith could exist that the word, which the Greeks thought of as a name (*onoma*), was not an arbitrary sound assigned to a thing but named the thing as what it really was. Sophism, however, achieves its rhetorical success precisely by dissociating words from reality and using them as tools to make the reality seem to be something it is not. This makes it appear that names and the thing named are not intrinsically one, but distinct. Thus at the very beginning of the *Cratylus* (383b) we find the name of a participant in the discussion, Hermogenes, singled out: in the "naive" sense his name does not name him, for he is neither rich nor inventive with speech as one "born of Hermes" ought to be (see 384c and 408b). But in another sense he is Hermogenes, for that is the name that has been assigned to him. Either way it appears that there first exist persons and things, who and which are what they are, and that our task is *subsequently* to give them a name that correctly (*orthōs*) designates their being and reality. *Orthotēs*, the correctness of names becomes the issue, not the truth of what they say about things.[3]

In what, then, does the correctness of names consist? *If we accept the tacit presupposition that names are given to people and things we already know*, two answers proffer themselves. Either we give them a name we simply agree to call them henceforth, as would seem to have been the case with Hermogenes, or we given them a name that in some way copies, imitates, what they are. Names can be correct either insofar as they are used in accordance with the convention (384d) or insofar as they correctly image the nature (*physis*) of what they name (391a ff.). For Plato both of these theories have their justification in explaining how names name *correctly*. However, a name conceived in either of these ways, which he assumes to be the only possibilities, cannot be trusted to yield *true* knowledge of the thing it names. Hence, any knowing that would be immune to sophism's playing with words must know the things themselves *aneu tōn onomatōn*, without any words or names at all (*WM*, p. 384).

Plato would lead us to this unstated conclusion by a dialectical *elenchus* or refutation of the truth claim of both theories of naming. He takes up the convention theory first and gives it short shrift: if words are merely conventional, it is clear that a word by itself can have no truth to it. We can even change it as we do the name of a servant (384d). Still, we claim that a *logos* or assertion made up of words can be true, and to make that claim there would have to be something true about its component words after all (385b–c). For Gadamer this would mean that "naming, as a part of speaking, is tied to the process of disclosure of reality [*Sein*] (*ousia*) that occurs in speaking" (*WM*, 386). But, he says, the anti-sophistic intent of Plato's argument blocks out this insight. And as a matter of fact the next step here in Socrates' refutation is to take up, as does the *Theaetetus*, Protagoras's contention that there is no truth and no reality apart from what each human being believes it to be (*Cratylus*, 385e ff.). Plato's aim all along, we see, has been to dispose of this thesis of sophism:

It is plain, on the contrary, that the things themselves have some steady reality of their own neither in reference to us nor dragged up and down by us in our fancy; rather, they stand by themselves in reference to their own reality, as accords with their nature. (386d–e)

In the argument of the *Cratylus* what things are in themselves is divorced entirely from what we say of them. This move makes it possible for Plato to defeat sophistic sleights of hand, but it blinds him to the possibility that what things are in the first place is originally "uncovered" (Gadamer: *aufgedeckt*) in what is said, that they come into their being only in speaking of them. For Plato they are what they are steadily (*bebaiōs*). They do not come into being at all, and least of all in speech, which only obscures them. The task, then, is to find a kind of speech that obscures them minimally, a speech whose word-names are as true as possible. With that we have passed beyond any "convention" theory to the idea of word-names as some kind of image, or so it would seem. And Socrates' *elenchus* is now directed to the second hypothesis, i.e., that words name by nature (*physei*).

But again the exposition is skewed from the start. Imaging is conceived of onomatopoetically, albeit in the widest sense. The word is taken to imitate in sound the reality it names—but not just an acoustical reality. Indeed the astonishing metaphorical capacity of speech is tacitly presupposed and simultaneously suppressed here, its capacity, that is, to transfer and carry over (*metapherein*) meanings from one range of our experience to another. To take the example of the *Cratylus*, the word "hard" (*skleros*) that initially names a tactile quality is carried over effortlessly into the acoustical realm when we name a sound "hard" or for that matter, a word from the optical realm, when we call it "bright" or even "white." (We will return to this point presently). *Skleros*, however, presents a problem that Socrates exploits in also refuting the theory that words could have their truth by nature. If *skleros* is to image in sound the reality it names, it must have a hard sound to it, which indeed it would were it not for its soft, liquid "l" sound or *lambda* (*Cratylus*, 434c–d). And to the extent we readily accept the soft letter in it, the fact that we understand *skleros* to name what is hard, can, it seems, only be attributed to convention (see *WM* pp. 386–87). So we are back where we started from and at an impasse (*aporia*).

Socrates' *elenchus*, we see, works like Zeno's dilemmas. Words, it is hypothesized, are true either by convention or by nature. The convention theory fails, so words must be true by nature. But that fails too. The only way out is to abandon words altogether—as Zeno would have us abandon motion since we can account for it neither in terms of space as continuous nor in terms of space as units. So too in Plato: if we are to know the truth, we must know the things themselves without words.

And where do we do that? "One comprehends," writes Gadamer,

> that not the word but the number is the proper paradigm of the noetic, the number which is obviously named by pure convention and whose exactitude consists in just this, that every number is defined by its place in the series and hence is a purely intelligible construct, an *ens rationis*. (*WM*, 389–90)

The being of things that pre-exists our speaking of them is, as we know from the discussion of the *koinōnia* or blending of the ideas in the later dialogues, a "Beziehungsgefüge" (*WM*, 389), a fitting together of the ideas in their interrelationships and segregation of them according to the principles of sameness and difference (see the *Sophist*, 254 ff.). And just as each of the numbers has its place in relationship to the others, so too would each of the ideas.

If we follow the paradigm of the number further, the word for any real thing, like the words "one," "five" or "twenty," would be reduced "to the mere *sign* of a being that is well-defined and hence known ahead of time" (*WM*, 390), namely "1," "5," or "20." This is to say that we would not know without words and use unequivocal wholly determinate signs to communicate our knowledge. The great advantage of the sign from the Platonic point of view—though importantly Plato himself never carries out the reduction of words to signs—is that unlike the word, which can always assert itself instead of what is meant and thereby introduce confusions, the sign has no reality of its own to assert. Its reality consists in its pointing to something other

than itself as, analogously, the letter in near complete self-efface-
ment and transparency points to the sound for which it stands
(*WM*, 390–91).[4]

In Plato, then, the switches are thrown that will determine
the course of all subsequent philosophy of language. In him it
becomes evident that the spoken word and speech will have to
be transcended in a thinking purified of their interference:

> Thought removes itself from the words' own reality, takes
> them as mere signs to such an extent that the word falls
> into a fully secondary relationship to the thing. It is a mere
> instrument of communication that brings out (*ekpherein*)
> what is meant and brings it forth (*logos proporikos*) in the
> medium of voice. It follows logically that an ideal system of
> signs, whose only point is [to secure] the univocal
> attribution of all signs [to what they signify], will make the
> power of the words (*dynamis tōn onamatōn*), the breadth of
> variation inherent in the contingency of concrete historical
> languages that have grown over time, seem a mere
> muddying of the their usefulness. What develops here is
> the ideal of a *characteristica universalis*. (*WM*, 391)

We should note too that in contrast to historical languages the
universal characters will be written, read silently, and spoken
out loud only as a last resort for communication. In this way the
particular sound English speakers make when they say "5," for
example, can be kept from getting in the way between the transparent written sign and the reality it was meant to signify. Unlike
ordinary letters the *characteristica universalis* will not signify pho-
nemes that signify reality, but reality directly. So too, Plato's
dialectic, though it even abjures the written sign too as a mne-
monic crutch that weakens the mind, would still raise us to a
pure thinking of the ideas without voice and sound (*aneu phonēs*)
(*WM*, 385; *Sophist*, 263e), to unspoken meanings we would not
hear but see. It would take us beyond all utterance (*logos*), i.e.,
beyond the mere "stream with voice coming through the mouth"
(*Sophist, idem*). For Plato what is made audible in voice has no
claim to truth. He "does not consider the fact that any carrying
out of a thought, if conceived of as a dialogue of the soul, implies
per se that the thought process is tied to speech" (*WM*, 385). In
his effort to overcome the sophistic misuse of the *dynamis tōn*

onamatōn, the power of words to equivocate and assert themselves instead of what they mean, Plato overrides the fact that our thinking first derives from just this "power of words," a power not only to obscure *but also to make plain* (Gadamer: *offenbar machen*); ". . . the discovery of the ideas by Plato covers up the proper nature of speech and language even more thoroughly than did sophist theoreticians" (*WM*, 385).

How is the tendency initiated in Plato towards a language of univocal signs to be reversed and what it obscures about *Sprache*, about language as speech, to be brought back into view? To begin with, it must be shown that, as opposed to the sign, the word is not a tool we use to get something done. *We* do not name things, rather words themselves do. Hence the nature of the word is distorted if we reduce it to an instrument with no cognitive value of its own that we use to signify a pre-existent reality. Of course taken by itself the word does mean something; it means (*meint*) something other than itself, and if we focus exclusively on this derivative function of it, as Plato has in the *Cratylus*, the split of the word from the reality it means will be the inevitable consequence. We are on our way to an understanding of words as signs. To reverse this, the original function of the word *within a logos*, within talking and speaking must be brought back to the foreground. Not the name itself, Achilleus, *achos* to the *laos*, grief to the warrior folk, is the starting point, rather an assertion in which it occurs: "This man is Achilleus."[5] There is an Aristotelian point here: whatever is said, is said of a "this something here," of a "tode ti" (see *DD*, 213). That does not mean at all that "Achilleus" *signifies* this *tode ti* and is separate from it. Rather in the assertion, "This man is Achilleus," what this man *is* is first laid in the open and made plain (*offen, dēlos*). The *logos* or assertion is a *dēloma* (*WM*, 389), a making plain, which is to say that the being or reality of this man which the assertion displays does not exist prior to the assertion, but rather is first brought out *in* the very saying of it.

Thus behind Plato's question of the *correctness* of words we find the original question of the *truth* of the *logos*, not truth as correspondence, of course, for that would be correctness again, but truth as the revelation of the being of a thing, of what it is. Cratylus cannot hold his own versus Socrates' arguments against the word, for it is not clear to him "that the *logos*, talking and speaking and the laying open of things accomplished therein, is something different from what the meaning (*Bedeutung*) inherent in the words indicates (*meint*)" (*WM*, 385–89).

With that, a way emerges past the impasse up to which Socrates has led Hermogenes and Cratylus. Rather than rejecting the word-name both as conventional and as some kind of natural image of reality and proceeding then to a knowing altogether without word-names, Gadamer returns to the image leg of the dilemma Socrates has posed, and calls into question the presumption Plato depends on to defeat it, namely that the *dēloma* or making plain of the thing in an image is by an imitation of the thing: as a matter of fact we are not dealing here at all, Gadamer maintains, with an imitative representation "such that the audible or visible appearance would be copied in an image" (*WM*, 387). Socrates, we saw, relied on the onomatopoetic model whereby what a thing is to begin with is imitated in the sound we make in meaning it. But this model falsifies the way words spoken in a *logos* work:

> An experience is not wordless at first and then turned into
> an object of reflection by naming it, say, by way of
> subsuming it under the universality of word. On the
> contrary, it pertains to the experience itself that it seeks and
> finds the words that express it. One seeks the right word,
> the word, that is, which really fits and pertains to the
> matter, such that in it the matter "gets in a word for itself
> [zu Worte kommt]". (*WM*, 394)

We are to think of the spoken word not as an imitation but as the perfection or completion of the thing's coming into being.

Hence unlike Plato's *eidos*, which is steadily (*bebaiōs*), the word, if I may bend customary diction, is eventual. It comes out in a process (vis. the Latin *evenit*). Plato is no help in thinking of the word in this way, but Christian theologians, who rely on the event of a word as an analogy for the coming of Christ, are—in particular, Aquinas. The question for him is how we are to think of the incarnation as the expression of a word out loud. Incarnation namely cannot be thought of in the way Plato thought of a soul inhabiting a body external to it, all the while remaining what it is in distinction from the body. Rather God becomes human, expresses Himself in human form. So too, if the analogy of the word is to be helpful, the word must not be thought of as Plato thinks of it, namely as an external sound with no cognitive value and used as an infelicitously opaque vehicle for communicating a pure cognition. Aquinas's Christological concern thus leads him to inquire about *ex*cogitation or how a cognition comes to be manifest in words said either to ourselves or to another (*ad manifestationem vel ad se vel ad alterum*) (*WM*, 399). Like God and Christ, the perfected thought and the spoken word are one. "All thinking is a saying to oneself" (*idem*), for the *species*, the *forma excogitata*, does not occur in our intellect as a second thing apart from the word, rather the cognition completes itself in the word (*WM*, 403). The process of thinking something out comes to its conclusion as the words for it come to mind—*per modum egredientis*, in the manner of coming forth (*WM*, 399).

Even Aquinas, however, does not circumvent Plato's distinction between the steady idea (Aquinas: *forma, species*) and the word that comes into being. Hence Gadamer argues against Aquinas that

> When what is displays itself in thinking intelligence, this is not the copying (*Abbildung*) of a previously given order of reality whose true relationships lie before the eyes of an infinite intelligence (the creator's intelligence). (*WM*, 433)

Aquinas perpetuates the Platonic ideal of an infinite divine knowing, transcending all contingency. Finite human knowing, which is discursive and speech-bound, thus continues to appear a deficient imitation to him too. It is a dramatic turn, therefore, when Gadamer abandons the divine paradigm of knowing and the system of fixed *eidē* or *species* as its object, and when he argues that the ideas themselves are eventual, that the very concepts of thinking come to be in an ongoing formative process. When Gadamer speaks of concept formation (*WM*, 404ff.), he radicalizes Aquinas's metaphor of an idea taking on form in a mirror (*speculum*). For the idea here, though like Aquinas's insofar as it is to be thought of as a result of a formative process, is, quite unlike Aquinas's, no longer an image or reflection of anything else. The *eidos, species*, concept, however it might be named, coalesces in Gadamer with speech. Hence he can refer to "a continual process of concept formation through which the life of meaning in speech goes on developing itself" (*WM*, 405).

What does Gadamer have in mind here? The classical, Platonic-Aristotelian conception of a *logos*, of saying something, works on the principle of subsumption of a particular under a universal: "Socrates is a human being"; "All human beings are mortal." The supposition is that "human being" and "mortal" each designate a fixed and steady concept of which we, insofar as we approximate divine knowing, have a clear idea, whatever word we might use to speak of it. Precisely this supposition Gadamer calls into question. When we say someone is a human being and mortal, not only the slot for that particular "someone" is a variable. The concepts "human being" and "mortal" vary too according to what goes into it. There is no fixed reality that the words "human being" and "mortal" mean, rather they display new shadings of sense on each new occasion for saying them in a *logos*. Hence, "the universality of the species and classificatory concept formation are entirely foreign to speech consciousness" (*WM*, 406). Our speaking and its formation of its concepts proceeds in a very different way, namely by metaphor taken broadly as a word's transferring, carrying over, of itself from its accustomed place to another. Metaphor thus includes many tropes, among them metonymy: "I have nothing to offer but *blood, toil, tears and sweat*"; anthimeria: "The thunder would not *peace* at my bidding"; irony: "For Brutus is an *honourable* man"; hypallage: "He took a *moody* spoonful"; and oxymoron: "O *brawling* love! O *loving* hate!" In each of these the words display new sense in their new context.

Here, then, is Gadamer's radical response to the Platonic tradition that takes the word to be an imitative copy: not the *Seinsgefüge*, the genus and species structure of reality, comes first and then the words we say to signify or designate it in our speaking, but the reverse. What is, is there first *in* an ever spreading, ever self-transforming speaking of it, there before we can abstract from speech in constructing a classificatory logic. Rhetoric underlies logic, not the other way around. Put another way, any logic of collection into a genus and division into species presupposes the rhetorical *loci* of similarity and difference, and the *loci* in turn presuppose the tropes, "the metaphorics of speech" (*WM*, 407). Aristotle, we know, gives priority over rhetoric to reasoning by syllogistic inference based on a classificatory logic; for example, inference from Socrates as a human being to Socrates as a mortal. But even he acknowledges, in his *Poetics* (1459a 8) and *Topics* (108

7–31), what Gadamer calls the *Vorrausleistung* of speech, namely what speech accomplishes in advance by transference of sense into what is different yet, as the transfer first shows, at the same time similar in some respect (*WM*, 407). It is metaphor, speech's transferring itself, that brings similarity and difference to light "in advance."

Once concepts and ideas are shown in this way not to underlie speaking but to evolve *in* it, the error in Plato's tacit assumption of the imitation of the word image is exposed. And with that, the criterion he uses to defeat the hypothesis of the word as an image becomes objectless. To be sure, an imitation can be judged with regard to its *correctness* in copying the original, and even judged this way, it will always be found to fall short (*apechei*) (*WM*, 386). *Skleros* with its soft "l" does not, it will be recalled, correctly render the reality of what is hard. But as Cratylus himself detects in Plato's dialogue, this criterion is somehow misplaced: if a word is to be a word at all it must "sit right" (*keisthai*) (*Cratylus* 429c; *WM*, 388). If it does not, it is not a misrepresentation but merely the empty sound of "ringing brass" (*Cratylus* 430a; *WM*, 388). The question is not one of discrepancy here, but of sense and senselessness. The word either displays something or falls flat like a joke that no one gets. Hence, in opposition to Plato, Gadamer speaks of the "absolute perfection of the word" (*WM*, 388). He means that there is precisely no question of an imperfect correspondence of the word to reality: "The 'truth' of the word most certainly does not lie in its correctness, in its correct commensuration with the thing. On the contrary, it lies in its perfected intelligibility, that is, in the word's sense lying in the open out loud" (*WM*, 388).

A word's perfected intelligibility does not imply, of course, that it is rid of all ambiguity, that what it makes plain about something in a *logos*, it makes unequivocally plain. Originally the truth of the word is not *bebaios*, not "steady" or fixed like the truth of the ideas to which Plato aspires, rather it shimmers. For the *dēloma*, the presentation of the thing in the *logos* makes the thing plain (*dēlos*) now in one way, now in the opposite. As we have seen, it was precisely this indeterminacy of ordinary speaking, its equivocation, that the sophists exploited and that Plato consequently set out to transcend in his projected "mathematization" of language. (There is nothing equivocal about

"1" or "5.") Hence in the third book of the *Republic,* for instance, Socrates asserts that gods and heroes should not be displayed in the chiaroscuro of Homer's speaking of them, not shown, that is, to *be* good and *not be* good concomitantly. A true representation of them would show the light and clear side only, their being truly noble (*kalos*) unadulterated by anything dark and even hideous (*aischros*). Only then would they, and the justice and good they stand for, no longer be susceptible to sophistic exploitation of ambiguity. But not only the shimmering of Homer's speech with its linking of *is* and *is not* and displaying of gods and heroes as good-bad, just-unjust, would have to be suppressed to attain this invulnerability to sophism, rather the original shimmering of speech as such. Speech itself would have to be systematically falsified, as it was in Plato.

Or was it? Gadamer, who comes to Plato with the *hermeneutical* concern of the interpreter's dialogical encounter with the "other" of the text uppermost in his mind, is able to see another side to him that his eremitic critics, Nietzsche and Heidegger, miss. Plato, it turns out, is true to the original nature of speech after all, true in the way only a dramatist who writes dialogue could be. Speech in Gadamer is, as we have heard, a center *between* speakers, and that means that the ever-widening formation of concepts takes place initially not in the thought of individuals but in discussion between them. If no one had ever spoken to us and engaged us in response, we could not think in the words of a spoken language. This is shown by the fact that even in thinking something through by ourselves we must carry on a discussion with ourselves as the partner. Far from cancelling the dialogical structure of speech, we only internalize it—something Plato, who speaks of the dialogue of the soul with itself, is well aware of (*Sophist*, 263e, *Theaetetus*, 189e–190a; *WM*, 399). *Sprache* is *Gespräch*, Gadamer insists: speech is speaking with someone else, discussion. Furthermore, since understanding (*Verstehen*) is based on speech and speech, as we now see, is speaking with someone, understanding turns out to be not something achieved on our own but *Verständigung* or coming to an understanding in discussion, in talking something through with another (*WM*, 422). Significantly, Plato's word dialectic derives from the Greek *dialegesthai*, which exactly translated means just this talking something through.

Now an understanding reached in *dialegesthai* is in fact very different from an understanding reached in mathematics about what sign to assign to a reality whose being we have already established. When in Plato's dialogues the question is asked, "What is it (*ti estin*)?" that is a very different question from "What name shall we agree to give it?" For with the former we are seeking to get clear in the first place about the nature and being of the matter itself and, what is most significant, seeking to do this by examination of the "things we say" about it, of the *logoi*.

Gadamer predictably places great emphasis on Socrates' "bracketing" in the *Phaedo* of naturalist assumptions about the world in itself and his "flight into the *logoi*" (*Phaedo*, 99e; see *IGPAP*, 15). For here the confirmation is to be found of Gadamer's own way through Husserl's phenomenology to an exploration of language as the mirror or *speculum*, in which, by the "speculative power of language," the world first takes shape for us (*WM*, 441ff.). And now the question becomes acute whether this flight to the *logoi* is only prefatory in Plato to a flight beyond the *logoi* to the pure ideas, as Gadamer has made it out to be in his criticism of Plato, or if the *logoi* are after all the final repose of all human inquiry and understanding. It is not surprising that even at the cost of weakening his critical arguments against Plato, Gadamer takes the latter to be the case. Indeed, as he himself points out, there are two traditional "Platos," one who prefaces the Galilean-Cartesian mathematical understanding of reality and another who "comes along like an undercurrent in the history of Aristotelian-Scholastic metaphysics" to whom we can turn for the vocabulary "needed to think the finitude of human existence" (*WM*, 461). It is in this other Plato that we find a theory of the finitude of human understanding and its corresponding inevitable bond to spoken language. Unlike a god's, human understanding, Plato shows, is always discursive: it involves running through thoughts verbally (vis. the Latin *discurrere*). Hence Gadamer, who is critical of the abstraction from the spoken word in Plato's dialectic of the ideas, can also refer at a crucial juncture in *Truth and Method* to "the paradigm of Platonic dialectic" for his hermeneutical theory (*WM*, 344). By dialectic he means here, of course, not Plato's method of collection into a genus and division into species, but the Socratic art of carrying on a discussion, the art, that is, of *dialegesthai* as Plato displays it in his dialogues.

35

It turns out that the very same Plato who seemed to want univocal meaning as the conclusive answer to the question what something is (*ti estin*), in fact never answers his questions about the real, the good, the noble, or the just conclusively. Instead he leaves them open, with what each *is* and *is not* pending or "in der Schwebe," as Gadamer puts it (*WM*, 345), thereby alluding to the fact that *is* and *is not*, this way or that, are left hanging in the balance—shimmering. Platonic dialectic is paradigmatic, we learn here, precisely because of the priority it assigns to the question over the answer. In its "laying open" of things, its *dēloma* (see above and *WM*, 387), it lays them open in their questionableness and ambiguity: "To question means to lay open (*Offenlegen*) and to pose as [an] open [question] (*ins Offene stellen*)" (*WM*, 349). This means, of course, that any understanding reached, far from being conclusive, is tentative and ongoing. Hence the Socratic art of dialectic, of "carrying on a real discussion," is the art not of giving fixed univocal answers at all but of raising further questions (*Weiterfragen*) (*WM*, 349).

This returns us to Plato's response to sophism. Is his defense really to establish, via the dialectic of collection and division (*Phaedrus*, 265d ff.), via the hypothesis of the *eidos* or form (*Phaedo*, 101c ff.), a certitude, an *answer*, that will withstand sophistic efforts to plunge everything into doubt? Certainly it is in part. The word *bebaios* that Socrates associates with the *eidos* means not only steady but also firm in the sense of providing the most secure (*asphalestaton*) footing from which we cannot be brought to a fall (*pesein*) by the wrestler's holds that sophism knows how to get on us (see the language of the *Phaedo* at 82d–e, and *IGPAP*, 84). It is not by chance that the master of confutation, Zeno, had the nickname of a great wrestler, Palamedes (*Phaedrus*, 261d). But at this earlier point in *Truth and Method* Plato's other response to sophism is brought to the fore, or better said, Plato's response to another sophism. For not the eristic sophists like Zeno who pervert dialectic are meant, but the masters of forensic rhetoric, the denizens of the law courts (see *Theatetus*, 172e ff.) who, blind to their ignorance of the truth, only serve up tasty morsels of what is likely to be believed (*Phaedrus*, 272d–e). These sophists, Tisias, Gorgias, Protagoras, have made a pseudo-art of the long harangue, but they cannot even engage in dialectic much less pervert it. For they are unable to pose real questions, and they look foolish when they try (*Protagoras*, 335a ff.; and *WM*, 345). Plato's defense against these sophists, as we see it in Socrates' art of carrying on a discussion, is precisely to establish the priority of the question over any answer. Socrates' negative midwifery, freeing his more willing interlocutors of their dearly held prejudices, is in fact nothing other than placing assumed certitudes in question. Not arguing the unshakeable answer but opening up the question is Plato's response to the sophism of the law courts and its tyranny of belief that would stifle all authentic talking anything through.

Plato's dialectic as exemplified in Socratic *dialegesthai* thus establishes a central point for Gadamer's hermeneutical theory: we learn precisely from Plato that an understanding of something is reached in a dialogical process, i.e., in discussion. Understanding occurs not in subjective thought but in an interrogative discursive exchange *between* speakers: "What emerges in its truth is the *logos* that is neither mine nor yours and thus exceeds the subjective beliefs of the partners in the discussion to such an extent that even the leader of the discussion remains unknowing" (*WM*, 350). The allusion, obviously, is to Socrates' "learned ignorance," which far from being a mere ploy, establishes the interrogative spirit of inquiry (*zētēsis*) needed for any *dialegesthai*. In not having an answer himself, in knowing that he does not know, Socrates calls the pat answers of his interlocutors into question too. In this way his partners in discussion are induced to let go of their private opinions and to open themselves to what will emerge for all out of the shared "center" of language. "Dialectic . . . is the art of concept formation as elaboration of what is meant in common" (*idem*).

Now if we consider Gadamer's hermeneutical concerns, we see that just this dialogical structure characterizes the understanding of texts. Here too understanding is reached in an interrogative discursive exchange, in this case, between the interpreter and the text. As interpreters who would understand, we enter into a discussion with the text (*WM*, 350). To be sure, the text is to be taken as an answer to a question raised by others, and our task will eventually be to reconstruct that question, but not initially:

On the contrary, there is to begin with the question the text puts to us, our being struck and affected by the word of the tradition. . . . What is transmitted traditionally and speaks to us–the text, the work, the trace–itself poses a question and opens our beliefs to question. To answer this question put to us we, the ones asked, must begin to question ourselves. (*WM*, 355–56)

As an art applied to the literary tradition, hermeneutics is modeled precisely on Socrates' art of talking something through "in question and answer, in give and take, in talking past one another and reaching agreement with one another" (*WM*, 350). "What is transmitted in literary form is thereby recovered from its condition of alienation and brought back into the living present of the discussion that originally is always carried out in question and answer" (*idem*).

With that a further convergence of Plato and Gadamer emerges and another way in which Plato may be said to have had a positive "effect" on him. I refer here to Plato's and Gadamer's conception of the relationship between written and spoken language. Literature, what is in letters, is, we have just heard, in the "condition of alienation." What is written, *Schriftlichkeit*, is an alienated form of what is spoken, *Sprachlichkeit*, and the overcoming of this self-alienation, "the reading of the text," is thus the highest task of understanding. "Even, for example, the pure content of signs in an inscription can be correctly seen and articulated when one is able to change the text back into speech" (*WM*, 368). There would seem to be a critique of writing implied here, one we know well from Plato's *Phaedrus*. But in fact the matter is more complex: though both Plato and Gadamer would change the written word back into speech, both see an "ideality" in writing insofar as writing, in contrast with oral transmission, detaches itself from any particular speaker. Indeed, "Everything written is in fact the privileged object of hermeneutics" (*WM*, 372). The issue is not at all whether writing should be replaced with speech, rather what sort of writing lends itself to being changed back into speech and understood. Plato is paradigmatic for Gadamer *not because he rejects writing but because he more than anyone has found the right form of it.*

Gadamer maintains that to understand Plato's apparent rejection of writing, a rejection that can hardly be the truth of the matter given Plato's own remarkable literary production (see *WM*, 370), we must take into account the kind of interpretation of texts cultivated by the sophists, in particular their use of poetry for their didactic purposes (*WM*, 350). When Plato says that the written word cannot come to its own defense (*Phaedrus*, 275a ff.), he is reacting to the sophistic tactic of making a text support now one point of view, now the opposite. In this way a text is worked into a long speech to lend authority to whatever position the author happens to be arguing, and thus far from raising a question, it then serves to fend off questions and silence the opponent. In his own *writing* Plato responds to this abuse of writing: "The literary form of the dialogue puts speech (*Sprache*) and concept back into the original movement of discussion (*Gespräch*). The word is thereby protected against all dogmatic misuse" (*WM*, 351). In other words, if read rightly, Plato's written dialogues keep open the question they address to us.[6] Far from giving us his answers, they draw us into the process of ongoing interrogative exchange.

Not surprisingly Gadamer finds the words for this occurrence in Plato: where Plato speaks of the *pathos tōn logōn* (*Philebus*, 15d), Gadamer speaks of the *Widerfahrnis der Reden* (*WM*, 441, see 433). By rendering *pathos* as *Widerfahrnis* Gadamer is emphasizing that the things we say (*logoi, Reden*) are not so much things we do as things that happen to us or even befall us counter to (*wider*) our expectations. We *experience* that "the word of speech is one and at the same time many. . . . The unity of this word explicates itself on and on in articulated talk" (*WM*, 433–34). Or, in the language of the *Philebus*, to which Gadamer is alluding here, "This [dispersion of the one into the many] is, . . . the immortal and unaging experience (*pathos*) in us (*en hēmin*) of the things we say (*tōn logōn*) themselves" (*Philebus*, 15d).

The *Theaetetus* gives an indication of how this self-unfolding of speech or the *logos* takes place, an indication, that is, of what speech does "in us": "But by virtue of what," Socrates asks Theaetetus, "is the capacity given that makes plain (*dēloi*) to you what is common to all things and to these [color, sound, taste], common to that which you name (*eponamazeis*) with 'it is' and 'it is not,' and concerning which we were just now inquiring?" (*Theaetetus*, 185c). The reference is to what "is" the same (*tauton*) and hence one (*hen*) and what "is not" the same but different (*heteron*) and hence two (*duo*) (185a–b), and the point is that these assimilations and differations are primal accomplishments in the mind (*psychē*) transcending any sensation (*aisthēsis*). For it is not by virtue of (*dia*) any sense organ that these assimilations and differentiations are made; rather it is by virtue of the mind itself (*autē di' hautēs hē psychē*) that the mind sees things in common (*ta koina*). The capacity referred to, then, is that of transferring what is said in one realm of our experience into what is said in another insofar as the latter though it "is not" the same but different, "is" nevertheless in some respect the same. But if like Kant we ask what is "the condition of the possibility" of the mind's being able to do this, we come back to what we have seen is the prior capacity of speech to transfer itself and proliferate, i.e., its *metapherein* not as something we do but as a *pathos*, as something that happens to us and "in us" (*en hēmin*). (See *WM*, 434 on the "virtuality" of speech.)

We could not say, then, that when Shakespeare writes, "The thunder would not peace at thy bidding," *he* first sees the similarity in different, initially wordless realities. And *he* does not proceed, in an act of poetic invention, to transfer the noun, peace, as a designation of the state without war, into the verb in order to give the thunder's ceasing a designation. Rather the occurring to him of the similarity of the two things and his hearing the transferred word are one and the same event. Gadamer's example is Hölderlin, who, in regard to finding the words of a poem, tells us of the total dissolution for him of accustomed words and ways of speaking and of the poet's feeling himself " 'grasped in the whole of his inner and outer life with the pure tone of his primordial emotions' " (*WM*, 445). In the experience of the eventual word there is no longer any inner and outer, no thinking subject and object known. Instead the poet's thought is absorbed in the feeling of what is happening to him, in the *pathos tōn logōn*.[7]

What bearing has this on hermeneutics and interpretation? Let us keep in mind that the transfer of sense in the poet's experience of speech ever further unfolding itself is paradigmatic for the interpreter's trans*lation* (vis. the Latin *ferre, tuli, latus*) of a written text back into heard speech on a given occasion (see *WM*, 363–64). What the speech of the text speaks to the interpreter of it will be yet another *dēloma*, a further self-explication of its sense as this unfolds in his or her discussion with the text. Hence the active side of interpretation, the *Auslegung* or laying out and applying the text on the occasion (*WM*, 291ff.), presupposes the *pathos* or experience of its own *Offenlegung* or making plain of its sense. Before we can say what it says, we must hear what it says to us.

Plato, it has turned out, is both an impulse and an obstacle for our getting clear about this dialogical, active and passive, nature of understanding something and interpreting it. Insofar as he stays with our experience of the *logoi*, to which his Socrates turns in the *Phaedo*, he impels us in the right direction. But insofar as he moves beyond what shows up in the speech we hear in our discussion with one another to a solitary vision of the pure form (*eidos*) of which spoken words are mere signs, he blocks our way.

Chapter 3

A RESPONSE TO
P. CHRISTOPHER SMITH

R. Nicholas Davey

As a quotation to preside over his paper, Christopher Smith's choice of George's line, "Where the word breaks off, there is no thing" is indeed finely judged. It is resonant with that conviction of Heidegger's that "Language is the house of Being," which not only permeates Part Three of Gadamer's *Truth and Method* but is also virtually restated in the latter's declaration that "Being that can be understood is language" (*TM*, 432).[1] It comes as somewhat of a surprise, therefore, when Christopher Smith suggests that "though Hegel's dialectic and Heidegger's destruction of metaphysics are certainly very important" in the development of his hermeneutics "the 'effect' of Plato's dialogues" informs Gadamer's thought "*more distinctive[ly] than any other*".[2] Without doubt Plato's dialogues have had a formidable impact upon Gadamer's hermeneutics. The penetrating essays within *Dialogue and Dialectic* not only attest to the excellence of Gadamer's Greek scholarship but also express themes concomitant with the hermeneutic principles enunciated in *Truth and Method*. None of this is in question, but what does demand redress is the specific claim that Plato's multifaceted approach to speech, language and writing has contributed to the building of Gadamer's hermeneutic "more distinctive[ly] than any other." It can be argued, not against but in supplement to Christopher Smith's paper, that Plato's dialogues are of importance for Gadamer not *per se* but because of what his Heideggerian philosophical inheritance allows him to bring to light within them. In what follows some comment will be made upon the Heideggerian presuppositions that shape Gadamer's approach to Plato. Furthermore, because his declared aim is to reveal "the strands of the philosophical tradition woven into "Gadamer's hermeneutic, Christopher Smith eschews any criticism of the conversational model of hermeneutic understanding Gadamer allegedly derives from the structural character of Plato's dialogues. Christopher Smith makes it perfectly clear that

> Plato's dialectic as exemplified in Socratic *dialegesthai* establishes a central point for Gadamer's hermeneutical theory; we learn precisely from Plato that an understanding of something is reached in a dialogical process, i.e. in discussion. Understanding occurs not in subjective thought but in interrogative discursive exchange *between* speakers.[3]

What Christopher Smith does not make plain, whereas Gadamer most certainly does, is that the conversational model of hermeneutic understanding has a specific philosophical entailment, namely, a devaluation of the status of the propositional statement or assertion (*Aussage*) within understanding. Amongst the very pages of *Truth and Method* that Christopher Smith discusses, Gadamer comments that

> . . . what Plato called dialectic depends, in fact, on subordinating language to the 'statement.' The concept of the statement, the dialectical accentuation of it to the point of contradiction is, however, in extreme contrast to the nature of the hermeneutical experience and the linguistic nature of human experience of the world. (*TM*, 425)

Indeed, earlier on in Part Three of *Truth and Method*, Gadamer notes that

> Greek ontology is based firmly on the factuality of language, in that it conceives the essence of language in terms of the statement. As against this, however, it must be emphasized that language has its true being only in conversation, in the exercise of understanding between people. (*TM*, 404)

For Gadamer, "the use of the statement in the process of communication between people distorts it" (*TM*, 427). Whatever "remains within the dimension of what is stated . . . does not attain the dimension of the linguistic experience of the world" (*TM*, 426).

The following comments on the Heideggerian dimensions of Gadamer's philosophy of language will illuminate this negative appraisal of the statement. Unless we are to remain solely within the realms of interpretive *exegesis*, the consequences of Gadamer's position must be opened to question. He might be accused, as Habermas has accused Heidegger, of completely blurring the connection between propositional truth and truth-as-disclosure, and of hypostatizing "world disclosing language" as "some sacral force fitted out with the aura of truth."[4] Even if such criticisms are warranted, let alone appropriate, there is not the space here to pursue them adequately. Yet Gadamer's evaluation of the statement is in need of adjustment. Suggestions will be proposed below; however, let us now turn directly to Christopher Smith's reading of Gadamer's interpretation of Plato.

I Gadamer, Plato and Heidegger on language

Christopher Smith correctly judges Plato to be both impulse *and* obstacle in the development of Gadamer's hermeneutics. Plato is accused of being a hindrance to the view that "what things are . . . is originally 'uncovered' in what is said."[5] By reducing them to instrumental signifiers of a pre-existent reality, Plato's doctrine of the Ideas covers up the proper nature of speech and language.[6] Yet at the same time, writes Christopher Smith, "Gadamer who is so critical of the abstraction of the spoken word in Plato's dialectic of the ideas can also refer . . . to the paradigm of Platonic dialectic for his hermeneutical theory."[7] As his dialectics imply a "talking something through with another, "that is, *Gespräch* and not merely *Sprache*, Plato "it turns out is true to the original nature of speech after all."[8] It is in and through the to and fro of discussion that what we talk of is laid open and thereby comes to be in our speaking of it. Indeed, Christopher Smith might have alluded to some of Gadamer's subsequent essays on Plato in support of his reading of the arguments in *Truth and Method*. In these essays, the following comments appear.

As dialectic, philosophy never ceases to be tied to its origin in Socratic discussion. (*DD*, 123)

To be sure, we must not overlook the mimetic character of Plato's dialogues. We are dealing here with a poetic

44

presentation, which should never be measured against a one-sided criterion of logical consistency. Rather, the presentation recounts a human discussion which must be understood as discussion. (*DD*, 21)

If we find in Plato's dialogues and in Socrates' argument all manner of violations of logic—false inferences, the omission of necessary steps, equivocations, the interchanging of one concept with another—the reasonable hermeneutic assumption on which to proceed is that we are dealing with a discussion. And we ourselves do not conduct our discussion *more geometrico*. Instead we move within the live play of risking assertions, of taking back what we said, of assuming and rejecting, all the while proceeding on our way to reaching an understanding. Thus, it does not seem at all reasonable to me to study Plato primarily with an eye to logical consistency, although that approach can of course be of auxillary importance in pointing out where conclusions have been drawn too quickly. The real task can only be to activate for ourselves wholes of meaning, contexts within which a discussion moves—even where its logic offends us. (*DD*, 5)

The latter passage is of considerable interest. Firstly, it exhibits the tension between propositional truth and truth-as-disclosure which will be discussed below. Secondly, it supplies ample evidence in favour of the correctness of Christopher Smith's reading of Gadamer's critical evaluation of Plato in *Truth and Method*. Indeed, it also suggests another interpretation of Christopher Smith's intention to enquire into that which informs "Gadamer's endeavours." Since the above passage is more lucid than equivalent statements in *Truth and Method*, what Christopher Smith may understand and present as Gadamer's "thought" has developed well beyond *Truth and Method*. The exploration of such developments would have been of major interest. However, though Christopher Smith declares that he will focus chiefly on *Truth and Method*, his own involvement in the translation of the essays *Dialogue and Dialectic* may have given rise to an element of back-reading in his interpretation of the approach to Plato in *Truth and Method*.

Though Plato may have simultaneously proffered, historically speaking, an impulse and obstacle to the development of Gadamer's hermeneutic position, it remains the case that the evaluation of Plato as "obstacle and impulse" already indicates a well articulated hermeneutic stance. After all, the passages that Christopher Smith comments upon commence, for the most part, a good twenty pages into Part Three of *Truth and Method*. The discussion of Plato's *Cratylus* is prefaced by a discussion of three themes: language as the medium of hermeneutical experience, language as determination of the hermeneutic object, and language as the determination of the hermeneutic act. In the discussion of these themes, Gadamer makes the following declarations:

> All language belongs in a unique way to the process of understanding. (*TM*, 351)

> Language is the universal medium in which understanding itself is realized. The mode of realization of understanding is interpretation. (*TM*, 350)

> All understanding is interpretation, and all interpretation takes place in the medium of a language which would allow the object to come into words. (*TM*, 350)

> Interpretation, like conversation, is a closed circle within the dialectic of question and answer. (*TM*, 351)

> It is characteristic of every true conversation that each opens himself to the other person, truly accepts his point of view as worthy of consideration and gets inside the other to such an extent that he understands not a particular individual, but what he says. (*TM*, 347)

These passages are not so much indicative of anything that Plato impels Gadamer towards as they are of a well-worked hermeneutic stance in which the spirit of Heidegger is clearly discernible. It is indeed just such a stance that can in effect determine what was an obstacle to and an impulse towards its own historical realization. It is, therefore, the attainment of an understanding of "the true nature of language" (*TM*, 369)—the perfection of a thing's coming into being within *Sprache* (see *TM*, 394)—which enables Gadamer to criticize Plato on the one hand for wedging language "in between image and sign" (*TM*, 378), and yet on the other to applaud him for a dialectical theory which begins to anticipate a proper understanding of the nature and significance of the spoken word within discussion. It is in other words Gadamer's normative laying down of "the true nature of language" which enables him to assess the development of language theory subsequent to Plato as either an obstacle or impulse towards the realization of a proper hermeneutic comprehension of language. The discussion of Plato's influence upon the development of concepts of language is thus an excellent instance of his notion of *Wirkungsgeschichte*. In this context Christopher Smith is quite correct to talk of the "effect" of Plato upon Gadamer. What remains in question is whether that "effect" is more influential than any other. Both Leibniz and Nietzsche have taught in their different ways that the degree of an "effect" depends upon the capacity to be affected in the effected. Gadamer can only effectively respond to Plato as "obstacle and impulse" because he is *already* sensitive to the alleged "true nature of language" and that understanding derives in large part from Heidegger.

The following passage in *Being and Time* reveals the enormous extent of Heidegger's impact upon Gadamer. It even anticipates the historical location of Gadamer's debate over the nature of language.

> The Greeks had no word for "language"; they understood this phenomenon "in the first instance" as discourse (*Rede*). But because the λογός came into their philosophical ken as assertion, this was the kind of *logos* which they took as their clue for working out the basic structures of the forms of discourse and its components. Grammar sought its foundations in the "logic" of this *logos*. But this logic was based upon the ontology of the present-at-hand. The basic stock of categories of signification which passed over into the subsequent science of language and which in principle is still accepted today, is oriented towards discourse as assertion. But if on the contrary we take this phenomenon to have in principle the primordiality and breadth of an *existentiale*, then there emerges the necessity of re-establishing the science of language on foundations which are ontologically primordial. (*BT*, sec. 34)

A close reading of sections 31 to 34 of *Being and Time* reveals that language is fundamental to Heidegger's existential hermeneutic.

Dasein—the nature of our being-in-the-world as creatures who understand—is constituted by discourse.

> As an existential state in which *Dasein* is disclosed, discourse is constitutive for *Dasein*'s existence. . . . Discoursing or talking is the way we articulate "significantly" the intelligibility of Being in the world. Being-with belongs to Being-in-the-world which in every case maintains itself in some definitive way of concernful Being-with-one-another. Such Being-with-one-another is discursive. (*BT*, sec. 34)

Heidegger insists therefore that *"Discourse or talk is the existential-ontological foundation of language"* and *"is existentially-equiprimordial with state of mind and understanding"* (*BT*, sec. 34). Not only do the dialogical dimensions of discourse (*Rede*) as a "being-with" anticipate the dialectical element within Gadamer's notion of *Gespräche*, but the ontological disclosure that discourse facilitates clearly foreshadows Gadamer's understanding of *Sprache* as that which brings things into being through the speaking of them. Though the emphasis in each argument is different, the relation is clear. Heidegger argues that

> In talking, *Dasein* expresses itself for in it Being-with becomes "explicitly" stated; that is to say, it *is* already, but it is unstated as something that has not been taken hold of. (*BT*, sec. 34)

Rather than talking of the structure of the human mode of being as disclosed through discourse, Gadamer speaks of the uncovering of the human world within language:

> Language is not just one of man's possessions in the world, but on it depends the fact that man has a world at all. For man the world exists as a world in a way that no other being in the world experiences. But this world is linguistic in nature. . . . Not only is the world "world" only insofar as it comes into language but language too has its real being only in the fact that the world is re-presented in it. (*TM*, 401)

Gadamer's privileging of conversation as a more authentic mode of linguistic communication compared to that of assertion, statement and proposition is also anticipated in Heidegger's writing. In section 33 of *Being and Time* Heidegger unequivocally maintains that the making of assertive, predicative or propositional statements is a derivative or secondary mode of interpretation.

All interpretation is grounded on understanding, that which has been articulated as such in interpretation and sketched out beforehand in the understanding in general is something articulate, is the meaning. Insofar as assertion is grounded on understanding and presents us with a derivative form in which an interpretation has been carried out, it *too* "has" a meaning. Yet this meaning cannot be defined as something which occurs in [a] judgment along with the judging itself. (*BT*, sec. 33)

It is plain that Heidegger is simultaneously striking out for one view of propositional statement whilst hitting out at another. Though he opposes that view which separates the contents of a statement from the vast deployments of meaning entailed by its words, he endorses that which holds the meaning of a statement to be anchored in—to be a derivative form of—(fore)-understanding. Language for Heidegger is a "totality of involvements" (*BT*, sec. 34), a "totality of words which is something we come across as ready to hand" (*BT*, sec. 34). It is "equipment ready-to-hand within the word, that can be used to accomplish . . . discursive sharing." "It is a means through which our common world can be made explicit among us."[9] To speak a language is thus already to be party to a nexus of fore-understandings which are "lit up" in the understanding of discursive statements. Speech is therefore the ordering and structuring power which dwells in our understanding and for that reason becomes the basis of interpretation and understanding.[10] It is for this reason that Heidegger argues as noted above that "insofar as assertion is grounded on understanding . . . it too has a meaning" (*BT*, sec. 34). The fullness of a statement's meaning lies not in its internal grammatical or logical structure but in its ability to illuminate the totality of fore-understandings which are the grounds of its intelligibility. It is, however, precisely where a statement is cut off from such connections that it begins to lose its full meaning. Heidegger makes a hostile reference to that "theory of judgment" which insists that the meaning of what is said resides within the predicative terms of the statement, its logical form or in the concepts to which it allegedly refers. His point is admirably put by Richardson:

> Because an assertion communicates, an involvement by means of a concrete predication, it is always possible for the hearer to retain and repeat this formula without himself ever sharing that relationship. Thus we may speak of the horrors of war because we have heard others do so. This way in which we may "pass the word along," without a genuine involvement in what is said . . . arises from the basic character of assertion.[11]

Heidegger's distinction between statements which have not been cut off from the totality of their involvement and those which have (inauthentic speech) is evidently the basis of both Gadamer's appraisal of conversation as the paradigmatic form of hermeneutical understanding and his interest in Socratic dialogue as a partial historical embodiment of such understanding. Christopher Smith may be correct to say that Heidegger does not perceive as Gadamer does, that element in Socratic dialectics which suggests a true understanding of the nature of language, but it is clearly Heidegger above all who permits Gadamer to perceive just that very element in Plato's thinking. Let us now turn to Gadamer's treatment of the statement.

II   Gadamer and the problem of statement

Though Christopher Smith's reading of Gadamer's veneration of Socratic *dialegesthai* is exemplary, it does not explore a key problematic entailed within the presentation of conversation as a paradigmatic form of hermeneutic understanding. Gadamer, however, is unequivocal in spelling out the fact that the conversational model of hermeneutic understanding must embrace the corollary of an unavoidable downgrading of the status of the predicative statement in linguistic intercourse. "The concept of the statement is," Gadamer insists, "in extreme contrast to the nature of human experience of the world" (*TM*, 425). "The dimension of the linguistic experience of the world" does not remain "within the dimension of what is stated" (*TM*, 426). To be sure, "the object of statements is already enclosed within the world horizon of language" but "the linguistic nature of the world does not include (as statements are wont to) making the world into an object" (*TM*, 408). Though Heidegger suggests that assertive or predicative statements can distort the fore-meanings upon which their intelligibility rests, he nevertheless accepts that, if properly interpreted, "they too can have a meaning." Gadamer, however, insists that the meaning derivable from statements can *only* be distorted meaning.

> A person who has something to say seeks and finds the words through which he makes himself intelligible to the other person. This does not mean that he makes "statements." Anyone who has experienced a law suit— even if only as a witness—knows what it is to make a statement and how little it is a statement of what one means. In a statement the range of the meaning of what is said is concealed with methodical exactness; what remains is the "pure sense" of the statements. That is what goes on record. But as meaning thus reduced to what is stated, it is always distorted meaning. (*TM*, 426)

Why is Gadamer so expressly hostile towards the statement? Let us return to Christopher Smith.

Christopher Smith uses Heideggerian terminology when in the context of discussing the intelligibility of a word, he speaks of "the original shimmering of speech."

> A word's perfected intelligibility does not imply . . . that it is rid of all ambiguity, that what it makes plain about something in a *logos*, it makes unequivocally plain. Originally the truth of the word is not *bebaios*, not "steady" or fixed like the truth of the Ideas to which Plato aspires, rather it shimmers. For the *deloma*, the presentation of the thing in the *logos* makes the thing plain (*delos*), now in one way, now in the opposite.[12]

It is this very indeterminacy of speech which is of crucial importance for Gadamer. Whereas for Plato the ability of a word to imply one thing and then another gives rise to the abuses of Sophism and his own subsequent attempt to rise above them through his projected mathematization of language, for Gadamer it is exactly speech's indeterminacy which invests words with the power not only to obscure but also to make plain. We are not talking here of a simple opposition; the power of a word to reveal a thing on the one hand and hide it on the other. Rather, what the thing is—the meaning of that which is spoken—is the simultaneity in language of its disclosure and concealment.[13] The equivocation between a word saying what "is" and what "is not" is precisely that quality which allows the meaning of the spoken to arise. As Gadamer argues,

> . . . there is another dialectic of the word, which assigns to every word an inner dimension of multiplication: every word breaks forth from a centre and is related to a whole through which alone it is word. Every word causes the whole of language to which it belongs to resonate and the whole of the view of the world which lies behind it to appear. Thus every word in its momentariness, carries with it the unsaid, to which it is related by responding and indicating. The occasionality of human speech is not a casual imperfection of its expressive power: it is rather the logical expression of the living virtuality of speech that brings a totality of meaning into play without being able to express it totally. (*TM*, 416)

Later in *Truth and Method*, the dialectic of the word is extended into a dialectic of the hermeneutical *per se*.

> Now the hermeneutical experience that we are endeavouring to understand from the centre of language is certainly not an experience of thinking in the same sense as this dialectic of the concept, which seeks to free itself entirely from the power of language. Nevertheless there is in the hermeneutical experience something that resembles a dialectic. . . . A thing does not present itself to the hermeneutical experience without its own special effort, namely, of "being negative" towards itself. . . . The unfolding of the totality of meaning towards which the understanding is directed, forces us to make conjectures and then to take them back again. The self-cancellation of the interpretation makes it possible for the thing-itself—the

52

meaning of the text—to assert itself. The movement of the interpretation is not dialectical primarily because the one-sidedness of every statement can be balanced by another side—this is, as we shall see, a secondary phenomenon in interpretation—but because the word that interpretatively encounters the meaning of the text expresses the whole of this meaning, i.e. allows an infinity of meaning to be represented within it in a finite way. (*TM*, 423)

The related notions of "every word" causing "the whole of language" to "resonate" and of the dialectical interplay between finite expressions of an infinity of meaning are at the root of what Gadamer describes as the "speculative" nature of language.

Language itself . . . has something speculative about it . . . as the realization of meaning, as the event of speech, of communication, of understanding. Such a realization is speculative, in that the finite possibilities of the word are oriented towards the sense intended, as towards the infinite. . . .
To say what one means . . . to make oneself understood, means to hold what is said together with an infinity of what is not said in the unity of one meaning and to ensure that it is understood in this way. (*TM*, 426)

The full extent of Gadamer's downgrading of the statement within hermeneutic understanding now becomes apparent. (1) Discursive speech expresses the ontological event of understanding achieved in and through language whilst propositional language is primarily concerned with the epistemological questions of predication and validity. (2) Discursive speech is "speculative," directing itself via the *said* to the unsaid, whilst propositional statements seek to eliminate semantic indeterminacy for the sake of methodological precision. (3) Through its speculative nature, conversational speech ushers up the infinite horizons of meaning which cradle humanity's being-in-the-world, whilst propositional language seeks to objectify the world by reducing it to a discursively constructed object. (4) The "truth" of conversational discourse lies in the fore-understandings which ground it, whilst propositional languages reduce the question of truth to methodological procedures licensed within and by a specific discourse.

Though deceptively simple in its structure, the problem of statement is a pivotal one in *Truth and Method*. On it hang themes which are fundamental to Gadamer's hermeneutic. The downgrading of the statement is not only part of Gadamer's opposition to objectifying methodologies which monopolize our understanding of the real and the true, but also explains his commitment to speculative speech with its specific hermeneutic entailment of the openness of all understanding. No wonder that Gadamer is so emphatic in his assertion of the priority of discursive speech over the exactitudes of propositional language.

Gadamer's position will evoke considerable sympathy from those reared within the Anglo-American analytic tradition of philosophy who know very well how the complex, philosophical, historical and linguistic strategems of Hegel, Nietzsche or Heidegger can be rendered as nonsense when reduced to judgmental assertions isolated from the horizons of meaning which underwrite them. In his hostility to the banality of such reductions, Gadamer clearly perceived an ally in Collingwood.

> He [Collingwood] clearly saw what was missing in naive
> hermeneutics founded upon the [then] prevailing
> philosophical critique. In particular the practice that
> Collingwood found in English Universities of discussing
> statements, though perhaps a good training for the
> intelligence, obviously failed to take account of the
> historicity that is part of all understanding. (*TM*, 333)

Yet the questions remain. Can Gadamer's downgrading of the statement within hermeneutics be justified? Two sets of issues can be identified: (1) the acceptability of the methodological polarity between conversational language and propositional statements and (2) whether assertive statements have no role in the interpretive process.

With regard to (1) Weinsheimer has cogently argued that Gadamer's attempt to stress the linguisticality of hermeneutic experience by weakening the claims of artificial propositional languages rests upon the false supposition that the propositions of a scientific methodology are both total and exclusive whilst their truth is internally validated by the methodology itself.[14] In his

DAVEY

discussion of Tarski and Gödel, Weinsheimer shows that artificial languages can never arrive at what Gadamer supposes they can, namely, the "totality of the knowable." If they could they would introduce paradox into themselves and thereby render all proposition within their discipline trivial. It follows that if any particular scientific or logical truth is to be meaningfully defined, neither it nor its definition can be the whole truth. Gadamer fails to acknowledge that "the advocates of method" know as well as he that "method never exhausts truth." What Weinsheimer might have gone on to say is that, if in certain respects statements within a scientific discourse are as logically "open" as conversational discourses and, like the latter, depend upon truths beyond the stated, then, as with the latter, scientific statements depend for their full intelligibility upon implicit unstated sets of conventions and modes of practice. In this respect, the very disciplines which Gadamer associates above all with objectifying statements—the natural sciences—have been shown in the work of Kuhn, Feyerabend and Hesse to work within hermeneutical fields analogous to those appertaining in the humanities. In other words, the methodological polarity which Gadamer insists upon between conversational language and propositional statement appears unsustainable. That the full meaning of scientific statements *also* rests upon underlying hermeneutic suppositions has a direct bearing upon (2): the question of whether statements have *no* role in the interpretive process.

Contrary to Gadamer's belief that the statement distorts meaning by obscuring the background horizon of commitments and assumptions upon which any discourse depends, Pannenberg argues that it is precisely the statement that allows "the infinity of the unsaid" to come into view. If the hermeneutic task is as Gadamer maintains, to restore the world of the transmitted text to its original unspoken context of meaning, such a task can only be realized if it begins with an exact grasp of what is said (*HUH*, 126). Pannenberg insists therefore that the implicit unspoken horizon of meaning is accessible to the understanding only on the basis of a statement as to a text's meaning and content (*HUH*, 126). That is not to say, however, that the statement will exhaust that meaning; to the contrary only that such foreground statements allow the unspoken horizons of meaning to come into view.

55

Everything (within interpretation) must be turned into
assertion; everything that was involved in the formulation
of a text—nuances, frames of reference of which the author
himself was partly unaware—must be made explicit. The
interpreted text is precisely the text which has been
objectified with respect to the previously unanticipated
propositions of its horizon of meaning. (*HUH*, 127)

Furthermore, unless the horizon of a text is fully thematized,
it is impossible to determine the appropriateness let alone the
correctness of an interpretation: "the comprehensive horizon of
understanding must be formulated so that one can test whether
or not it is capable of including both the horizon of the text
and the contemporary horizon of the interpreter" (*HUH*, 128).
Pannenberg even goes so far as to insist that conversational
practices are not an appropriate paradigm for hermeneutic understanding. Firstly, he suggests that conversational language
cannot really be separated from propositional statements.

Even conversation, which Gadamer takes as the paradigm
of the hermeneutical event, always operates in statements
and sets of statements and indeed without this there can be
no communication about the same thing between parties to
a conversation. (*TPS*, 179)

Secondly, the everyday understanding attained by conversational partners rests upon an acknowledged (but perhaps unstated) horizon of assumptions and meanings which defines
the boundaries of their conversational practices and allows, as
Wittgenstein might put it, a conversation to "go on." That horizon rarely comes into the foreground of analysis. Only when
challenged or endangered does it become an object for reflection.
Unlike conversational exchanges, however, hermeneutic interchange with a text constitutes only a *metaphorical* conversation.
The text cannot itself speak. Accordingly, it is necessary in the
process of interpreting a text (where it is not in conversational
interchange) to fully thematize or objectify the horizon of that
text. "The interpreter," Pannenberg argues, "must see that the
peculiar form, the alien horizon of the text, is allowed to assert
itself in contrast to the horizon that he brings with him" (*HUH*,
118). Objectifying thematization is therefore crucial to establish-

ing those differences of horizon between text and interpreter which even Gadamer insists are crucial to the process of understanding. According to Pannenberg then, the predicative and assertive statement has a central role in the interpretative process.[15]

III Conclusion

In response to Christopher Smith's paper two issues have been discussed: firstly, the extent to which Plato's dual approach to language affects the historical parameters out of which Gadamer's hermeneutic arises, and secondly, the downgrading of the statement implicit in Gadamer's evaluation of Socratic discourse as paradigmatic of hermeneutic understanding. The discussion has not sought to repudiate Christopher Smith's reading of Gadamer or Gadamer's understanding of the objectifying function of statements but to suggest that both thematics are in need of certain redress. There is no question that Plato's metaphysics and philosophy of language had an enormous hold upon how post-Greek philosophies of language evolved and upon what subsequent thinkers were and were not capable of perceiving in language. It is, however, Heidegger who alerts Gadamer to what lies implicit in Socratic dialectics. Gadamer's responsiveness to Plato as impulse and obstacle is above all facilitated by the hermeneutic he derives from Heidegger. This reveals the pressing need for an intensive comparative study of Heidegger's and Gadamer's philosophy of language.

Gadamer's acceptance of Socratic *dialegesthai* as *the* model of hermeneutic understanding has as its consequence a downgrading of the propositional function of language. In this context Weinsheimer questions Gadamer's supposition of a methodological polarity between the truth disclosing discourses of the humanities and the propositional methodologies of the sciences. Exposing the falsity of this assumption has the positive consequence of revealing the extent to which scientific enquiries also operate within the horizons of meaning, tradition and convention. Pannenberg on the other hand does not accept as Gadamer appears to, that statements can be isolated from the wider horizons of meaning upon which their intelligibility and meaning depends. He accepts the correctness of Gadamer's insight into the infinite horizon of meaning which structures and informs any hermeneutic exchange, but insists that statements as well as conversational utterances derive their full meaning from such horizons and are not hermetically sealed within the confines of pure methodology. Method is neither ahistorical, nor unconnected to social and cultural projects. Even the application of "method" implies a wider "hermeneutic" understanding of when it is and is not appropriate for a methodological approach to be applied. What Pannenberg's position implies, then, is an important shift of emphasis. Once Gadamer can be freed from the supposition that the objectifying function of propositional language inevitably distorts the background horizon of meanings upon which a given discourse depends, the possibility of using the language of statement in a tactful and focused way to illuminate background horizons of meanings comes into sight. In this respect Plato continues to be a negative effect upon Gadamer. Because Gadamer persists in associating the propositional form exclusively with the doctrine of ideas or modes of methodological analysis, he fails to see what Pannenberg clearly can, namely, that lighting and being lit up by the "infinity of the unsaid" is not the sole purview of the spoken utterance. Pannenberg therefore tries to establish within hermeneutic discourse a necessary interdependence of statement and background meaning. He insists that what remains implicit in conversational discourse—the unspoken but tacitly referred to horizon of assumptions and meanings grounding the conversation—must be made emphatically explicit within any hermeneutic exchange with a text. But it can only be made so once the content of a text has been objectified in a statement or assertion, the appropriateness of which can then be judged against what it brings into view. The force of Pannenberg's amendment to Gadamer's stance is illustrated in cases where conversations break down. Because it supposes an implicitly accepted horizon, or continuity of horizons, of meaning between two parties in a "conversation," Gadamer's hermeneutic cannot readily cope with instances of open disagreement as to what the constitutive norms or universals of a grounding horizon actually are. It is not enough to suggest that disputants listen more carefully to each other or open themselves more fully to the central concern (*Sache*) of their dialogue, for such disputes can be about not only the subject matter of a dialogue but its very terms. In other words, only when what is taken as implicit in a conversational dialogue is fully thematized in explicit statements can either party come to understand the nature of the disagreement, let alone reflect upon the possibility of its resolution.[16] In a post-modern epoch where a sense of rupture and discontinuity in and between cultures is more manifest than any sense of continuity, Pannenberg's corrective of Gadamer's position is a very necessary one. Insofar as the Platonic "practice of subordinating language to the statement" (*TM*, 425) blinds Gadamer to the hermeneutic dimensions and functions of the statement itself, does Plato indeed remain an obstacle to the continued development of Gadamer's hermeneutics?

PART III
RICOEUR/GADAMER

Chapter 4

DIALOGUE, TEXT, NARRATIVE: CONFRONTING GADAMER AND RICOEUR

Gary E. Aylesworth

The works of Gadamer and Ricoeur offer distinctive paradigms for contemporary hermeneutics. The most immediate difference between them is their diverging positions in regard to the text. Where Gadamer develops a dialogical model of interpretation, in which the text is a "thou" with whom we are engaged in conversation, Ricoeur insists upon the reflective distance of the text as a linguistic object. This entails a broader difference in their understanding of the relation between philosophical hermeneutics and the practices of the human sciences. For Gadamer, philosophical hermeneutics is more fundamental than the methods of the *Geisteswissenschaften*, and provides a corrective for the methodological alienation of their subject matter. Ricoeur, on the other hand, believes that philosophical hermeneutics must serve an epistemological function vis-à-vis the human sciences, and must incorporate their critical practices into its own discourse.

Taking Heidegger's ontological hermeneutics as his point of departure, Gadamer develops a dialogical model of understanding and interpretation that diverges, nevertheless, from the Heideggerian problematic. Where *Being and Time* stresses the futural orientation of *Dasein* as being-towards-death, Gadamer emphasizes the role of the past in constituting any present or future understanding. Any understanding whatsoever, he argues, is conditioned by the affections, concepts and practices of a cultural heritage.

Furthermore, where Heidegger sees in Plato the incipience of a dark age of *Seinsvergessenheit*, Gadamer finds in the Platonic dialogue an authentic mode for understanding the "thing itself," the subject matter of historical texts—which is the same subject matter for the present and future. Gadamer believes that a text is best read as a response to a question, so that the key to interpretation is an understanding of the question that the text presupposes.[1] Moreover, he suggests that the text is best regarded as a "thou," who is contemporaneous with the reader.[2] In this respect, Gadamer is more in agreement with Romantic hermeneutics, and with Schleiermacher especially, than with Dilthey, who thinks of the text as an object to be deciphered. However, where Schleiermacher takes dialogical understanding to be a reconstruction of the interlocutor's psychological processes, Gadamer insists that the dialogue provides an understanding of what the discussion is about. Rather than the genesis of the other's beliefs and assertions, Gadamer's hermeneutics seeks to understand the truth of their subject matter. Indeed, only through the mediation of the subject matter is mutual understanding possible between interlocutors.[3]

Although Dilthey begins from the premise of an affinity between a text and its interpreter, Gadamer believes that he betrayed this affinity by reducing it to a similarity between a subject and its object. Hence, says Gadamer, "in spite of the diversity of methods, the 'differences' with the natural sciences no longer exist—since in both cases we address questions to an object already fully present, to an object which contains every answer."[4] His objection is that Dilthey's distinction of a difference in method between the human and natural sciences precludes the question of method *per se*. Gadamer reasons that whatever says something to us speaks, and whatever speaks is ontologically the same as we ourselves. Following Heidegger, he finds in speaking a moment of belonging (*Zugehoerigkeit*), in which we are already claimed and constituted by/as a tradition, a tradition that is never, as such, objectifiable.[5] Thus, just as we cannot objectify ourselves insofar as we belong to and are a tradition, so too with the text. As something that speaks, it is inalienable from its tradition and its concomitant historicality. The dialogical model, then, does not alienate the affinity of belonging between the text and its reader, but preserves it from any objectifying moment.

Because Ricoeur seeks to continue the epistemological project of hermeneutics after Dilthey, he includes a moment of textual objectification within his more general theory of narrative. Ricoeur criticizes Heidegger and Gadamer for abandoning the epistemological project and giving philosophical hermeneutics over to what he takes to be a self-contained problematic, from which there is no way back to the legitimate methodological concerns of the human sciences.[6] An exclusively ontological hermeneutics, he believes, divorces philosophy from its integrative function and leaves the humanistic disciplines without a general hermeneutics to mediate their differences. Without such mediation, the human sciences are left to an irresolvable "conflict of interpretations."[7] Ricoeur accepts the proliferation of methods among the human sciences as fundamental to contemporary modernity, and sees here a challenge for philosophical hermeneutics and a possibility for the renewed relevance of philosophical discourse in general. By the same token, he believes that the narrative practices of history and fiction can resolve certain "aporias" concerning temporal experience that philosophy engenders. Philosophy, therefore, stands to gain by incorporating narrative practice within its own discourse.[8]

Although Ricoeur defends Dilthey's epistemological mission for hermeneutics against its radical ontologization in Heidegger and Gadamer, he differs from Dilthey on the issue of understanding and explanation. Where Dilthey insists upon a separation of the interpretive methods of the human sciences, grounded upon understanding (*Verstehen*), from the explanatory methods (*Erklaeren*) belonging to the natural sciences, Ricoeur believes that this opposition is no longer valid. He suggests that Dilthey's injunction against importing the methods of natural science into the humanistic disciplines can be observed without sacrificing the rigor of scientific explanation, as long as hermeneutics incorporates the methods of semiotics and structuralist linguistics. In this way, the text can become an object for explanation without becoming a "natural" object, since its explanation will be strictly linguistic rather than causal.[9] Ricoeur's difference with Dilthey is that he takes speech (discourse) to be the key to understanding, where the latter characterizes understanding as a mental intuition. Since structural linguistics became paradigmatic for the human sciences (at least in France), Ricoeur claims to have advanced beyond his predecessor by exploiting the new sense of explanation that modern linguistics makes available. Instead of simply opposing understanding and explanation, Ricoeur insists upon a dialectical relation between them.[10]

Ricoeur asserts that explanation is not only possible for the human sciences, but that a valid interpretation must include an explanatory moment. Conversely, however, textual explanation is bound to understanding, which is complete only in reference to a human self and its life-world.[11] The text is a moment of distanciation within a more general narrative model, a model that includes the subject as narrator/reader and which terminates in a re-constituted life-world that offers the subject new possibilities for being.[12] On Ricoeur's model, then, philosophical hermeneutics is a rehabilitation of the reflective tradition, and of Husserlian egology in particular.[13] Structural explanation, made possible by the distanciation of the text, is a critical moment that exposes the subject to the techniques of psychoanalysis and the critique of ideology.[14] These are for Ricoeur techniques for overcoming the naiveté of a first reading, or for exposing the illusion of false consciousness. Without such methods, he believes that hermeneutics would be given over to the self-validation of unconscious motives and concealed interests.

Where Ricoeur sees the methods of linguistic explanation as a weapon that hermeneutics can employ against false consciousness, Gadamer sees the subjugation of discourse to method *per se* as a capitulation to the unbridled calculative interest that prevails in the technological age.[15] Furthermore, he holds that

> The articulation of the world in which we live through
> language and communicative cooperation is neither a
> completely conventional dimension nor the residue of a
> perhaps false consciousness; it is constitutive of what is and
> is for the most part sure of its legitimacy precisely because
> it has to be assumed by every protest, contradiction, and
> critique.[16]

Thus the truth about ourselves is not revealed by a critical objectification of the text, with all its techniques of disillusionment and demystification. For Gadamer, the truth about ourselves is not a matter of reflective knowledge, and the achievement of self-understanding is not the constitution of a subject-ego. Indeed, Ricoeur's reflective tradition is implicated in the alienation and bureaucratization of life which hermeneutics is to oppose.[17]

Gadamer takes the Platonic dialogues to be exemplary for hermeneutic practice. In them, he maintains, we see Socrates giving himself over to the *logoi*, that is, to the meanings conveyed by words—the subject-matter of the discussion.[18] There is, however, another classical source for Gadamer's dialogical model: Aristotle's notion of practical judgment or *phronesis*.[19] Aristotle sets practical reason off against theoretical and productive reason (*theoreia* and *techne*), in that the latter are concerned with either the contemplation or methodological application of universal principles. *Phronesis*, on the other hand, is the non-methodological application of general principles to particular situations. While moral principles, like theoretical principles, can be taught, the application of moral principles is a matter of character, formed by cultural and social habituation (*ethos*). Since *phronesis* is an application of principles, it resembles *techne*, but where *techne* is guided by method and a pre-given object, practical reason is guided by the particulars of the situation, and has no pre-determined end. It must reconstitute itself in every concrete application. In this way, Gadamer views the dialogue as an application of traditional habituations (prejudices) to new and unpredictable situations.

The Platonic and Aristotelian antecedents to Gadamer are similar insofar as they are non-methodological. Where Aristotle opposes *phronesis* to *techne*, Plato opposes dialectic to the methods of rhetoric and mathematics. Gadamer interprets Plato's criticism of rhetoric as a response to the danger of sophism: the manipulation of the words, sounds and images of discourse, to the neglect of its subject-matter. The rhetorical *technai* of the sophists threaten to destroy understanding when they are employed for their manipulative power, rather than placed in the service of dialectic. Dialectic always attends to the thing itself, to that which discourse is about, rather than the means of saying it. Moreover, Plato also opposes dialectic to the deductive procedures of mathematics. Where mathematics proceeds from assumptions and definitions, dialectic questions everything. Nor is its questioning on a par with Cartesian doubt: it does not arrive at a moment of certainty that can serve as a foundation for an apodictic science. Rather, its truths are always open to further interpretation and revision.

Clearly, for Gadamer, Cartesianism is the sophism of the present age. The two ancient methodologies that Plato opposed to dialectic have joined forces: mathematical apodicticity now serves the interest of planning and calculation. As Heidegger had shown earlier, the technological control over human life is as anonymous as it is pervasive. Its unspoken, but imperative, interest is managerial control and systematic efficiency. It thus constitutes a kind of "bad faith" vis-à-vis the particularities of experience and the openness of understanding. Furthermore, Gadamer believes that the human sciences, insofar as they comprise a body of methods and techniques, are not distinguishable from technology and its totalizing agenda.[20] Philosophical hermeneutics, on the other hand, offers a more fundamental understanding of experience in terms of practical reason.[21] Here, experience does not terminate in a moment of reflective knowledge a *posteriori*, nor is it ruled by a reflective concept a *priori*, but remains open to *further experience.*[22]

Ricoeur, of course, believes that the methods of the human sciences can and must be incorporated into hermeneutics if the latter is to retain its epistemological relevance. Furthermore, since Ricoeur sees hermeneutics as a continuation of the tradition of reflection, in which self-knowledge is simultaneously the constitution of the subject as an ego, the critical methods of psychoanalysis and Neo-Marxism are needed to expose the illusions of subjectivity that would otherwise become self-validating in interpretation. For Ricoeur, the critique of subjectivity is possible only via the objectivity of the text. While Ricoeur agrees with Gadamer that text and reader belong together unreflectively, he insists that hermeneutics must overcome "mere belonging" through reflective distanciation.[23] Moreover, the encounter between reader and text, according to Ricoeur, is anything but dialogical. As he writes in *Interpretation Theory*: "The right of the reader and the right of the text converge in an important struggle that generates the whole dynamic of interpretation. Hermeneutics begins where dialogue ends."[24] And again, he says in "Appropriation" that "Nothing is less intersubjective or dialogical than the encounter with the text."[25] But here, as in his critique of "belonging," Ricoeur is already interpreting these notions in terms of the reflective tradition. This is clear where he characterizes "belonging" as an adherence to "lived experience," or *Erlebnis*.[26] In the reflective tradition, this is a purely epistemological term that denotes the foundation for objectivity. For Ricoeur, "lived experience" pertains to a prelinguistic noetic plane, corresponding to what Hegel calls the substance of objective spirit. This would include the unreflected heritage of customs, mores, practices, affections, etc., in relation to which Ricoeur believes linguistic meaning to be derivative. Gadamer, on the other hand, is careful to characterize experience as *Erfahrung*.[27] Unlike *Erlebnis*, *Erfahrung* includes a moral relation to an other, an other who speaks and calls upon us to respond.[28] Thus for Gadamer, experience is always already "linguistic," and does not constitute a substratum that is only brought to language reflectively and secondarily: the relation of belonging to a cultural heritage is itself thoroughly linguistic, and does not require a secondary act for its articulation.

For Ricoeur, dialogue is an exchange of speech acts between interlocutors, where meaning is determined by ostensive reference to things present in a shared "here" and "now."[29] Hence, the dialogical relation is not ontological; it is an epistemological relation between two subjects. Furthermore, according to Ricoeur, dialogue is derivative upon discourse. Following Benveniste, he describes discourse in terms of a linguistics whose basic unit is the sentence.[30] The sentence, in turn, refers to a speaker, a world that is spoken about, and an interlocutor to whom it is addressed. In addition, discourse is an event in time whose meaning must endure. The fleeting event itself is not understood: only what surpasses it is intelligible and can be historically handed down. This distanciation of meaning from event is precisely what Gadamer denies. For him, language is an emanation of the word (*verbum*), an event where meaning "occurs".[31] The word is a linguistic totality, from whose multiplicity all discursive speech is derived. It "emanates" through works, traditions and historical epochs. Hence, its historicality is of a different order than that of the sentence or narrative.

In Ricoeur's view, reading a text is not an instance of dialogue, for "the reader is absent from the act of writing; the writer is absent from the act of reading."[32] The text therefore replaces the relation that Gadamer seeks to preserve. However, although Ricoeur insists that the text surpasses the event of discourse, he agrees with Gadamer that the appropriation of the meaning of the text is historical. The difference is that for Ricoeur the text is not a "thou" for the reader, since the text is a distanciation of meaning from event.

Ricoeur also agrees with Gadamer that hermeneutics should not approach the text from a theoretical position à la Descartes. Like Gadamer, he appeals to Aristotle for an alternative to the Cartesian model of reason. The Cartesian model has prevailed in the reflective tradition as continued by Hegel and Husserl, but has also been sharply attacked by Freud, Marx and Nietzsche. In Aristotle's notion of *poiesis*, Ricoeur believes he has found a model of understanding that allows for the reflective constitution of the subject while accommodating the critical insights of the latter three thinkers. By appealing to productive reason, he hopes to mediate the opposition between the hermeneutics of belonging and the hermeneutics of suspicion. Working from Aristotle's discussion of tragedy in the *Poetics*, Ricoeur adapts the terms *poiesis* and *mimesis* to his own theory of narrative. These concepts of productive reason are "grafted" on to his appropriation of sentential linguistics and speech-act theory to achieve a dialectic between explanation and understanding.

In Ricoeur's formulation, a narrative is a larger unit of discourse analogous to the sentence.[33] Where the sentence refers to its speaker and to the world about which it says something, the narrative also refers to a speaker and a world. However, given the larger scale of the narrative and its distanciation, qua text, of meaning from event, its "speaker" is an idealized and imaginary subject rather than an existential individual. Moreover, the world of the narrative is not the world of immediate perception, but a world of imaginative possibilities that the reader understands as possibilities for being.[34]

Working from Aristotle, Ricoeur describes the act of narration as an "emplotment" (*mise en intrigue*), where characters and events are given a configuration within a whole.[35] The plot must have a beginning, middle and end, while the narrative text must be construed according to culturally sedimented rules of genre and composition. In keeping with the reflective tradition after Kant, Ricoeur characterizes emplotment as a power of schematization, albeit on a cultural-historical level. Furthermore, for Ricoeur, the intelligibility of the narrative "has more to do with imagination than with reason."[36] For him, Kant's notion of productive imagination is restored to its praxical, rather than theoretical, sense. Since the schematism of productive imagination is part of the unreflected historical tradition, the most characteristic narratives are "anonymous"—the individual identities of their authors are irrelevant, even when known.

With his shift from theoretical to productive reason, Ricoeur characterizes understanding a narrative text as a reconstruction of the operations that produced it.[37] To do this we must, in a sense, "know" the plot. The sense of closure afforded by the plot is such that we already understand the events of the story to be leading to a certain end or outcome, an outcome that need only be acceptable rather than logically necessary. Beyond the moment of emplotment, Ricoeur argues that the narrative refers back to the pre-given world of action, from out of which the text was produced. On the other side, the narrative, as a work, refigures the world of action as a world of possibilities that a reader might appropriate. There are, then, three moments of understanding on the narrative model: pre-figuration, configuration (emplotment) and refiguration. Each corresponds, in turn, to a moment of *mimesis*.[38]

Ricoeur characterizes *mimesis* as a presentation of action. This holds not only for the action of the poet, but also for the world of action from which the plot emerges, and the transfigured world of action that is afforded to the reader through appropriation. Hence Ricoeur speaks of a three-fold *mimesis*, in which the pre-reflective understanding of the world of action (*mimesis* 1) and the appropriative refiguration of that world as a world of possibilities for being (*mimesis* 3), are mediated by the objective moment of the text (*mimesis* 2). In this way, Ricoeur expands his reading of Aristotle via Hegel. Having alienated itself in the text, the subject returns to its life-world, now developed and transformed, in a moment of appropriation.[39] Of course, the text can be read and re-read, with the possibility of new appropriations in each case. Contra Hegel, there is no final *Aufhebung* or total appropriation, and so the reading subject never fully recovers itself from the alienation of the text. Its self-interpretation, or self-constitution, is an infinite task.

Thus, while Gadamer and Ricoeur agree that hermeneutical understanding is always self-understanding, their notions of the self and its constitution are not reducible to one another. This is evident in their different adaptations of Aristotle.

Gadamer emphasizes *phronesis* as the paradigm for hermeneutical understanding. Through *phronesis* the self is constituted in its moral character (*ethos*). As the practice of moral reason, *phronesis* involves an other or others with whom I interact, and whose claims upon me cannot be codified into a set of rules or laws. On the contrary, moral judgment is specific to each situation and its application cannot be guided by any schema or concept. *Phronesis* remains open to the contingencies of experience. The moral self, therefore, is nothing definite or fixed: it is a general disposition to act that is reconstituted in every concrete application. Strictly speaking, then, the moral self has no individual identity. It is an habituated openness that is always in transition. Although this seems close to what Ricoeur has in mind, and although he suggests that the intelligibility of the plot "neighbors" on *phronesis*[40], his emphasis upon productive reason leads to a different notion of the self.

True to the reflective tradition, identity rather than character is the issue for Ricoeur. Though Ricoeur agrees that we belong ontologically to the world of action and to a tradition, he emphasizes the individuation of the subject through the production and appropriation of the text as an individual work.[41] The moment of individuation does not follow from moral reason, but from productive reason (*poiesis, technē*). Indeed, for Ricoeur, the text is discourse that has been worked upon and given shape according to the rules of genre, etc.[42] As a linguistic work, the text is an individual—a singular totality, with a circular relation of parts to the whole.[43] This circularity, or closure, is provided by the plot. We understand the work insofar as we understand the end in the beginning and vice versa. This teleological feature reflects the nature of productive reason. For Aristotle, *techne* is the application of rules of action to achieve a pre-given end, and involves judgment only as to the choice of means. This sets *techne* off from *phronesis*, for it indicates a closure of purpose that is absent in moral judgment. *Poiesis*, the highest form of *techne*, is distinguished by its mimetic function. *Mimesis*, however, is predetermined by its object: nature. By substituting "action" for "nature" in his own discourse, Ricoeur does not thereby render *mimesis* free from its predetermined end. The individuality of the self as an agent is its end and standard for coherence. For Ricoeur, the production and appropriation of the text constitutes the self as an individual, i.e., as a singular totality. To understand one's self is, in this sense, to have an identity. Ricoeur characterizes identity in practical, rather than logical or theoretical terms: the subject understands itself as an agent who has acted or can act in certain ways.[44] It can thus understand itself as morally responsible for those actions, etc. But this is the responsibility of an individual agent, and pertains to a reflective conception of moral reason. It is, in fact, derivative upon the productive reason that forms the singular totality of the text.

Of course, the identity of the subject is not fixed, but enlarged through the encounter with the text.[45] The reader experiences an imaginative variation upon his or her ego by playing the role of subject to the text's ideal meaning. As Ricoeur says: "it is always a question of entering into an alien work, of divesting oneself of the earlier 'me' in order to receive, as in play, the self conferred by the work itself."[46] Insofar as appropriation is tantamount to a return of meaning to the event of speech, however, it can never exhaust the possibilities of its object. The reading subject cannot make the meaning of the text entirely its own: reading is temporal and processive, the ideal meaning of the text is not. Nonetheless, the ideality of meaning accomplished by the text provides a teleological ground for the process through which the subject comes to know, and to be, itself.

On Gadamer's model, there is no distanciation of meaning from event. Rather, meaning itself is temporal and processive. As the subject-matter of the dialogue between text and reader, meaning is produced in an event of disclosure, not as something fixed by the text, i.e., not as an ideal object, but as a third moment that neither the reader nor the text already contains. As Gadamer writes in *Truth and Method*:

> In as much as the tradition is newly expressed in language, something comes into being that had not existed before and that exists from now on. We can illustrate this by any historical example. Whether what is handed down is a poetic work of art or tells us of a great event, in each case

73

what is transmitted emerges newly into existence just as it presents itself. It is not being-in-itself that is increasingly revealed when Homer's *Iliad* or Alexander's *Indian Campaign* speaks to us in the new appropriation of tradition but, as in genuine conversation, something emerges that is contained in neither of the partners by himself.[47]

Thus for Gadamer appropriation itself produces meaning, where for Ricoeur appropriation actualizes a meaning already produced. Moreover, in Gadamer the production of meaning is, in an important sense, non-teleological; it is not an instance of *techne*. Rather, production is derivative upon *phronesis* and so remains without a predetermined end. Nor is understanding a matter of relating the parts of a text to the whole, or the text to the reader or author. For Gadamer, the "hermeneutic circle" relates the thing itself to the process of dialogue between the text and reader. This helps to account for the differing notions of historicality at work in narrative and dialogue, respectively.

Gadamer and Ricoeur agree that interpretation is temporal, and that the best model for hermeneutic understanding is the one most adequate to the experience of time. However, both are aware that time is a deeply contentious issue in the philosophical tradition. Indeed, the tradition is in many ways one of difference over the nature of time and its intelligibility.

Gadamer suggests that one of our most fundamental experiences of time is that of a discontinuity, or a becoming-other.[48] This stands in contrast to the "flowing" nature of time, thematized by Aristotle and Augustine, that has dominated the Western tradition. According to Gadamer, there are at least three "epochal" experiences that introduce temporal discontinuity into our self-understanding.[49] First, there is the experience of old age, which occurs as a sudden revelation rather than a gradual progression. Second is the transition from one generation to another, often accompanied by revolution or dynastic succession. Finally, there is what Gadamer calls the "absolute epoch." This is a reference to the new age occasioned by the advent of Christianity, where history itself is understood in a new sense. Where the Greeks understood history "only as a deviation from the order of things," the Christian believes that "there is no recognizable order within history, but there is an order of provi-

AYLESWORTH

dence, a plan of salvation."[50] For Gadamer, the absolute epoch
is not the Christian understanding of history, so much as the
break that this understanding represents in relation to the classical view. Indeed, he indicts the modern result of the Christian
position: it has led to the technological conception of the future
as plannable and controllable.[51] The epochal understanding of
time that Gadamer wishes to develop opposes this secular result
of Christianity, and he looks to Hölderlin for an alternative.

In the essay "Concerning Empty and Ful-Filled Time," he
states: "An epoch-making event establishes a caesure. It establishes that which preceded as old, and everything which now
comes as new."[52] Gadamer characterizes the epochal experience
as a transition that simultaneously separates and conjoins past
and future. It is both a departing and a beginning "that brings
the flow of time to a standstill."[53] Here, he develops his understanding of transition through a reading of Hölderlin's essay
"Über das Werden im Vergehen." He finds in Hölderlin an experience of the "now" that breaks up the double-relative "now" of
classical ontology, which is a dialectical mediation of the old and
the new. Hölderlin's notion of transition is distinguished from
the classical view in that it is not both a passing away and a
developing at the same time, but "the new comes to be as the
old is recollected in dissolution."[54] In recollection, the dissolution
of the old becomes *ideal*, i.e., an opening of possibilities for the
new. Thus one must take leave of the past in order to have a
future, and the moment of leave-taking, or recollection, is a
discontinuity in the flow of time. This break makes possible a
new totality of relations—a new world.

The notion of ideality at work here is to be distinguished from
that in Ricoeur. For the latter, ideality pertains to an atemporal
objectification of meaning that is accomplished when discourse
is fixed in writing. Following Hölderlin, Gadamer characterizes
ideality as an event, albeit an event that interrupts the serial flow
of time. Though it occasions a rupture and a break in time, the
ideal for Gadamer is not an atemporal objectification, and it does
not entail the critical distance from temporality that is so crucial
for Ricoeur. It is, instead, an opening within temporality itself.
Such an event is occasioned by the poetic word, which dissolves
language in its conventional forms and opens the possibility for
saying something new. For Gadamer, the word calls upon us to

75

take leave of our "prejudices and prior attitudes" and to hold ourselves open to the future, which is yet indeterminate.[55] Gadamer believes that a word from the historical tradition addresses us in the same way. Language provides the continuity of the tradition along with the discontinuity of the epoch. This means that language is fulfilled when "one word yields another," i.e., in the give-and-take of a dialogue. As dialogue, the event of discourse carries within itself the possibility of overcoming prejudice and arbitrariness in interpretation. The surpassing of prejudice is not predicated upon an objective meaning, but an openness to the new. The word is both a fusion of horizons between epochs and an epochal event itself. The achievement of continuity among previously discontinuous moments is something "new," and thus presents a discontinuity of its own. In this way, the dialogical process remains open and without a preordained end. Ricoeur, on the other hand, insists that "the objectification of meaning is a necessary mediation between the writer and reader."[56] Moreover, his treatment of temporality is derived from the very sources that Gadamer rejects.

Ricoeur argues that temporality must be understood as a dialectic between "lived time," as in Augustine, and "cosmological time," as in Aristotle. The problematic he develops is precisely an attempt to think time as a succession or "flow." In the third volume of *Time and Narrative*, Ricoeur claims that Augustine's attempt to derive the measurement of time from the distension of the soul, and thus to derive cosmological time from lived time, is unsuccessful.[57] It fails because the object whose duration is to be measured must be passively received by the mind through an impression. The impression is the focal point for the relations of "before" and "after," without which the three ecstases (past, present, future) of the soul would have no common reference. On the other hand, Aristotle's attempt to think time in terms of cosmic motion also fails. Ricoeur argues that the motion of the universe requires the presence of the soul in order to introduce the distinction of past, present, and future into the undifferentiated continuity of movement. Thus Ricoeur concludes: "the problem of time cannot be attacked from a single side only, whether of the soul or of movement. The distension of the soul alone cannot produce the extension of time; the dynamism of movement cannot generate the dialectic of the threefold present."[58] This relation between lived time and cosmic time, he argues, continues to operate in the works of Kant, Husserl and Heidegger.[59]

For his part, Ricoeur proposes to "resolve" the dialectic of lived time and cosmic time productively, via narration. Historical narrative, in particular, can mediate between them according to the scheme he develops in the third volume of *Time and Narrative*.[60] Historicality, he believes, is the bridge between lived time and the time of the external world.

There are three features of historical time that allow for its mediating role. First, history is narrated chronologically, via references to specific dates and places. The specificity of chronological time is accomplished in its relation of physical occurrences to lived events. Second, historical narrative involves a relation of contemporaneity between the private time of an individual and the public time shared anonymously with one's generation. The individual is thus joined to the succession of generations on the cultural-historical level. Third, the historian follows the traces of collective memory in documents, archives, monuments, etc. The trace, for Ricoeur, is an effect-sign. It brings together relations of causality and significance, pertaining to cosmological movement and lived presence, respectively. Besides these relations of succession, the trace also indicates something essentially and irrevocably absent. "The trace signifies without making appear."[61] In this sense, the trace constitutes a relation to what lies beyond the temporal order per se, that is, to eternity.

For Ricoeur, the relation of time to its "other" is a relation of significance, a function of lived time and its structures. On his reading, fictional narratives offer imaginative variations upon these structures and their aporias.[62] These include variations upon the "fault" between lived time and cosmic time, and the hierarchization of temporal modalities within lived presence, for whom eternity is the upper limit. Ricoeur interprets *Mrs. Dalloway, The Magic Mountain* and *Remembrance of Things Past* as exemplary instances of fictional narrative vis-à-vis these relations.[63]

Furthermore, he argues that, where phenomenology fails, fiction can make time "appear" through mythologization or personification,[64] achieving a material representation of time via imagination rather than perception. A fictive construction can stand in for a missing intuition.

Ricoeur's culminating thesis is that there is an intersection (*l'entrecroisement*) between history and fiction. Just as fiction can provide a poetic construction in place of a perception, there is a fictive element in history, since the historical past is, strictly speaking, non-observable.[65] History presents a past that "has been" as if it were present—a function of poetic imagination. Moreover, fictive narration imitates history, in that it presents events as if they had happened, i.e., as if they occurred in the past.[66] This intersection between history and fiction constitutes what Ricoeur calls "human time" (*le temps humain*) from where an historical consciousness might develop, for whom time can be understood as a singular totality.[67] Only thus, as historical consciousness, can there be a *self*-consciousness.

However, in keeping with the reflective tradition, Ricoeur insists that time can be understood only if we can think its limit, namely, eternity. While fictional narrative can "present" eternity through mythologization and personification, there is no end to the possible worlds for whom it is the limit. There is no totality of possible representations of time and its other. Thus, time remains inscrutable because eternity escapes the totalization and closure of any particular narrative.[68] The representation of time as a singular totality is inachievable, yet it is the guiding end for *poiesis*.

The theological import of Ricoeur's position is quite evident. Clearly, eternity is the ideal *telos* of historical consciousness and the identity of the individual. Its analogue is the meaning fixed by the text, ideally separated from the flux and contingencies of time. Although unrealizable, the anticipation of eternity must promise the ultimate coherence of narrative and the final determination of individual identity, whose eschatological significance cannot be denied. This result, along with the entire problematic of lived time and cosmic time, contrasts with Gadamer's exposition of the epoch within the context of Neo-Platonic and Romantic ontology.

Gadamer, too, includes eternity as a backdrop for his thesis on epochal discontinuity. However, he declares that "I will try to adhere to the fact that time is conceived from the perspective of the world's life-time and to keep aloof from all implications which intend an eternity that would no longer be temporality."[69] Instead, he develops a notion of "organic time," based upon Plotinus' reading of Plato's *Timaeus*, and extended by von Baader and Schelling. On this view, organic time is conceived as the *Aion*, or 'the temporal structure of that which endures as one and the same in every alteration and articulation of life's phases, namely liveliness."[70] The *Aion* is the duration of the life of the universe, and constitutes an immanent eternity within the "flow" of time. Gadamer insists that the self-sameness of an identical ego is not the issue here, for "*Aion* is . . . the complete identity of life within itself, which fulfills the present by the constant virtuality of its possibilities."[71] Thus the *Aion* is not conceived as an individual organism, with its circular relation of parts to whole, but as the self-sameness of life without the continuity of an ego. Here, there is no dialectic between lived time and cosmic time, as in Ricoeur. Organic time does not differentiate between the soul and the cosmos; it is a continuity that is prior to their reflective difference.

Eternity, for Gadamer, is not a principle of individuation, nor is it an atemporal limit within which time must be understood. It is an immanent continuity that makes possible the fusion of horizons between epochs, without subsuming epochal disconti- nuity to a parts-whole dialectic. Its analogue is the emanation of the "word," the process through which one word emerges from another. This process is non-totalizing and non-teleological; it is, instead, a pluralizing movement in which the "one" becomes "many," where each word is the "whole" and not merely "part" of an ideal totality. Each word is complete in itself, yet, because of its temporality, its meaning is realized only in its historical application. Hence organic time, as developed by Gadamer, makes for the continuity of discourse without reflecting that continuity into the identity of an ego.

The differences between Gadamer and Ricoeur as to the nature of temporality and understanding are of a piece with their respec- tive anxieties over the role of hermeneutics in relation to the human sciences and the dominant position of science and its methods in contemporary life.

Ricoeur is anxious about the "irrelevance" of a discourse that does not appreciate the epistemological and praxical legitimacy of methods and techniques that have developed independently of any ontological grounding. Furthermore, he believes that any such grounding must be *constructed* from the various discourses as they are, that no mediating ground between discourses can be supposed *a priori*. He is concerned that a philosophical hermeneutics that is already and exclusively ontological would become just another self-contained discourse, and thus part of the proliferation of discourses that philosophy is supposed to ameliorate. Philosophical hermeneutics is, for him, a secondary act that mediates the differences between the discourses of the human sciences, and it is predicated upon the de facto legitimacy of those discourses as it finds them.

Moreover, Ricoeur's philosophical hermeneutics is an act of reflection upon the works of the human self, and is an attempt, on a cultural-historical level, to recover the self from its dispersion among an otherwise bewildering plethora of languages, signs, symbols and texts. As he remarks in *Freud and Philosophy*, *"Reflection is the appropriation of our effort to exist and of our desire to be, through the works which bear witness to that effort and desire."*[72] He thus understands hermeneutics as an appropriation of the "will to be," and for him this means the will to be an *individual*. The unity and closure of an individuated ego is therefore the ideal telos that guides hermeneutical practice and its mediating constructions.

Gadamer, on the other hand, is anxious about the technological co-option of any discourse that is methodological in nature. He is concerned that a methodological hermeneutics would become implicated in an instrumental totalization of experience, such that openness to the new, and thus the authentic recovery of the past, is precluded. He believes that the integration of the discourses of the sciences is achieved, if at all, through their rootedness in a common context of experience. This context, more basic than any epistemology, is ideally one of "solidarity" in the moral-political sense.[73] Thus philosophical hermeneutics must distinguish itself from the methodological disciplines, rather than perform a secondary mediation at their own level of discourse. As he states in "Hermeneutics and Social Science":

Both rhetoric and the transmission of scientific knowledge are monological in form; both need the counterbalance of hermeneutical appropriation, which works in the form of dialogue. And precisely and especially practical and political reason can only be realized and transmitted dialogically. I think, then, that the chief task of philosophy is to justify this way of reason and to defend practical and political reason against the domination of technology based on science.[74]

Gadamer is not concerned to demonstrate how epistemological-technological discourses are grounded upon a more basic, ontological, understanding, for any such demonstration must be guided by method. He is willing to risk "epistemological irrelevance" in order to preserve a discursive domain apart from technological totalization, a domain that he believes all other discourses must presuppose.

For Gadamer, philosophical hermeneutics is not an attempt to recover an individual "self" from the proliferation of discourses, but the preservation of a level of discourse that is ultimately self-less. On his model, the philosophical appropriation of texts is not a "becoming self" but a "becoming other." It is not a reflective recovery of the desire to be, but a response to a question, that is, the question of the subject-matter of the historical tradition. That subject matter is, of course, we ourselves. But our identity is not fixed in eternity, it is instead the continuity of our becoming-other in every response, in every application of the preunderstanding that we have of ourselves in new and unpredictable situations.

Chapter 5

THE DIALECTICAL UNITY OF HERMENEUTICS: ON RICOEUR AND GADAMER

Leonard Lawlor

Unlike the numerous comparative readings of Ricoeur and Gadamer, Aylesworth's paper, "Dialogue, Text, Narrative," presents them in striking opposition. Within their overlapping themes and projects he uncovers differences in their views of the human sciences, the text, dialogue, technology, the subject, and reflection. It is only because Aylesworth has focused the difference between Ricoeur and Gadamer in its sharpest resolution that we can examine their unity more precisely here. Their unity lies in the attempt to recover, from the Greeks and Hegel, the dialectical nature of understanding (*MV*, pp. 40–43, 292–93; *HHS*, p. 132; *TM*, pp. 407–08; *HD*, pp. 32–34). The perfection or purpose (*telos*) of the understanding and interpretation of linguistic expression lies in making something present. As both have pointed out, the nature of hermeneutical experience is presentation (*HHS*, p. 193; *TM*, p. 410). *Darstellung* consists of a differentiating event in which something that remains the same, the *Sache*, for Gadamer (*TM*, p. 363), *l'intenté*, for Ricoeur (*MV*, p. 74), comes to presence. The interplay of event and repetition, difference and sameness, is indicated, for Ricoeur and Gadamer, by the "fundamental metaphoric," by the poetizing, that animates language (*MV*, p. 22; *TM*, pp. 75, 429).

What I shall try to show therefore is that *both* Ricoeur and Gadamer think sameness and difference *together* in the notion of presentation. Taking Ricoeur and Gadamer in turn, I am going to proceed in two steps. In Ricoeur, I shall focus on what he calls the "dialectic of event and meaning," the basis of his metaphor theory. Then in Gadamer I shall focus on the dialectical process of concept formation, the basis of his claims about the poetical word. When one examines Ricoeur's dialectic of event and meaning and Gadamer's concept formation, one sees that both these notions oppose the type of teleology in which a pre-existing, static meaning encloses the process of understanding from the outside. This type of teleology is not found in either Ricoeur or Gadamer.[1] Metaphorizing keeps language incomplete and open. Nevertheless for both, understanding exhibits a "naive" teleology (*TM*, pp. 453, 459; cf. *MV*, p. 40). The dialectic which is language points to presentation as the nature of language. Thus we shall see finally that the dialectical unity of hermeneutics is presence.

I

As is well known, Ricoeur opposes the reduction of language, as in French structuralism, to differentially determined codes or synchronic systems.[2] The problem, for Ricoeur, is not the universal structure of language, but communication (*HHS*, p. 131). How is it possible for particular linguistic systems to bridge the gap between humans? In order to answer this question, Ricoeur appropriates the structural linguistic notion of message (*INT*, pp. 2–6; *MV*, pp. 66–69). What the structuralists call message Ricoeur calls discourse. Ricoeur does not, however, simply identify the message with discourse. Rather, discourse is what takes place *between* speaker and hearer. This "between" is nothing other than dialogue. Discourse consists therefore in what Ricoeur calls a "dialectic of event and meaning" (*INT*, pp. 8–12; *MV*, pp. 70–72; *HHS*, pp. 132–36).

Discourse can be characterized as an event because discourse possesses temporal existence. Temporal existence gives discourse "ontological priority" over the codes, which, having no existence apart from their actualization in speech, possess only "virtual existence" (*INT*, p. 9; *MV*, p. 70). Ricoeur clarifies the event's temporal existence by saying in *The Rule of Metaphor* that "The present is the very moment at which discourse is being uttered. This is the present of discourse. By means of the present, discourse qualifies itself temporally" (*MV*, p. 75; cf. *HHS*, p. 133; *PPR*, p. 114). The temporal existence of the discursive event then is the *present*.

Discursive presence implies that every discourse is singular or unique and whole (*INT*, pp. 9–11). An utterance (or a dialogue or a text) is discrete, because the discursive event is always innovative (*PPR*, p. 111). Ricoeur recognizes that ordinary conversation must repeat codified formulas such as a word's polysemy (*HHS*, p. 133). Every discourse, however, is prevented from being a mere repetition of the codes, a mere message, by linguistic units called shifters or indexicals (*INT*, p. 13). As the name "shifter" indicates, words such as "I" have no permanent meaning. Their sense *shifts* with every occasion. Thus, according to Ricoeur, their function lies in referring the entire discourse back to whoever is speaking at this moment, to "me, here and now" (*INT*, pp. 13–19; *HHS*, p. 135; *MV*, pp. 72–73). A discourse is a whole because the discursive event consists of sentences. A sentence (and any larger unit composed out of sentences such as dialogues or texts) results from synthesizing activity and thus consists of a synthetic "configuration" or structure (*INT*, p. 11; *MV*, p. 70).[3] In fact, in a sentence's synthetic structure, for Ricoeur, one cannot even actually speak of separable parts. The sentence simply forms a discrete whole unit (*INT*, p. 10; *MV*, p. 179). Because every discourse is singular and whole, it is, for Ricoeur, understandable or intelligible.[4] In ordinary conversation, the singularity and wholeness of the utterance provides a "code" of pertinence that directs the hearer to "screen" unintended polysemy (*MV*, pp. 130–31, 151–52; *PPR*, pp. 126–27; *INT*, pp. 16–17). Univocity, the "work" of all understanding for Ricoeur, is then achieved (*RM*, p. 302; *HHS*, p. 44; *PPR*, p. 127).

In metaphorical discourse, understanding achieves the same aim of univocity in a somewhat different way. Unlike ordinary discourse, metaphorical discourse is not simply singular, but novel (*MV*, pp. 130–33, 154; *PPR*, pp. 131–32; *HHS*, p. 169).[5] Even as it appropriates words' polysemy and certain literary forms or genres, a "living metaphor" leaps away from these codes in the present instance. Although polysemy always exhibits a certain outline of order which provides a trajectory for the poet, he or she nevertheless breaks away from the trajectory (*MV*, p. 299). The poet breaks the rules, creates a novel sentential configuration in which none of the appropriated words' accepted meanings are pertinent (*INT*, p. 50; *HHS*, p. 174; *MV*, p. 151). A poem at first glance therefore appears to be nonsense because its sentential configuration is radically singular, radically discrete. Someone who reads a poem then must treat it entirely in terms of its novelty, not in terms of the genres to which it may allude. On the basis of its novel whole configuration, the reader must *create* meanings for the appropriated words. Such a creation comes about by imaginatively searching for a new similarity among the possible meanings accepted for the words (*MV*, p. 214).[6] In discovering this similarity, the reader therefore creates a meaning for the metaphor as a whole which never before existed in any linguistic code. This new meaning saves the poem from being hopelessly impertinent. Thus, when the reader saves the poem from nonsense, he or she attempts to determine the poem univocally. Although metaphorical interpretation, like ordinary understanding, directs itself at one unified and identical meaning, it is nevertheless, for Ricoeur, an event in the strongest sense: a discontinuity or deviation (*écart*). As Ricoeur would say, it productively overcomes distanciation in appropriation; it makes the new meaning present (*HHS*, p. 132).

This analysis of Ricoeur's discursive event does not fully disclose its dialectical nature. The event's dialecticity comes to light, for Ricoeur, when one considers its meaning, what Ricoeur calls *"l'intenté"* or *"the said"* (*HHS*, p. 134). The event, being temporal or present, is transitory and vanishes. The meaning (or configuration), however, is *omnitemporal*, reidentifiable across time, repeatable. Appropriating Husserl, Ricoeur says that meaning is an ideality (*INT*, pp. 20, 90; *PPR*, p. 114; *HHS*, pp. 134–35, 184; *MV*, p. 174). Ricoeur's appropriation of Husserl is entirely compatible with discourse's dialecticity.[7] As he says in *The Rule of Metaphor*,

> Such, then is the instance of discourse: an event which is eminently repeatable. This is why this trait [of discourse] can be mistaken for an element of *langue*; but what we have here is the repeatability of an event, not of an element of a system. (*MV*, p. 70)

This is not the repeatability of an ideal *form*, like a code, but that of the original expressed *content*, the same event of meaning.

Meaning achieves universality by cancelling and preserving the event's singularity (*IT*, p. 12).

Following Husserl, Ricoeur sees ideal meaning as an Idea in the Kantian sense.[8] Husserl articulates Idea in the Kantian sense most precisely in relation to the sense of a physical thing.[9] Even if consciousness were infinite (even if we could imagine God's consciousness), a physical thing's sense would still be presented finitely. Essentially, the sense of a physical thing can be given only in perspectives, in what Husserl calls "closed appearances." Although the sense is essentially incomplete, its "Idea," its kernel of sameness, comes to presence in its own type of evidence. Our intuition of an Idea is an insight, a finite insight, into the Idea's infinite repeatability (sameness) *and* infinite possibility of redetermination and reversal (difference). In short, the evidence of an Idea in the Kantian sense is an insight into its incompleteness. This insight predesignates or prescribes the *task* of completeness. The "Idea," being infinitely repeatable, is open to progressive determination. The Idea in the Kantian sense, therefore, is teleological in a very precise sense. Although the Idea is irreducibly incomplete, the evidence of the Idea presents merely a direction for possible completeness.

For Ricoeur, meaning, as an Idea in the Kantian sense, is infinitely repeatable (the same) and limitlessly plurivocal (different). It is open to constant redetermination, renewal, more events. Meaning never stands outside the process of time and interpretation. Because of the "structure" of meaning, Ricoeur always qualifies his claims about univocity. He always says that the communicated meaning is "relatively univocal" (*PPR*, p. 127; *HHS*, p. 44). There is, for Ricoeur, always a certain overabundance of meaning which outstrips any attempt to understand it. Every dialogue is incomplete. Yet, any experience of meaning overcomes distanciation in an insight. This insight is the experience of meaning as a horizon, that is, its infinite repeatability (sameness) and infinite novelty (difference) (*INT*, p. 93). Understanding therefore exhibits a "naive" teleology. It always *aims* at univocity, at complete determination, at perfect presence.[10]

II

As is well known, any experience of language, for Gadamer, is an event. According to Gadamer, anyone who speaks directs his or her speaking towards what is particular or occasional in the dialogical situation. In doing so, the speaker, however, must conform his or her speech to the universality of the pre-established meanings of words. This conformation does not imply simple repetition. In the occasionality of the speaking event the intended universal meaning (or concept) is, according to Gadamer, "enriched by the transient intuition of the thing, so that what emerges finally is a new, more specific word formation that does more justice to the intuited thing [*Sache*]" (*TM*, pp. 428–29). In speaking therefore the word not only participates in the universal, but also comes to participate in the particular of the situation. For Gadamer, enrichment and novelty take place not only in speaking and hearing, but also and especially in the production and interpretation of works of art and poetry. This process, in which the universal meanings of words are particularized or differentiated, is what Gadamer calls concept formation, "in which the life of a language develops" (*TM*, p. 429).

With concept formation, Gadamer appropriates three Hegelian insights. First, all thought, in order to be itself, must be expressed in statements, poetic words, works of art, in language in general. The fundamental shortcoming of all philosophic speculation prior to Hegel lies in "the untruth of pure inwardness" (*HD*, p. 32; *TM*, p. 467). Thought, the universal applicability of concepts to the world, must present itself in a statement in order to demonstrate its truth or validity. The statement, or expression, is the presentation (*Darstellung*) of the infinite in the finite. The word is the *actualization* (*Wirklichkeit*) of the speculative (*HD*, p. 32). Second, in the movement of language generalization and concretization (or differentiation) of concepts take place (*HD*, pp. 13–14). Presentation is the event of this differentiation. Third, the finite form of the presentation or expression can mislead. The word's permeability permits sophistical utilizations. Thus, in Hegel (as in Plato and Aristotle), thought occurs only when one attends not to the associative senses that cling to any word, but to the thing itself (*HD*, p. 25). In presentation, the word or statement disappears before what is presented or expressed.

Unlike Hegel's subjective interpretation of dialectic, concept formation for Gadamer does not imply an absolute beginning. The process is not simple passage from potency to act, from a perfected thought or pre-existent universal to speech in the here and now (*TM*, pp. 423–24). Gadamer points out that even internal thought is a process (an emanation). Thinking (not thought) is irreducibly mixed with memory (*TM*, p. 425). Memory does not function as some sort of "treasure chest" from which perfected thoughts can be "plundered." Rather, it presents an aspect to which or from which thinking can turn as the thought comes about. When externalized, the word reflects and continues this process. As Gadamer says, speech "is the fulfillment [*Vollzug*] of knowledge itself. Thus, the word is simultaneous with formation [*formatio*] of the intellect" (*TM*, p. 424).

Concept formation also does not imply an absolute end. The Greek idea of *techne* (as Aylesworth points out well) lies behind the standard concept of teleology. In the *technai* the concept of a product must pre-exist the actual production. Without this concept, it would be impossible to determine the means necessary to produce that product (Cf. *TM*, p. 459). In language (and in history), however, no such concept pre-exists (Cf. *TM*, pp. 342–43, 346).[11] The infinite applicability of concepts (or, to be more Hegelian, of the concept) implies the infinity or the openness of presentation (*HD*, p. 33). Language remains available for everyone to use in unforeseen ways. The future is unpredictable. More events can happen. Hermeneutical experience therefore, according to Gadamer, discloses and recognizes an "unclosable openness" in its own process. Because of this "unclosable openness," the Hegelian type of "circular perfection" (*runde Vollendung*) in which beginning and end are mutually determined is forbidden (*TM*, p. 472).

The lack of "circular perfection," however, does not stop Gadamer from asserting some sort of perfection for hermeneutical experience. Gadamer asserts that not only in hermeneutical experience, but in all experience, something can occur that marks the experience as "genuine" or "authentic" (*echte* or *eigentliche*) (*TM*, pp. 355–58, 362). Authentic experience, for Gadamer, possesses not only the recognition of what really is at this moment, but also the recognition of the future's ambiguous openness. The future not only provides the time for the successful completion of plans, but also contains the unknown that makes the success of all plans uncertain (*TM*, p. 357). Any plan can fail; prediction is limited. Authentic experience is, as Gadamer says, the insight into "human finitude" (*TM*, p. 358). This insight forms the basis of what is meant with the phrase, "experienced person." The experienced person has suffered. On the basis of prior experiences, this person now lets himself be open for new and more experience. He or she is "radically undogmatic" (*TM*, p. 355). As Gadamer says, "The dialectic of experience has its own perfection [*Vollendung*] not in closed knowledge, but in that openness to experience that is encouraged by experience itself" (*TM*, p. 355). In hermeneutical experience, the parallel to this openness is the insight that language remains. More events can always reverse any particular understanding. Within this insight, however, something else can happen. Gadamer speaks of "an absolute perfection [*Perfektion*] of the word, inasmuch as no sensible relation, i.e. no gap, exists between the word's sensible appearance and its meaning" (*TM*, p. 410). In other words, the perfection of the word is an image, not a copy or a sign (Cf. *TM*, pp. 117, 134–144); or, better still, it is a presentation (*TM*, p. 410). As image, the word possesses a sort of tangibility or sensibility that can be cancelled. When the listener (or reader) attends only to the thing itself and not to the significations associated with the sensible word, then the word's tangible quality "disappears" (*TM*, pp. 398, 473–74). As Gadamer says, "the word is a process in which the unity of what is meant is brought to perfect [*vollendenten*] expression" (*TM*, p. 434). Perfection as disappearance here means that the word, on the one hand, brings about a creative event in which a new determination of the thing or meaning discloses itself. On the other, it presents finitely or sensibly what is infinite, universal, or intelligible (*TM*, p. 473). Presentation does not imply that the insight of the experienced person is overcome. It is the perfect understanding of a finite person into the thing itself (Cf. *TM*, p. 473).

Thus, we can say paradoxically that the perfection of experience in general and hermeneutical experience in particular, for Gadamer, lies in the insight into its irreducible imperfection (Cf. *TM*, p. 425). Nevertheless, this insight occurs only when the sensible word disappears and the thing itself comes to presence in a new determination. This sort of "double perfection" of the finite and the infinite gives hermeneutics its precise task. The purpose (*Zweck*) of hermeneutics lies in unlocking a "whole of sense" without forgetting that understanding is always partial (Cf. *TM*, pp. 459, 471). In order to illuminate the nature of perfect hermeneutical experience, Gadamer ultimately returns to Plato (*TM*, p. 477):

> The idea of the beautiful is truly present [*wahrhaft anwesend*], whole and undivided, in what is beautiful. . . . Presence [*Anwesenheit*] belongs in a convincing way to the being of the beautiful. . . . In the use of words what is intuitively given is not put at our disposal as a particular case of the universal, rather in being said it is itself made present [*gegenwärtig*]—just as the idea of the beautiful is present [*gegenwärtig*] in what is beautiful. (*TM*, pp. 481, 490)

Perfect hermeneutical experience resembles then the experience of the beautiful. When the word expresses the thing without distortion, the word presents an idea, the idea of the beautiful, *beautifully*.[12] For Gadamer, and it seems to me that Ricoeur would agree with this too, beauty is the task of hermeneutics.

Therefore what unifies Ricoeur and Gadamer beyond any difference is the *dialectical* nature of language, the dialectic of nature itself. As in Hegel and the Greeks, this movement goes from the singular, finite, and partial to the universal, infinite and complete. The linguistic event, a singular difference, presents sense, the thing itself, which remains the same. Unlike Hegel, however, for Ricoeur and Gadamer the movement itself postpones completeness; language's very nature is to be open to more events. Ricoeur and Gadamer have remembered the lesson of Aristotle and not forgotten those of Kant and Heidegger.

And yet, the task of hermeneutics, open as it is, lies in an appropriation of meaning, an overcoming of distanciation, a disappearance of the signifier, an event of presentation. A direction is outlined, an end is projected, a destination given, perfection promised. Language works for Ricoeur and Gadamer; it has a purpose; it makes sense. What happens however when the word distorts, deviates, errs, wanders from its path? Doesn't this open the hermeneutical horizon beyond any dialectic, no matter how naive? What if the beautiful were not only the presence of an idea, but also "dissemination, the pure cut without negativity, a *sans* without negativity and signification"?

PART IV
BARTHES/GADAMER

Chapter 6

READING THE TEXT

James Risser

The text is experienced only in an activity, a production.

—Barthes

A text is not a given object, but a phase in the execution of
the communicative event.

—Gadamer

It is now well established that contemporary literary criticism
(seen primarily through the work of the Yale critics and the *Tel
Quel* group) has radically transformed the idea of text.[1] No longer
is the text to be considered essentially simple, essentially present
to the reader depending on a proper methodological access. No
longer is the text to be considered insular to itself, defined by its
markings: title, margins, beginning, end, authorship. In turn,
the task of criticism and reading is no longer seen to be one of
deciphering meaning, at least the meaning that "sticks" to the
text by virtue of its markings. The search for principles that
would allow one to grasp the real idea of the text has been
abandoned. What has been recognized is that the text, as a
repository of meaning, as centered, cannot, like the statues of
Daedalus, be tied down. In critical reading one enters a linguistic
hall of mirrors where the master text has disappeared. *Being and
Time*, authored by Heidegger, remains a text permeated by the
texts of Dilthey and Kierkegaard, and is itself a text that is subsequently effaced in every text that writes about it. In every text
there is an intrusion of intertextuality that constantly dissemi-
nates the text. With its markings gone the text remains open to
a fundamental multiplicity of meaning, which, for all intents and
purposes, must be produced.

In this way deconstructive criticism sees itself as moving decisively beyond hermeneutics as a theory of understanding texts.[2] Roland Barthes, in particular, is quite explicit about this "post-structuralist" advance over hermeneutics. For Barthes hermeneutics is of an older order. It regards the text as a treasure chest of the signified, something that is secretly there and thus something to be sought out by interpretation. The task of hermeneutics is to decipher meaning, to reproduce the text in explanation.

But the matter is not as simple as it seems, for contemporary hermeneutics also insists, in its own way, on effacing the markings which serve as borders to a text. In the case of the border of signature, of author, this is most obvious. For Gadamer, the normative notion of author's intention represents only an empty space, for what is fixed in writing always frees itself for a new relationship. The author is always decentered in the act of reading, and the reader, in turn, is decentered in the act of textual production. For Gadamer, this decentering is what the event of understanding is all about. The reader *participates* in an event in which the text is made to speak again. The act of reading becomes, as it does for post-structuralism, an act of production.

How far can we extend this similarity? Perhaps the question of the limit is not the important one. More important, it seems to me that hermeneutics—and I mean here Gadamer's hermeneutics in particular—should be defended against a misreading. Gadamer does not want to *reconstruct* the text, to find *the* meaning of the text. Although this could be said of nineteenth-century hermeneutics, this is not the case with Gadamer. Nor do we want to confuse Gadamer's philosophical hermeneutics with Ricoeur's investigations into methodological questions of textual interpretation. A philosophical hermeneutics does see the activity of reading as a quest for meaning rather than a kind of play that carries out a series of dislocations, but, at the same time, it also regards the fixation of meaning as precisely what is problematic of reading. Properly understood, a philosophical hermeneutics is not of the old order, but then again, it is not quite of the new order. If Gadamer is correct, the relation between hermeneutics and post-structuralism is not a matter of the old and new, but of the two movements of play that perform the text.

I   The death of the author

Let us give the Barthesian version of the post-structuralist text a clearer definition. In two brief essays[3] Barthes marks the space of this text in terms of a subversive move within two sets of terms: from author to reader and from work to text. The two sets of terms clearly intersect: at the heart of the movement from work to text—from that which is held in hand to that which is held in language—is the death of the author.

Barthes rightly points out that the author is a modern figure, "emerging from the Middle Ages with English empiricism, French rationalism, and the personal faith of the Reformation." (DA, 142–43) The author is a product of a society that has discovered the prestige of the individual. Consequently, the text is always the text *of someone;* the text is always authored, centered and unified through the speaking of someone. Under the sway of individualism and capitalism, the text is a personal expression of the author, a glimpse into someone's inner state. The reader of such texts is left to participate in a form of filiation; the author, as father and owner of the text, is the final signified which all reading is directed towards.

But who really *owns* the text? Barthes thinks we do not have to search far for our answer, for it has already appeared in the work of Mallarmé. The French symbolist poet suggested that because of the possibilities adhering in the poem, the poet is often surprised to find more has been written than was known by the author. The author as well as the reader can take pleasure in discovering new extensions of meaning. Consequently, Mallarmé tells us that we must "cede the initiative to words." To write is to reach the point where it is not me who acts, but language. Language is potentially live material; language speaks, not the author. Accordingly, Barthes finds one of his essential tenets for reading in Mallarmé: we must suppress the author in the interests of writing. Linguistics too has contributed to the derision of authorship by showing that the whole of the enunciation is an empty process that does not require a filling with the person of the interlocutors. According to Barthes:

> Linguistically, the author is never more than the instance writing, just as *I* is nothing other than the instance saying

I: language knows a "subject," not a "person," and this subject, empty outside of the very enunciation which defines it, suffices to make language "hold together," suffices, that is to say, to exhaust it. (*DA,* 145)

If it is language that performs rather than the author, then courage requires an act of patricide to set the matter straight. Once the patricide is committed the text is decisively transformed in several ways. First of all, the temporality of the text is different. Previously, as father to a child, the author stood in relation to the text as a before and after. The author, existing before the book, is the *past* of his own book. Writing itself is a form of delay: a hand too slow for thought. But now, without the author to direct the work from behind, without a being preceding the writing, the "modern scriptor" is born simultaneously with the text. Writing is now performative: the hand "borne by a pure gesture of inscription" traces a field without origin other than language itself. (*DA,* 146).

Secondly, the transformed text takes on a multidimensional space. With the demise of the author the text is no longer a direct line of a single message bearer which imposes a limit on the proliferation of signification. Hermes, if you will, has not been given the message. The text, in other words, is no longer the expression of one meaning, the meaning intended by the author to the reader. The author is certainly allowed to enter the text, but only (to change the metaphor) as a guest. "If he is a novelist, he is inscribed in the novel like one of his characters," another figure sewn into the rug. "He becomes, as it were, a paper-author: his life is no longer the origin of his fictions, but a fiction contributing to his work" (*WT,* 161). "The modern scriptor, writing 'intransitively' infinitely deferring the signified, can only imitate a gesture that is always anterior, never original" (*DA,* 146). The text becomes a "tissue of quotations," an irreducible plurality of meaning that does not depend on the ambiguity of its content, but on the plurality of signifers that weave the text together.

Consequently, the attempt to decipher a text is futile. With the death of the author, the final signified, which holds the key to the secret of the text—its ultimate explanation—vanishes. Rather than deciphering, the critic must disentangle: "the space of writing is to be ranged over, not pierced; writing ceaselessly posits meaning ceaselessly to evaporate it, carrying out a systematic exemption of meaning" (*DA*, 147). In refusing to fix meaning and assign a secret to the text, writing becomes a form of liberation, an anti-theological activity refusing God and his hypostases—reason, science, law. Traditional criticism, whether biographical, historical, or formalist, is undermined.

Finally, despite the fact that the text is made of multiple writings, one can still speak of the unity of a text. In the transformed text the unity is displaced from origin to destination. The death of the author makes way for the birth of the reader. The reader becomes "the space on which all the quotations that make up a writing are inscribed without any of them being lost." (*DA*, 148) The reader, unlike the author, is not personal: "the reader is without history, biography, psychology; he is simply that *someone* who holds together in a single field all the traces by which the written text is constituted" (*DA*, 148).[4]

In holding the text together in this way, the reader no longer regards the text as an object of consumption, but "gathers it up as play, activity, production, practice" (*WT*, 162). The text is that which is opened out by the reader in play. But playing must be understood in all its polysemy. The text itself plays like a door on its hinges, a device that moves, operates, works. And the reader is caught up in a double play. The reader not only plays the text as one plays a game in the attempt to re-produce the text, but also, in order to keep the play from being reduced to an inner *mimesis* plays the text in the musical sense of the term as a co-author of a score.[5] The text demands of the reader an active collaboration for its very execution. Where interpretation simply "reads off" the musical score, the new reader completes the musical score. Consequently, reading, directed towards the future of a text, is *performative;* it opens it out, sets it going. The text is experienced only in an activity of language production.

II On text and interpretation

The imagery of musical performance that Barthes gives for text and reading is striking for one obvious reason. Gadamer employs a similar imagery in his discussion of the hermeneutic signifi-

97

cance of the work of art in *Truth and Method*.[6] Gadamer insists that the experience of art is comparable to the enactment of play in which the spectator—the one who stands at a distance from the work of art—is transformed by the participatory character of play.

In the play of art, what is captured is an image. But such image-making is not imitating, that is, the production of a semblance of a prior original. The play of art is a self-presentation, not a re-presentation (see *TM*, 97–99). Gadamer uses an analogous example to make his point: when the child plays at dressing up, the imitation is not a disguise but a presentation of such a kind that what is presented exists. Gadamer would have us understand the imitation in art in general in a similar fashion. The spectator, who like the player of a game gives oneself over to the play itself (and thus decenters subjectivity as a "final signified"), is caught up in the presentation in such a way that interpretation is the *recognition* of what is. The spectator belongs to the work because of what speaks to the spectator through the presentation. For Gadamer this invitation extended to the spectator in the presentation effected by play is most obvious in a religious rite where the relation of community to the performance of the rite is essential to religious truth. Gadamer thinks that this is precisely what occurs in the experience of art. The being of art—most notably in drama and music—has this character of performance. The work of art is nothing other than its appearance just as the performance cannot be detached from the play itself.

How are we to understand this concept of play in the context of text and reading? Certainly it is not enough to say that Gadamer shares with Barthes the notion of a reader who activates the text in the present moment. We have not yet seen how the reader's activation of the text is anything other than a recreation of the text. What is required is a further analysis of the play of understanding that occurs in reading the text.

To begin, we should recall that for Gadamer it is the *fixation* of meaning that is problematic for the question of interpretation. Such is the case because of the fundamental dialectical character of hermeneutic experience. At one place Gadamer writes:

> In order to locate my first attempts at thinking, I could in fact say that I took it upon myself to save the honor of

"bad infinity" [*der "schlechten Unendlichkeit"*]. Of course, in my eyes I made a decisive modification here . . . [for thinking] is not to be characterized as an endlessly continuing determination of an object-world waiting to be recognized.[7]

If thinking is not the *logos* of the world situated in subjectivity (as it is for Hegel), then what is it? For Gadamer, instructed by Heidegger, thinking has its context in language, and consequently the overcoming of every fixation of meaning occurs through the future development of conversation. In conversation there is always a "potentiality of otherness that lies beyond every coming to agreement about what is common."[8] The fact that a potentiality of otherness remains suggests that for Gadamer the text remains plural and not for reasons of an ambiguity of its content. Rather, the text remains plural by virtue of the structure of interpretation itself. This structure is such that, in a way similar to Barthes, Gadamer argues that the text emerges in its performative character. The difference here is that the performative character of text takes its direction from what Gadamer calls the "communicative situation" (*Verständigungssituation*) in which the text, as a hermeneutic concept, is located.

According to Gadamer, the history of the concept of text shows us that it does not occur outside the interpretive situation; it refers to "all that which resists integration in experience" (*TI*, 35). Even the "book" of nature is something that becomes readable from out of its interpretation. From the perspective of interpretation, the text is "the authentic given which is to be understood," and "remains the firm point of relation" over the possibilities of interpretation which are directed towards the text (*TI*, 34). It is always the same text presenting itself to us that is understood in different ways.

But it is not enough to say that the concept of text as a hermeneutical concept is that which is open to interpretation. This broad characterization of text is ultimately too inclusive. Gadamer wants to narrow the concept of text in order to bring the "eminent mode of textualizing [*Textierung*]" into view (*TI*, 41). He does this by distinguishing three forms of opposition or resistance to textualization: antitexts, pseudotexts, and pretexts. Antitexts are texts that cannot stand on their own because they only make sense in the context of interactive speaking. Texts which are ironic are antitexts in this sense. To say the opposite of what one means and still be understood in writing presupposes the existence of a "supporting mutual understanding." Pseudotexts are texts that serve as rhetorical bridges over the flow of speaking. Gadamer insists that every translator has encountered such pseudotexts in the performance of translation; the translator will recognize what is filler material and deal with it in an appropriate way. Pretexts, by far the most significant oppositional form, are texts that do not mean what they say. The understanding that occurs with pretexts must always push through a wall of pretense precisely because what comes to expression is masked. Both dreams and ideological statements are examples of such texts. In both one finds a masking of interests that distort the communicative event while at the same time both presuppose the possibility of non-distortive understanding. Thus, in principle Gadamer objects to privileging the forms of distorted communication as the normal case in textual interpretation. One cannot, in other words, take the hermeneutics of suspicion as the paradigmatic case of textual interpretation. But more importantly, the point that Gadamer indirectly makes here directs us back to the post-structuralist criticism of hermeneutics that hermeneutics wants to decipher meaning. As Gadamer sees it, it is not a matter of decoding, of deciphering at all, and yet, it is still a question of meaning.

What is other than decoding shows itself in the "eminent mode of textualizing," for which the literary work is the paradigmatic case. Such a text is not simply open to interpretation, but in *need* of interpretation in a special sense. The interpreter steps in when the text is not able to do what it is supposed to do, namely, to be heard and understood on its own. But such a text does not disappear in our understanding of it, for it continually stands before us continually speaking anew. Hermeneutic repetition is at work in the self-presentation of the word:

> Interpretation in [the case of a literary text] is not a mere
> means of getting back to an original expression. The literary
> text is text in the most special sense, precisely because it
> does not point back to an originary act of linguistic
> utterance but rather in its own right prescribes all
> repetitions and acts of speaking. No speaking can ever

completely fulfill the prescription given in the poetic text. The poetic text possesses a normative function which does not refer back either to an original utterance nor to the intention of the speaker, but is something which seems to originate in itself, so that in the fortune and felicity of its successful coming-forth, a poem surprises and overwhelms even the poet. (*TI*, 46–47)

Thus for Gadamer, (in a way similar to what Mallarmé has already said) the eminent text is something in itself that can always say something more to the reader in its interpretation precisely because language itself comes to appearance in its own way.[9] The eminent text is not simply understood and left behind.

With such a conception of text, the nature of interpretation can never be a matter of deciphering that would reproduce the text in explanation. Text and interpretation, it would seem, coalesce into one movement of departure and return. The departure must be understood in the context of writing's ideality. In an obvious way a text attains an ideality in the way it stands apart from the necessary repetition, which links the past with the present, of oral tradition. Writing, unlike speech, is freed from the contingencies of origin. But the issue here is not one of understanding writing on the basis of its supplement, for writing, despite the loss of oral immediacy in which intonation and accent lends itself more readily to human communication and understanding, has, in Gadamer's words, an "astonishing authenticity." Just as a literary text is not just the rendering of spoken language into a fixed form, writing is more than a mere fixation of what is said. Ideality, Gadamer tells us, "befits not only the written structure but also original speaking and hearing insofar as their content can be separated from the concrete speech act and can be reproduced."[10] The written structure is essentially a separation from the original language-event. "Reproduction," which can be more or less adequate, is always possible. Thus, the real issue here is to see that written texts present the real hermeneutic task. "Even the pure signs of an inscription can be seen properly and articulated correctly only if the text can be transformed back into language" (*WM*, 368; *TM*, 352). The ideality of writing, which makes it contemporaneous with every present, is an abstraction from the event (of language itself).

Interpretation, as that which brings written fixed language once again into speech, is, consequently, the event of overcoming the self-alienation, the departure, of writing. The return is to what is meant. But this return is not a reconstruction, for the thing meant is nowhere else than in the appearing word. Speaking is, for Gadamer, dialogical, an endeavor that continually modifies itself and as such it leaves behind the intended meaning of the speaker; consequently, the return is the hermeneutic event of speaking again in a new voice. For different reasons than others, Gadamer too recognizes the distinction between *langue* (language) and *parole* (speech). The spoken word is not to be confused with the system of symbols that constitute language. The activity of language in dialogue is not a system of signs, but "real exchange and work."

The consequence of this notion of language as speech-event for a theory of text is decisive. Interpretation does not proceed on the basis of a free-floating attitude that can discuss the statements of the text as objective information.[11] The text, in other words, "is not to be viewed as an end product the production of which is the object of analysis whose intent is to explain the mechanism which allows language as such to function at all" (*TI*, 35). The functioning of language, which is the concern of the linguist, is merely a pre-condition for comprehending what is said. The text must be readable. And then, from out of its readability, it is the subject matter of the text and not the text itself that is the point of concern. Writing needs to be transformed into speech, i.e., the communicative event. "The text is a mere intermediate product [*Zwischenprodukt*], a phase in the communicative event [*Verständigungsgeschehen*]" (*TI*, 35).

III   The text as between

The communicative event would seem to be problematic for a theory of text interpretation since the written text, by virtue of its ideality, is something cut off from the give and take of living conversation. What would a conversation with a text amount to? Above all, it would be a conversation that places a certain demand upon the reader as locus of the "real exchange and work." In spelling out the character of this work we are able to rejoin our comparison with Barthes's reader. For Gadamer as well a performative dimension is at work in every interpretation.[12]

With respect to the communicative situation, Gadamer emphasizes how both partners in a conversation must have a "good will" to try to understand one another. This phrase, not to be confused with the will in Kant, captures the overall sense of the conditions for conversation. But in the exchange between the text and a nameless reader the "good will" seems all the more problematical. Is it not simply a matter of recognizing that the writer of a text wants to impart meaning and thereby has in mind the preview of the other with whom he/she shares presuppositions? Knowing full well that we cannot resurrect the author, the answer to this question would seem to be both a yes and a no. Yes, because what is our writing and speaking if not a community of speakers and writers who wish to be understood. And although this implies that in an exchange we are able to bring about a real understanding—that rupture and break can be brought back to unity, that one can "say the same"—we have not made a naive return to a metaphysics of presence,[13] for the event character of understanding means precisely that there is no mere repetition of the text nor a mere recreation of a text, but a new creation of understanding. The sense of the good will is Socratic: "one attempts . . . to make the other as strong as possible so that his statements obtain some intelligibility" (TI, 59). Gadamer considers this essential for every understanding.

But the moment we attempt to probe this dimension of a partner in conversation more deeply, the "no" to our question arises. The intention of a reader is simply to grasp what is spoken of in the text. In Gadamer's hermeneutic theory this presents a special problem in as much as the reader is always guided in advance by anticipations of meaning. The good will, in this context, is simply the projection of truth, of intelligibility of the text on the part of the reader, that is necessary for the text to speak at all. Without this projection, one enters a circle of having only one's own prejudices confirmed. Gadamer insists that interpretation always fails as the will to mastery.

In Truth and Method this projection of intelligibility was characterized as the "anticipation of completion" (Vorgriff der Vollkommenheit).[14] In order to understand at all, a reader presupposes that the subject matter of a text has a perfected unity of meaning.

The subject matter, in other words, is regarded *initially* as neither incoherent within itself ("immanent unity of meaning") nor inconsistent with what is true concerning the subject matter ("transcendent expectations of meaning which proceed from the relation to the truth of what is being said") (*WM* 278, *TM* 262). Naturally a text could be otherwise, but if a text is not regarded as having a perfected unity of meaning there would be nothing to call into question the prejudices guiding the interpretation. A text would say whatever the reader wanted it to say. The perfected unity of meaning thus enables the text to stand as a self-presenting and authoritative whole. From the point of view of the reader, the negative experience which causes the anticipation of completion in a text to fail is simply the change that would not allow the text to speak "be it that we find it boring, empty or ridiculous, sentimental, imitative or simply not working."[15] A text thus cannot say anything it wants to and at the same time Gadamer eschews a methodology of a correspondence theory of meaning. The anticipation of completion is more regulative than constitutive of text and reading. A text must be followed according to its meaningful sense (*Sinnsgemäss*) and this is what the communicative situation is directed towards.

Granted, then, that the good will is a condition of the communicative situation and that the understanding of a text is dependent upon the communicative situation, what can we now say about the notion of text? In the coalescing of text and interpretation, the text only emerges in its effect (*Wirkung*). In interpreting a text, the text has an interpretive free space precisely because what is followed is the "meaningful sense" and not the text itself (as literal). Judicial hermeneutics—one of Gadamer's favorite examples of the practice of hermeneutics—convincingly displays this feature of interpretation. The mediating of the universality of the law with the concrete material of the case before the court is a hermeneutical problem whenever the legal text is no longer the authentic expression of our experience of the law. But notice that here, as well as in the interpretation of literary texts, it is always a matter of making univocal understanding possible. The free space amounts to a free space of meaningful concretization.

And yet, it remains true that the text always holds within itself a fundamental openness. This is the sense of the performative dimension of reading.

[I]n writing the openness which is implied in seeking the words, cannot be communicated, because it is printed. Therefore a virtual horizon of interpretation and understanding must be opened in writing the text itself, one which the reader must fill out. (*TI*, 39)

Reading, for Gadamer, is similar to the active involvement of spectators of a performance: a reshaping produced by its actualization. This performative character means that there is ultimately no determination of meaning that is originary or even reproductive; the determination of meaning remains productive. Although Gadamer argues that everything that is fixed in writing refers back to what was originally said, what is fixed in writing is always open to the future, "for all that is said is always already directed towards communication and includes the other in it" (*TI*, 39). The performative character is directed toward the future of the text. But unlike Barthes's reader, Gadamer's reader remains personal. In the performing directed toward the future of the text, there is a thickness to the performing—by virtue of the event of understanding—that produces a doubling of the future: at stake in the performing is the future of the reader as well as the future of the text. For Gadamer, to reach an understanding is not so much the successful assertion of one's point of view, but a transformation into a communion in which we do not remain what we were.

Chapter 7

REREADING GADAMER:
A RESPONSE TO JAMES RISSER

Deborah Cook

The invitation to write this paper is tantamount to a request to dialogue with a dialogue on dialogue. The work of Gadamer, focused as it is on the dialogic form of textual understanding, is a reflection on that authentic conversation which allows one to approach the text as a speaker in a tradition in which both text and reader participate. The invitation to converse with James Risser's text, in which he compares Gadamer's ideas on reading with those found in poststructuralism, obliges this reader first, to renew a dialogue with Gadamer's text; second, to read a dialogue concerning Gadamer's views on dialogue and third, to dialogue with this latter dialogue. A brilliant and poetic rendering of this task can be found in Italo Calvino's *If on a Winter's Night a Traveller,* where the reader dizzily circles in a nightmarish spiral of reading about reading about reading. . . . There is no end to this obsessive and narcissistic reflection. If I thought, therefore, that I was obliged to write about writing about writing (or read about reading about reading), I would not accept the invitation. In order to avoid this infinitely regressive dialogue, I shall interpret the request as an invitation to rework my own understanding of Gadamer's texts. This rereading of Gadamer will form the basis for a dialogue with Risser on Gadamer's views about dialogue. It is to be hoped that our readers will see this dialogue as an example of that Socratic good will towards a text which, according to Gadamer and as Risser notes, should accompany all understanding of texts.

Risser neglects to devote a section of "Reading the Text" to the problem of the reader. Apart from some remarks about the personal reader (versus the impersonal one?), Risser concentrates on the author, the text and the act of interpretation. To open this dialogue, then, I shall complement Risser's comparison with a discussion of the poststructuralist and hermeneutic conceptions of the reader who engages in textual interpretation. The relationship between Gadamer's hermeneutics and poststructuralism with respect to their ideas about the reader is mediated by phenomenology. It is Husserl and Heidegger who make it possible to view hermeneutics and poststructuralism as intrinsically (because historically) related. In Heidegger's work, *Dasein*—the reader who understands—is not a substance.

> The person is no Thing-like and substantial Being. Nor can the Being of a person be entirely absorbed in being a subject of rational acts which follow certain laws. The person is not a Thing, not a substance, not an object.[1]

On the contrary, *Dasein* is radically temporal. Heidegger's investigation of temporality discloses the ground for textual understanding. Understanding a text is always temporal and, by extension, historical. Heidegger's idea of temporality is drawn from Husserl's *Zur Phänomenologie des inneren Zeitbewusstseins*.[2] *Dasein's* temporality is manifested in its being-ahead-of-itself (future), being-alongside (present) and being-already-in (past). Dasein's fundamental mode of being is to be outside of itself in the "ecstases" of past, present and future. We can therefore make a preliminary sketch of the reader in both hermeneutics and poststructuralism as a radically temporal and nonsubstantial being.

Following Heidegger, Gadamer's reader is a finite being whose understanding of a text is a temporal process. Yet, in Gadamer's work, *Dasein's* temporality, which is the basis for its historicity, also grounds a tradition. This modification of Heidegger's work may be seen as Gadamer's interpretation of the last sections of *Being and Time* in which Heidegger claims that the embodiment of temporality can be found in *Dasein's* historicality. To this idea of historicality, Gadamer adds a linguistic dimension, which the later Heidegger also introduced, and which makes language the medium for the understanding, the community (*Gemeinschaft*) and the tradition. Both the tradition and the community are grounded in *Dasein's* temporality but also surpass it to form the court of appeal for every understanding of a text. Reading, for Gadamer, is a trans-subjective and trans-objective process in which the reader eliminates subjective prejudice in order to merge with the tradition as it is given to the linguistic community. Reading involves a form of *parousia* in which the reader goes beyond everyday praxis and returns to it with an understanding that can then be applied to that praxis. The circle of understanding, interpretation and application

> is neither subjective nor objective but describes
> understanding as the interplay of the movement of the
> tradition and the movement of the interpreter. The
> anticipation of meaning that governs our understanding of
> the text is not an act of subjectivity but proceeds from the
> communality that binds us to the tradition.[3]

It is not, therefore, clear why Risser calls Gadamer's reader a "personal" one. The reader must assume the prejudices of the community to which he or she belongs because only these prejudices are productive enough to permit an authentic understanding of a text.

Risser confines his comparison of hermeneutics and poststructuralism to a discussion of the similarities between Gadamer's work and that of Roland Barthes. Although the comparison is instructive, it might also be of some value to compare Gadamer to other poststructuralists such as Derrida.[4] In Derrida's work, the reader is tied to a temporal framework which Derrida also derives from Husserl's *Phänomenologie*.

> We must then *situate*, as a simple *moment of the discourse*,
> the phenomenological reduction and the Husserlian
> reference to a transcendental experience. To the extent that
> the concept of experience in general—and of transcendental
> experience, in Husserl in particular—remains governed by
> the theme of presence, it participates in the movement of
> the reduction of the trace. [. . .] But that must come to
> terms with the forces of rupture. In the originary
> temporalization and the movement of relationship with the
> outside, as Husserl actually describes them, non-
> presentation or depresentation is as "originary" as
> presentation.[5]

Derrida locates the "forces of rupture" in Husserl's notion of the *reell*, as opposed to the *real*, component of experience. The *reell* is the "nonreal component of lived experience" (*OG*, 54) and is described by Husserl in the *Ideen* as the noetic and proper component of intentional experience. The *reell* exists neither in the world nor in experience. Derrida claims that, by introducing this component, Husserl makes possible a philosophy which is not based on presence. Combined with Husserl's theory of internal time consciousness, the temporal relations between *reell* components become the set of relations governed by the trace in Derrida's work.

The reader is also inscribed in the relations governed by the trace. By virtue of his or her temporality, the reader is nonsubstantial. Writing or reading can

> never be thought under the category of the subject;
> however it is modified, however it is endowed with
> consciousness or unconsciousness, it will refer, by the
> entire thread of its history, to the substantiality of a
> presence unperturbed by accidents, or to the identity of the
> self-same [*le propre*] in the presence of self-relationship.
> (*OG*, 68–69)

To arrive at his idea of the nonsubstantial reader, Derrida preserves Husserl's theory of time consciousness but unhinges this theory from its privileging of presence to make of time a trace of an endless deferring or differing. This deferring or differing (*différance*) is what constitutes the reader.

Barthes' relationship to phenomenology can be traced via Sartre to Heidegger and Husserl. The reader, for Barthes, is simply the grammatical "I." It has no substantial reality. What we call the reader is simply the empty repetition of the contentless "I."

> Does one not have the right to ask *who then* it is who
> interprets? It is the interpretation itself, a form of the will to
> power, which exists (not as a "being," but as a process, a
> becoming), as a passion.[6]

This quote, which can be found in Nietzsche's 1880 notebooks with different emphases and in the declarative form,[7] refers to the desire for mastery which characterizes, for Nietzsche and for Barthes, all interpretation. It is also clear that for both Barthes and Nietzsche, the question of *who* interprets must be answered with reference to a process and not an individual being. Barthes goes on to say that the reading subject as an individual is a fiction. The reader derives a "certain pleasure" from "imagining him or herself as an *individual*" (*PT*, 98). Barthes distinguishes this fiction from the illusion of unity to which Risser refers in his quote from "The Death of the Author." In this quote, Barthes writes that the reader is "*someone* who holds together in a single field all the traces by which the written text is constituted." This remark must, however, be reconciled with Barthes' idea that the individual is a fiction and that unity is an illusion. Both are equally misleading when it is a question of understanding *who* interprets. As Barthes' quote from Nietzsche's work illustrates, the individuality and unity of the reader are belied by the reading process itself. It is the process (here, the process of mastering the text) which defines the subject-reader (cf. Sartre and Heidegger) and not the subject who controls the process.

The similarities between Gadamer's hermeneutics and post-structuralism with respect to their conceptions of the reader are striking. The basis for these similarities lies in the philosophical sources which are common to both. Although the influence of Nietzsche is not marked in Gadamer's work as it is in the work of the poststructuralists, the temporality of the reading process—its essential characteristic—and the idea that the reader is non-substantial can be traced back to Husserl's pathbreaking work on time consciousness. Further, the rootedness of both hermeneutics and poststructuralism in Husserl's theory of temporality affects not only their conceptions of the reader but also their ideas about the text.

As Risser notes, in Gadamer's work, the text does not have a fixed meaning which the reader would discover like the figure in Henry James' carpet. Meaning can only be apprehended temporally and historically. This implies that the meaning of a given text will change as the temporal and historical context changes. Gadamer defines what he calls "the true nature" of this interplay as the transformation into structure. This structure is the structure of play itself. The players (text and interpreter) must assume the structure of play if the text is to come "into existence" (*TM*, 105). "Interpretation is probably, in a certain sense, re-creation, but this re-creation does not follow the process of the creative act, but the lines of the created work which has to be brought to representation in accord with the meaning the interpreter finds in it" (*TM*, 107). One should note here that there is a difference between poststructuralist theory and Gadamer's hermeneutics with respect to interpretation as creation. As Terry Eagleton remarks: "There is no clear division for poststructuralism between 'criticism' and 'creation': both modes are subsumed into 'writing' as such."[8] In Gadamer's hermeneutics, what is produced by understanding is new and original but the reader must not think that he or she is writing another text. Misreading and misunderstanding are still possible for Gadamer as they are not for the poststructuralists. A misunderstanding will arise if the reader is not experienced and does not hold him or herself open to the voice of the tradition.[9]

What the voice of the tradition reveals is Being. Gadamer remains faithful to Heidegger's idea that intelligible Being is what is disclosed in an authentic act of understanding. "Being that can be understood is language" (*TM*, 432). What accedes to language in the play of text and interpreter is truth as the disclosure of Being. Being that comes to be represented in play is defined as the transformation of reality into truth or speech. This idea is drawn from Heidegger's "The Origin of the Work of Art." *"Art then is the becoming and happening of truth."*[10] Lest it be thought that this truth ties the reader to a fixed meaning, it should be added that Gadamer explicitly states, following Heidegger, that the truth of Being as disclosed in an act of understanding is only possible in language, and language is finite and situated. Truth is therefore rooted in the historico-linguistic context in which it is uttered. It arises as the tradition and the prejudices of the community merge in that act of understanding whose temporal distance from the text is the condition for the disclosure of any truth whatsoever. Hence, although Gadamer denies that the text has a fixed meaning, he does not deny that one may misread. A misreading would involve an inability or a refusal on the part of the reader to remain open to the truth of Being which is revealed in play. Such misreading is impossible for the poststructuralism of Derrida and Barthes.

One of the major differences, then, between hermeneutics and poststructuralism can be found in their conceptions of the text. From the same philosophical sources, each draw different conclusions. Derrida is seeking the forces that would rupture the privileging of presence in Husserl's work. This critical moment is absent in *Truth and Method*. Much like the goal of hermeneutics itself, Gadamer's aim is to reappropriate the tradition in aesthetics, hermeneutics and the philosophy of language in order to allow it to speak to his own concern of reformulating hermeneutics. For Derrida, texts are not to be reappropriated but deconstructed. His comments on the *reell* component of lived experience exemplify the deconstructive manoeuvres he is attempting to ground in *Of Grammatology*. In Derrida's work the text is a tissue of contradictions which, by themselves, transgress the logo-phono-phallocentric oppositions of Western metaphysics. Derrida endeavors to overcome the tradition, by force if necessary. He accomplishes this by employing operations he derives, by way of deconstruction, from that tradition.

Terry Eagleton's synopsis of Derrida's theory of textual meaning in *Literary Theory* is probably the most condensed and precise of any one might read. On Eagleton's reading, meaning for Derrida

> is not immediately *present* in a sign. Since the meaning of a sign is a matter of what the sign is *not*, its meaning is always in some sense absent from it too. Meaning, if you like is scattered or dispersed along the whole chain of signifiers: it cannot be easily nailed down, it is never fully present in any one sign alone, but is rather a kind of constant flickering of presence and absence together. Reading a text is more like tracing this process of constant flickering. [. . .] There is also another sense in which we can never quite close our fists over meaning, which arises from the fact that language is a temporal process. When I read a sentence, the meaning of it is always somehow suspended, something deferred or still to come: one signifier relays me to another, and that to another, earlier meanings are modified by later ones, and although the sentence may come to an end, the process of language itself does not. (*LT*, 128)

To quote Risser, "the master text has disappeared." What remains is a temporal movement, controlled neither by the reader nor by the author, in which meaning is deferred and differed according to the operations that govern the transcendental field of arch-writing. In this context, meaning is plural. Every sign is radically polysemous which means that every reading, every interpretation will necessarily be different. There is no author, no reader, no figure in the carpet which could exercise authority over the meaning produced by a particular reading. Misreadings are therefore impossible, although Derrida does refer to protocols of reading in *Positions*[11] and to bad readers in *La Carte Postale*.[12] Unfortunately, I do not have the opportunity in this paper to deal with the apparent contradiction. What should be emphasized at this point, however, are the *differences* and not the similarities in the hermeneutic and poststructuralist conceptions of the text. Gadamer believes that an authentic understanding of a text discloses an historical truth. Derrida rejects the idea that a truth can be wrestled from a reading. Gadamer, as Risser remarks, treats the text as an Other which must be respected as intelligible. This is the basis for an authentic and dialogic understanding. For Derrida, the very notion of Otherness needs to be deconstructed. The text produces its own readings and never discloses a truth, historical or otherwise.

Risser's treatment of Barthes' conception of the text is excellent. In most respects, Barthes' views on the text are similar to those of Derrida. In both writers, the idea of a language which would be wholly present to things, and thus the notion of representation, must be transformed. Language cannot be defined by its supposed representational function: it refers, if to anything at all, ceaselessly to itself. The text is a tissue, a web (like a spider's web) of meanings (*PT*, 100–101) which refer to other meanings intra and intertextually. Derrida speaks in a similar fashion of the texture of the text.[13] The 'writable' text, usually a modernist one, has no determinate meaning, no settled signifieds, but is plural and diffuse, an inexhaustible tissue or galaxy of signifiers, a seamless weave of codes and fragments of codes, through which the critic may cut his own errant path" (*LT*, 138). Although Derrida, Barthes and Gadamer all insist that the text has no fixed meaning, Derrida and Barthes take a more radical step with respect to the problem of textual meaning. For Gadamer, it is the linguistic community (via the reader) which determines the meaning of a text by virtue of holding itself open and listening to the tradition. For Barthes and Derrida, it is the temporality of language that makes such an authentic understanding impossible. Even though both hermeneutics and poststructuralism see time as the ground for reading, the poststructuralists have divorced time definitively from subjectivity. With his notion of arch-writing, Derrida ensures that time and subjectivity are not correlatives. Gadamer's reading subject has a temporal foundation but, in his work, temporality merely remains a more precise rendering of subjectivity. Temporality does not operate in a transcendental realm as it does in Derrida's work. Derrida goes beyond the situated temporality of *Dasein* and its community to disclose an autonomous temporal sphere. Derrida insists that "writing is other than the subject, in whatever sense the latter is understood" (*OG*, 68). The poststructuralists remove the operations of time from the subjective (or intersubjective) realm to a transcendental realm the processes of which make possible not only "the constitution of subjectivity" (*OG*, 69), but the constitution of anything whatsoever.

Risser's discussion of the problem of the author in poststructuralism and hermeneutics shows quite well that "the normative notion of the author's intention represents only an empty space, for what is fixed in writing always frees itself for a new relationship." The presumed authority of the author with respect to meaning gives way to interpretations which the text itself produces or which are produced in the interplay of text and interpreter. For Gadamer, the author's intention must yield to the meaning the text acquires in play.

> The real meaning of a text, as it speaks to the interpreter,
> does not depend on the contingencies of the author and
> whom he originally wrote for. It is certainly not identical
> with them, for it is always partly determined also by the
> historical situation of the interpreter and hence by the
> totality of the objective course of history. [. . .] Not
> occasionally only, but always, the meaning of a text goes
> beyond its author. (*TM*, 263–64)

In Derrida's work, it is because the temporality of language constitutes subjectivity that meaning cannot be referred to an author. The author must be referred to meaning produced by the operations governing language in the sphere of arch-writing. Once again, then, for both poststructuralism and hermeneutics, it is temporality or time which makes the author's intention of little or no consequence. Since reading is temporal, we can never disclose an author's intention, only our own prejudices. Since language as temporal constitutes subjectivity, the author's so-called intention is just another text or a plurality of meanings produced by the operations of arch-writing. Nevertheless, given the differences between the two ideas of temporality, it is necessary to note that there are also differences between the two ideas of what one author has called "the eclipse of the author." "[T]he eclipse of the author is not announced in the hermeneutic privilege of a simultaneity (*Gleichzeitigkeit*) of a kind of eternal presence of a meaning submitted to the vicissitudes of temporality, but in the 'specific temporality' of the text."[14] The specific temporality of the text must be distinguished from the temporality of subjectivity or intersubjectivity. For this reason, the idea that the author's intention has no authority over a reading must be qualified with reference to the distinct ideas that hermeneutics and poststructuralism have of temporality.

To end this dialogue, I shall refer to an interesting and important text which, to my knowledge, has not yet been translated into English. *Herméneutique et Grammatologie*, written by Jean Greich and published in 1977, treats both the similarities and differences between Gadamer's hermeneutics and Derrida's grammatology. Greich views both as "fundamental philosophies" that "surpass all regional problematics in philosophy" (*HG*, 111). In the fourth chapter of his book, entitled "Programmes," Greich makes an important contribution to any comparison of the work of the poststructuralists and Gadamer's hermeneutics. This comparison concerns the reading process. So far, I have discussed the hermeneutic and poststructuralist conceptions of the reader, the text and the author's intention. It is fitting, therefore, to end with an overview of the reading process itself. I shall use Greich as my guide.

Reading, for Gadamer, is ultimately a problem related to self-understanding. The reader who engages in play gains an understanding of him or herself in the deployment of the community's effective historical consciousness (*Wirkungsgeschichte*) and in disclosing a meaning that can then be applied to the praxis of everyday life. For Derrida and Barthes, of course, the problem of self-understanding does not arise. What can be gleaned from the tradition of Western metaphysics are operations which undo the tradition as opposed to understanding it. Self-understanding must therefore be contrasted with critique if one wishes to understand what is at stake in the reading process. Greich encapsulates the differences between critique and self-understanding when he claims that hermeneutics involves the reduction of the text to meaning and poststructuralism is concerned with the reduction of meaning in the text. Gadamer

> defines philosophy as a whole as *Erinnerung* in the sense that Hegel and Heidegger gave to this word. Philosophy is the gathering [*receuillement*] of meaning, which must not be confused with the reconstruction of a past meaning. What is thus gathered did not yet exist and is manifested for the first time. (*HG*, 157)

Deconstruction, on the other hand, follows Nietzsche "much more than Heidegger." Deconstruction is "what Nietzsche described as *aktive Vergesslichkeit*, active forgetting" (*HG*, 159). Derrida does not simply reject the tradition, he transforms it so that "active forgetting may have its effects on the level of language" (*HG*, 161). Gadamer wants to make the tradition speak to us as readers so that we may use it to understand ourselves as historical beings. Derrida, on the contrary, wants to make the tradition "die laughing" (*HG*, 159). It is the Nietzschean *fröhliche Wissenschaft* which accounts for the differences between the two. When poststructuralism and hermeneutics are understood with reference to their Husserlian/Heideggerian roots, similarities may be discovered. However poststructuralism may also be understood with reference to Nietzsche and it is Nietzschean laughter that makes a comparison of similarities more difficult. The source of this difficulty is pinpointed by Nietzsche himself who wrote: *"Der Fehler steckt in der Hineindichtung eines Subjekts"* (*AN*, 489).

PART V
DERRIDA/GADAMER

Chapter 8

BEYOND SERIOUSNESS AND FRIVOLITY: A GADAMERIAN RESPONSE TO DECONSTRUCTION

Gary B. Madison

I In search of a strategy

In the preface to his grandiose *Phänomenologie des Geistes*, in which, like some hired ghost writer, he narrates the autobiography of the Absolute itself, the arch-metaphysician Hegel asserted that philosophy is "serious business." Unlike the artist or the craftsman who merely toys around with things, the philosopher is a *scientist* who penetrates to the very heart of *die Sachen selbst*. In saying this G. W. F. Hegel was merely reasserting what mainline, serious-minded philosophers—whom I shall simply call "metaphysicians"—have always maintained, from Plato through Descartes and Kant to Husserl and beyond. Philosophy's claim to the status of Science is, however, one which has always been contested by those thinkers who go to make up what I call the Counter-Tradition: the Greek sophists and rhetoricians, the Pyrrhonian skeptics, Montaigne, Kierkegaard, Nietzsche. . . .[1] And the metaphysicians have always retaliated by accusing the counter-traditionalists of "not being serious," of, in fact, being frivolous. It certainly cannot be denied that many of them have indeed delighted in being intellectually playful: Think for instance of Gorgias' tongue-in-cheek anti-Parmenedian treatise, *On Non-Being*, Kierkegaardian irony, Nietzschean wit. . . . The principal target of the dialectical fireworks of writers such as these has been precisely what Sartre would call "l'esprit du sérieux" of orthodox philosophy.[2] However, does being an anti-metaphysician, an anti-foundationalist, necessarily entail being frivolous? This is in effect the background question I would like to raise in this paper by way of comparing the intellectual endeavors of Hans-Georg Gadamer and Jacques Derrida. When Gadamerian hermeneutics is compared to Derridian deconstruction, the answer to the question appears to be a "No." One can quite well reject metaphysical seriousness without courting frivolity.

A comparative analysis of these two key figures of our postmodernity is by no means an easy undertaking. While, as a result of many years of close personal association, I feel I understand Gadamer fairly well and have a pretty good idea of what he is up to and of the significance and import of his philosophical project, I cannot say the same for Derrida, even though I first encountered both the man and his work back in the late 1960s when I was teaching as an assistant to Paul Ricoeur at the University of Paris (at that time Derrida was interested among other things in finding out more about Peirce). In fact, directly contrary to my experience with Gadamer, I almost feel I have progressively understood Derrida less and less as the years go by, in the sense that each new work of his has been less and less intelligible to me. It may be because (and I do not mean this frivolously) there is less and less to understand in each new work of his. So I do not pretend to know what Derrida means, wants to say, and am not surprised when he intimates that there is nothing he wants to say, that the *vouloir-dire* is a hopelessly metaphysical notion.[3] Not only is Derrida not a "serious" philosopher, his irony is so extreme that in his case it is not, or so it would seem, a matter of saying one thing and meaning something else thereby, but rather of saying this and that and the other thing and not really meaning anything at all. In any event, I can only say of him what Gadamer himself has said: "I will not say that I was extremely successful in understanding him."[4]

To be more precise, I believe I understand fairly well the negative or critical significance of Derrida's deconstructive attack on the "metaphysics of presence." This is in fact something I sympathize with wholeheartedly. But this aspect of his undertaking is as fully characteristic, as I shall be arguing, of Gadamer's hermeneutics as it is of Derrida's own deconstruction. What I fail to understand in Derrida is precisely what I fail to understand in Richard Rorty as well: the positive, *philosophical* significance of the critique of metaphysics and epistemology. Where does it all get us? What future, if any, is there for philosophy after the end of Philosophy (in Rorty's sense of the term, which is also that of Derrida, i.e., Platonism)? Is there nothing left for the philosopher to do, after the demise of metaphysical seriousness, but to be an intellectual "kibitzer," a concern-free creator of "abnormal" discourse, an insouciant player of deconstructive and fanciful word games, an agile figure skater on the thin ice of a "bottomless chessboard"?[5]

According to Rorty, the new breed of "intellectuals" who are to displace the traditional "metaphysicians" should not, it appears, have any fixed views on anything. Although Derrida does not quite say this, it often seems to me to be what he implies by his intellectual practice and his approach to texts, as well as by his near-total silence on the ethical and political dimensions of the philosophical enterprise.[6] Rorty's distinction between metaphysicians and intellectuals ("intellectual dilettantes") furnishes me in fact with the interpretive strategy (and the *tertium comparationis*) I need if I am to make some meaningful comparison between Gadamer and Derrida, which otherwise could be as difficult as comparing apples and oranges. Accepting this distinction, I wish to argue the following: while Derrida embodies the traits of Rorty's carefree "intellectual," Gadamer, equally as anti-metaphysical as Derrida, does not; he transcends the distinction and in fact provides us with an alternative to it. Whence the title of this paper: "Beyond Seriousness and Frivolity."

The intertextual allusions (or "parasitism") of this title will not fail to be noted, and they in fact provide the reader at the outset with the substance of my argument (which is indeed a Gadamerian *response* to deconstruction).[7] With Richard Bernstein's *Beyond Objectivism and Relativism* in mind, I wish to argue that while Gadamer successfully leads us beyond both objectivism (metaphysics, epistemology) and relativism, Derrida's critique of metaphysics lands us, for all practical purposes, in a debilitating relativism, a kind of philosophical nihilism. I would like to say of Derrida what Bernstein says of Rorty, that from a Gadamerian perspective Derrida's hermeneutics, his handling of texts, is "mutilated or castrated, for it is a hermeneutics without the claim to knowledge or truth."[8] It seems to provide only for auto-affectional "suppléments," not the kind of "knowledge" which is achieved through genuine intersubjective intercourse. It is, to use Derrida's words, the "adventurous excess of a writing that is no longer directed by any knowledge."[9] In contrast, what Gadamer's work shows is that it is not at all necessary to abandon the notions of knowledge and truth, that it is in fact fully possible to extricate them from any and all metaphysical/epistemological contexts. To so extricate them is to point the way beyond both objectivism and relativism, beyond both "seriousness" and "frivolity."[10]

II Hermeneutics

One of the major motivations of Gadamer's hermeneutical project is to overcome or displace what he has called "l'ère de la théorie de la connaissance," the age of epistemology.[11] His critique of classical hermeneutics in the person of Dilthey is directed primarily at the fact that it remains caught up in the modern epistemological, foundationalist project.[12] Phenomenological hermeneutics is thus a thoroughly postmodern form of thought which understandably appeals to an anti-foundationalist like Rorty. What is surprising is that Derrida appears unwilling to recognize the post-epistemological and post-metaphysical significance of Gadamer's enterprise.

In *Spurs/Eperons,* Derrida does, however, make a number of pejorative references to "hermeneutics." It seems that by "hermeneutics" ("le projet herméneutique") he understands the attempt to get at "the true meaning of the text".[13] The implication seems to be that "hermeneutics" presupposes that a text has a definite, in-itself sort of meaning that it would be the business of interpretation to *reproduce* in as accurate a form as possible, this meaning being the author's intended meaning.[14] In opposition to hermeneutical naïveté of this sort, "la question de la femme" (as Derrida calls it) reveals that there is no "decidable opposition of true and not true"; "philosophical decidability" falls by the wayside (*S/E,* 106). Just as it cannot be decided what Nietzsche meant when he scribbled on a scrap of paper, " 'I have forgotten my umbrella,' " so it cannot be denied that, "in some monstrous way," the meaning of the totality of Neitzsche's text might be

undecidable. "The hermeneut cannot but be provoked and dis-
concerted," Derrida tells us, by the freeplay (*jeu*) of the text (see
S/E, 132–33), the endless play of signifiers devoid of decidable
meaning which makes of reading itself not interpretation aiming
at truth but free, parodying play.

What actually provokes the "hermeneut" and what he finds
disconcerting in all this is Derrida's failure to say what *he* means
by "hermeneutics," i.e., exactly who or what he is referring to.
The text itself leaves the issue undecided. If by hermeneutics
Derrida means the classical hermeneutical tradition stemming
from Schleiermacher (whom he alludes to) up to Betti and Hirsch,
then Derrida is, whether he likes it or not, stating something
"true" when he characterizes it as the attempt to reproduce
objective, determinate meanings. If, however, the term is a blan-
ket one meant also to cover Gadamer, and phenomenological
hermeneutics in general (the various references to Heidegger
and "phenomenology" in the text seem to indicate as much),
it is manifestly false. Any meaningful confrontation between
Gadamerian hermeneutics and Derridian deconstruction would
require that this matter be set straight.

For the sake of the record (or to set it straight), let us simply
take note of some of the central theses of Gadamer's hermeneutics. For the sake of the present discussion I shall single out
three: (1) *To understand is in fact to interpret* ("All understanding is
interpretation . . ." [*TM*, 350]). Understanding must not, therefore, be conceived of "epistemologically," as the "correct" *representation* of some "objective" state of affairs. It is not so much
reproductive as it is productive, transformative ("understanding
is not merely a reproductive, but always productive attitude as
well" [*TM*, 264]). (2) *All understanding is essentially bound up with
language* ("Being that can be understood in language" [*TM*, xxii];
"language is the universal medium in which understanding itself
is realised" [*TM*, 350]). (3) *The understanding of the meaning of
text is inseparable from its application* (". . .understanding always
involves something like the application of the text to be understood to the present situation of the interpreter" [*TM*, 274]).

These main theses[15] have some important implications, especially in regard to the notions of meaning and truth, as we shall
see in the remainder of this paper. Suffice it for the moment to
remark on how they entail a decisive break with the logocentric

metaphysics of presence in that they render meaningless the metaphysical notion of meanings that would be timeless and invariant, free from the unsettling play of language, and which would simply have to be intuited or otherwise directly reproduced in order to be grasped (for there to be "truth").

One thing which makes a comparison between Gadamer and Derrida difficult is that they are not out to do the same kind of thing. Whereas Gadamer outlines a general philosophical theory, Derrida mainly presents us with a technique for reading.[16] Derrida's interpretive tactic or reading strategy consists in showing how what an author actually does in his text tends to subvert in one way or another what he says, what he *intends*. A deconstructive reading seeks to discover "blind spots" in a text around which it organizes itself (such as the usage of the word "supplément" in Rousseau) with the aim of discrediting the metaphysical and epistemological assumptions held by the author (in particular the assumption that philosophy is a form of pure reason— and not just another form of "writing"—free from the metaphorical and rhetorical play of language), of discrediting, ultimately, the entire metaphysical or onto-theological project. Derrida's work pretty much exhausts itself in this sort of activity; it is, borrowing his own words, a "strategy without finality" (See *Dis*, 7). That it should not be able to do any more is understandable, given the fact that Derrida appears to equate philosophy with metaphysics ("Philosophy" in Rorty's sense), and thus is led to say that deconstruction seeks to determine "from a certain exterior that is unqualifiable or unnameable by philosophy" that which philosophy has dissimulated or forbidden (See *Pos*, 6). It is not too much to speak of nihilism if that on the basis of which or in terms of which we criticize the tradition and seek to overcome it is "unqualifiable or unnamable" by us. It is hard to know where we stand and what we are left with when the deconstructive enterprise turns around and, as we are told it must, deconstructs ("erases") itself.[17] Deconstruction, as Derrida rightly observes, is essentially a *critique*. Unlike ordinary, run-of-the-mill critiques (e.g., Marxism), it is, however, a critique from, so to speak, nowhere. But because it is from nowhere, it leads us nowhere, and this is precisely why it is basically nihilistic. If there is not a good philosophical *reason* for deconstructing metaphysics that can be stated and argued for, if, for instance, there is not some justifying theoretical-political point to it (such as arriving at a less mythical conception of *truth* or furthering the cause of *emancipation*), the activity itself becomes purely and simply *destructive,* a kind of theoretical vandalism.

Although it too is critical (as Gadamers's *Auseinandersetzung* with Habermas makes clear), Gadamerian hermeneutics on the other hand, is not primarily a method or technique for reading and interpreting texts. This, of course, is where it differs from classical hermeneutics as well. As Gadamer is at pains to point out in the forword to the second edition of *Truth and Method,* what he is proposing is not (unlike Hirsch, for instance) a new and better method for determining the correct meaning of texts. His phenomenological hermeneutics does not propose a method of understanding to be used in order to avoid misunderstanding or to make the unfamiliar familiar, as Schleiermacher would have said. It is not, indeed, concerned with the epistemological questions of methods and methodology at all. Rather, its goal is properly philosophical (whence the term "philosophical hermeneutics") in that it seeks to determine what is involved in the understanding process itself, what it is that has actually happened whenever we claim to have arrived at an understanding of things, the world, ourselves.[18] Since Gadamer is building on Heidegger's insight that understanding is not something we "have" but, rather, is what as existing beings we *are* (an *Existentiale*), the scope of hermeneutics conceived of in this way is indeed *universal.* This claim to universal scope is reflected in Gadamer's literary style, as when he says typically that *all* understanding is of such-and-such a sort. The purpose of his investigations has been, quite simply, "to discover what is common to all modes of understanding"; it is concerned with "all human experience of the world and human living" (*TM,* xix, xviii).

Because of its claim to universality, Gadamerian hermeneutics is properly *philosophical* in its intent, and in this regard it contrasts sharply with the equivocal position in regard to philosophy taken by deconstruction which does not seem to know quite where it stands (inside still, outside already, or, like Derrida's own signature, only "on the edge"?). Because it makes universal claims, ones, moreover, which are completely at odds with traditional logocentrism (as we shall see in more detail in what follows), it amounts in fact to a displacement or overcoming of the metaphysics of presence. Precisely because it so displaces traditional foundationalist thinking, it is in its results at least as "deconstructive" as deconstruction.[19] A consideration of the way Gadamer approaches the subjects of "meaning" and "truth" should confirm all of this.

III Meaning

Deconstructive freeplay (*le jeu*), Derrida tells us, "is the disruption of presence."[20] This is to say that it discredits meaning in the traditional metaphysical sense, for metaphysics "considers in a way meaning as a presence (*vorhanden*) to be exhumed,"[21] as, in other words, an objective state of affairs of one sort or another that it would be the function of epistemological "knowing" to reproduce, mirror. But for Derrida meaning is nothing other than the ephemeral play of language itself. Language does not refer to anything outside of itself; it refers only to itself, in an endless, disseminating deferral of any definite referent.

Derrida arrives at this view by capitalizing on the structuralist notion that the "value" (i.e., meaning) of any given linguistic unit is (like that of a piece in a chess set) determined solely by its differences from all the other units in the language (*la langue*, the linguistic code). What any given sign "means" or "signifies" (its meaning, the "signified") is a function solely of its diacritical oppositions to other signs or "signifiers." Meaning is thus a wholly intra-linguistic sort of affair; there is no "transcendental signified," something outside of the play of signifiers themselves whose function it would be to confer on them their meaning, be this an empirical or ideal state of affairs or a psychological meaning-intention. We can never step outside of language, and since, moreover, any present linguistic meaning is a function of absent signifiers, meaning itself can never be fully present, determined.[22] To Saussure, who said that in language "There is nothing but differences,"[23] Derrida adds: there is nothing but *différance* (a term which, if it refers to anything at all, must remain without meaning).[24] Derrida draws from the semiological view of language[25] the conclusion that language is nothing but a differential system of slippage and dissemination and that meaning (as something decidable) is something that is forever deferred:

meaning "is infinite implication, the indefinite referral of signifier to signifier" (*WD*, 25).

Thus for Derrida there is no exit from the labyrinth of a text, no finished, decidable meaning, merely an endless play of signifiers. There is, quite simply, nothing outside the text: *Il n'y a pas de hors-texte* (*G*, 158). What are the results of all this for the business of textual interpretation, which is, one would think, the attempt to articulate the meaning of a text? What, in this view of things, is there to interpret? Not much, it seems.[26] Because for Derrida a writer does not dominate his language but can use it only by letting himself be used by it, the aim of reading cannot or should not be that of recapturing, re-producing the author's signifying intention, of "doubling the text" (see *G*, 158).[27] We seem to be faced here with a kind of either/or: Either we are constrained in our interpretations by a pre-existent meaning which we seek merely to double ("hermeneutics" in Derrida's sense) or we are set free to engage in an "active interpretation" (*WD*, 292), one which is, so to speak, *dechaînée*.[28] Freeplay does away with all decidable meaning; the interpretive game engenders an endless series of proliferating interpretations. In our interpretive efforts (our attempt to understand the text, to get at its meaning), we are condemned to an "abyss," a perpetual oscillation between conflicting interpretations with the impossibility of making any decisive choice.

Just as language is not about anything, so it would appear neither is interpretation. "For Derrida," Rorty says, "writing always leads to more writing, and more, and still more."[29] Derrida is one of Rorty's heroes because he is what Rorty would call a "strong textualist," who is in the interpretation business "for what he can get out of it, not for the satisfaction of getting something right."[30] Derrida himself is not quite so cavalier about the matter. He does recognize that there must be constraints on reading (one must recognize and respect the "classical exigencies"—although, he adds, these have always only *protected,* never *opened* a reading [*G*, 158]), and he does say that although "reading is transformation," "this transformation cannot be executed however one wishes" and that it requires "protocols of reading" (*Pos,* 63). He does not, however, tell us what these protocols should be. (Why not say it bluntly: "I have not yet found any that satisfy me.") Given the way he has misrepresented hermeneutics, and given also his misreading of Peirce (to which I shall turn in what immediately follows), one wonders what usefulness these unspecified "protocols" might have (unless it be that of helping to engender what Harold Bloom would call "strong misreadings").

Let us consider for a moment Derrida's handling of Peirce, as this particular "blind spot" in his text can light up for us the way hermeneutics escapes the deconstructionist either/or. Peirce appeals greatly to Derrida ("Peirce goes very far in the direction that I have called the deconstruction of the transcendental signified, which, at one time or another would place a reassuring end to the reference from sign to sign" [G, 49]), but Derrida ignores about as many important things in Peirce as Rorty does in Gadamer. What appeals to Derrida is Peirce's "semiotic," as he called it, specifically his notion of the "interpretant," i.e., Peirce's theory that the meaning of one sign is simply another sign that can be substituted for it.[31] It all sounds like Derrida's endless play of signifiers in which meaning is forever deferred ("every signified is also in the position of a signifier" [Pos, 20]). But there is, nonetheless, a différence (avec-un-e).

Peirce maintains, as Derrida says he does, that we think only in signs. But he does not maintain, as Derrida says he does, that "there are nothing but signs" (G, 50). Derrida has no grounds for enlisting Peirce's support for his notion of freeplay. The fact of the matter is that in texts that Derrida passes over in silence, Peirce speaks of a *final* interpretant. At first glance this might seem to contradict his theory that the meaning of one sign is another sign (its "interpretant") and that this interpretive process is without end. But it does not. When Peirce says that the process of interpretation is endless, he means that it is potentially endless; no given interpretant can ever be final in the sense that it is not open to further interpretation. This is why Peirce says that the meaning of a sign is something "altogether virtual." If this were all Peirce had to say, we could no doubt view him as a proto-deconstructionist. But he fully realized that to leave things at this point would land us in a form of nihilism; it would mean that *at no time* do we ever have access to decidable meanings. Peirce realized the need for something which, here and now, at any given moment, will provide for meaning, even though this meaning will not be immune to further change. He called this "the living definition, the veritable and final logical interpretant."

The important thing for us to note is that Peirce locates this "final logical interpretant" not in the order of language or textuality but in the order of *praxis*. He writes: "Consequently, the most perfect account of a concept that words can convey will consist in a description of the habit which that concept is calculated to produce." This, of course, fully reflects Peirce's pragmatic bent: his linking of belief to habit, and habit to action. Meaning is not something which is free-floating; if we wish to determine the meaning of a particular belief or concept, and do not wish to get caught up in endless word-games, we must take into consideration the kind of action to which it gives rise. It is in habit and action that we discover the true meaning of beliefs (our own as well as those of others).[32]

If I have taken the time to recall a crucial element in Peirce's semiotic, it is because there is a striking parallel between it and a crucial element in Gadamer's hermeneutic: the latter's notion of *application*. While both Peirce and Gadamer reject any notion of a transcendental signified, they do not conclude from this that we have to do only with an endless play of signifiers. They realize quite well that although we are always in the process of producing texts, and that although there can never be any final text, there is nevertheless always something outside of the text and the order of textuality, and that it is this which allows for decidable meanings. Let us focus on this crucial difference, on the real difference between deconstruction and hermeneutics.

Deconstruction maintains that because writing exceeds the signifying intention of the author, the object of reading should not be that of rediscovering and reduplicating this meaning. This, it says, is what "hermeneutics" seeks to do. Consider, however, some of the things Gadamer has to say: ". . .the sense of a text in general reaches far beyond what its author originally intended" (*TM*, 335). "The mens auctoris is not admissible as a yardstick for the meaning of a work of art" (*TM*, xix). "Does an author really know so exactly and in every sentence what he means?" (*TM*, 489). "Not occasionally only, but always, the meaning of a text goes beyond its author" (*TM*, 264).

For Gadamer understanding is not only thoroughly *linguistic* in character, it is also *transformative, productive* of new meanings ("It is enough to say that we understand in a different way if we understand at all" [*TM*, 264]), and in insisting on these two characteristics of understanding his hermeneutics overlaps with deconstruction. However, the act of reading is not for him a form of free-floating play. It is always tied to a concrete situation. This is why, unlike Derrida, he also maintains that understanding is inseparable from *application*, i.e., from the reading subject's reaction to and appropriation of the text. While all understanding is ultimately linguistic in character, in a very important sense writing does not simply give rise to more writing (". . .there will never be anything but texts" [*G*, 29 n. 38]) but has its fulfillment (end) outside of itself, in the realm of the existential-practical, in the transformation it produces in the reading subject (in his or her world orientation). The task that phenomenological herme- neutics sets itself is not, contrary to what Derrida would have us believe, that of reconstituting a past, originating meaning but is, instead, that of explicating the possible senses that a text has for us today, what it says to us, here and now.

Gadamer's central thesis that meaning is inseparable from application is thoroughly postmodern and is *at least* as anti- or non-metaphysical as anything to be found in deconstruction (it is one of Hirsch's main targets for criticism), for it is one of the central tenets of the metaphysics or epistemology of language (one that Derrida has sought expressly to deconstruct) that there is a radical distinction between sense and reference, between meaning (what words invariably mean) and application (how they are applied in particular situations). However, we do not find in Gadamer the blind spot which is so salient in Derrida's work. Derrida quite simply omits to take into account in his theorizing (if it can be called that) the fact that texts have *readers*.[33] And these readers are always *particular individuals* existing in *particular situations*, in the light of which and by application to which the text assumes, by means of what Gadamer calls a "fusion of horizons," a particular, decidable meaning. Given his animus towards the "subject," it really is no wonder if Derrida can find no decidable meanings in texts, for it makes no sense to speak about the meaning of a text apart from our reading of it. No reading, however, is context-free, and it is precisely this *phenomenological fact* that there is always a context that serves to anchor the text in our actual living and to allow it to have a decidable meaning.[34]

Deconstruction tends to issue in relativism, interpretive arbitrariness, because while it maintains (as Gadamer himself does) that there is no meaning *present* in the text, one that it would be the task of interpretation simply to re-present (there is no original, fixed, hidden meaning to be uncovered), it maintains, at the same time, in accordance with its structuralist inspiration, that there is nothing but texts, that meaning is nothing but the interplay of signs which are themselves without intrinsic meaning. The deconstructionist project is a hopeless venture because it cannot, in accordance with its anti-phenomenological bias against "subjectivity," allow for the moment of appropriation (to use the term favored by Paul Ricoeur)—no doubt because it links this to the supposedly metaphysical notion of the *proper*, i.e., that which is "absolutely *proximate* to itself" (*G*, 50).[35] There is no reason, however, why subjectivity should be viewed, metaphysically, as pure self-presence (and accordingly rejected *en bloc*), and, indeed, it is one of the positive accomplishments of phenomenological hermeneutics to have decentered the subject, to have, so to speak, de-subjectivized subjectivity.[36]

To the deconstructionist notion of undecidability should be opposed the quite different hermeneutical notion of *inexhaustibility* (see *TM*, 336). In contrast to deconstruction, hermeneutics maintains that there is always the possibility of meaning, but, in contrast to logocentrism, it maintains that it is never possible to arrive at a final meaning: "the discovery of the true meaning of a text or a work of art is never finished; it is in fact an infinite process" (*TM*, 265). Unlike "undecidability," "inexhaustibility" points not to the eternal vanity of all human endeavor but rather to the limitless possibility of interrogation, expression, and understanding.[37] "Inexhaustibility" means that in the already acquired we can always find that which can serve to renew our lives and to break the metaphysical circle of the eternal repetition of the Same.[38] Nor does the fact that we never have access to a transcendental signified mean that our interpretations are free-floating and "groundless"; they are anchored in our effective history which they also serve to reshape and which, although it is a ground without a ground (i.e., not a foundation in the metaphysical sense, a Cartesian *fundamentum inconcussum*), is yet sure and stable enough to allow for a viable and enduring *human* community.

If "knowledge," once deconstructed, is reconstructed nonfoundationistically to mean "understanding" in the hermeneutical sense (the generation and possession of viable meaning), then hermeneutics gives us what deconstruction cannot give us and does not even claim to give us ("we know something here which is no longer anything, with a knowledge whose form can no longer be recognized under the old name" [*Dis*, 21]), namely knowledge. That is, it leaves us with something more than the cacophony of everyone's parodying, fanciful interpretations of things, and it allows us to construct a society which is something more than a deconstructed Tower of Babel.

IV Truth

As philosophy has always maintained, the notions of meaning and truth are intimately related. In Gadamer's case, if interpretation does not work with the expectation of encountering both meaning and truth in that which is to be interpreted, understanding is quite simply impossible (see *TM*, 261–62). Thus, what was said above about Gadamer and Derrida in regard to the subject of meaning contains implicitly most of what needs to be said about them in regard to the subject of truth. Here too the crucial difference, "the difference that makes a difference," as Bernstein would say,[39] has to do with Gadamer's notion of application. Just as the meaning of the text is realized in the reader, in the history of its effects, so also is its truth.

Although the notion of truth is perhaps the least explicated of Gadamer's key concepts, it is nevertheless one of, if not the most central of them, as is instanced by the appearance of the term in the very title of his *magnum opus* and by the fact that it also forms the very last word of the book (there is a parallel here with Proust's monumental *A la recherche du temps perdu* which, in a similar fashion, posts its key term in its title and which ends with the words "dans le temps"). We can say of it, however, what we said of meaning. Just as it is meaningless to speak of meaning if there is nothing outside of the play of signs (Derrida is, like Lévi-Strauss, quite right on this score),[40] so also it is utterly vacuous to speak of truth *if*, as Gadamer indeed has, one has abandoned the metaphysical/epistemological conception of truth as the representation of an "objective" state of affairs *and* one maintains that all there is is the free-play of signs. Then indeed we enter into "the epochal regime of quotation marks" (*S/E*, 107) in which everything, being without "reference," is also without truth, and philosophy, seen now to be a form of fiction, reaches its end. There can be truth only if there is something *outside* of the linguistic code and outside of "quotation marks," and only if there is something more than just "a play of traces or differance that has no sense" (*Dif*, 154). And indeed, as we have seen, there is, in a sense, an "outside" for Gadamer, although this is in no way a Derridean, metaphysical Origin. Language, for Gadamer, is not, as it is for the (post)structuralists, a kind of self-enclosed, self-subsisting entity, even if this entity which has no outside has, as it is said, no internal self-centeredness either (see *Dis*, 35–36). While it is all-encompassing and, as he says, "ubiquitous," language nonetheless is not a prison (however much an internally decentered and Kafkaesque hall of mirrors this may be).[41] It is nothing other than the universal medium of our *experience* of the world, the form in which the *play of experience* realizes itself.[42]

The notion of play (*Spiel, jeu*), which is as central to Gadamer as it is to Derrida, is one of the more notable instances of the overlap between hermeneutics and deconstruction. And yet, as is to be expected, it is one in which is revealed most clearly the crucial difference between these two instances of postmodern thought. Derrida joyfully embraces a Nietzschean notion of play, a groundless and aimless play in which all standards and distinctions are meaningless, a form of play which rules out in advance any notion of "progress" (progression) and in which meaning is forever deferred in an endless supplementarity.[43] Derrida's "jeu" is "the Nietzschean *affirmation*, that is the joyous affirmation of the play of the world and of the innocence of becoming, the affirmation of a world of signs without fault, without truth, and without origin which is offered to an active interpretation" (*WD*, 292). It is a form of play which is both pointless, i.e., without goal, and meaningless. For Gadamer, however, the play of linguistic experience is, to borrow a phrase from Huizinga, *zwecklos aber doch sinnvoll*.[44] It is "goal-less" in that, unlike metaphysical progression, it does not aim at a final, ultimate meaning or understanding in which would be revealed the ultimate truth of things. It is not, however, without meaning, this meaning lying in the enhanced self-understanding the player receives as a result of the play of understanding.

Gadamer's concentration on play as a metaphor for the understanding process is not meant as a Nietzschean rejection of rules or of the subject; its purpose is, rather, to enable us to conceive of subjectivity anew, in a postmodern, post-epistemological fashion. Differing in a salutary way from his mentor Heidegger in this regard, Gadamer does not direct his deconstructive critique against subjectivity and traditional humanism as such. His purpose (certain ill-chosen remarks of his notwithstanding) is not to abandon subjectivity, as if it were some dreadful metaphysical construct which gets in the way of the advent of Being (*Ereignis*), but to arrive at a less "subjectivistic," less Cartesian conception of it. Play, for Gadamer, whose thinking is fully a part of the classical tradition of *humanitas*, is not, as it is for Derrida and other such contemporary anti-humanists, an attempt to "pass beyond man and humanism" (*WD*, 292). Play for Gadamer is most definitely not *eine Spiel ohne Spieler*.[45] The very meaning of Gadamer's notion of the fusion of horizons is that what we have to do with in the play of understanding is the transformation of one subject in his or her encounter with another. We have to do with a self which, in and by means of the dialogical encounter with the other, comes to a greater realization (in the concrete sense of the term) of itself, becomes, as Kierkegaard would say, who or what he or she is. In this context, truth does not mean correspondence with reality (truth as presence)—what possible meaning could that have?—but refers rather to the disclosure of possibilities for being and acting that emerge in and by means of the playful encounter. Truth refers not to a static, mirroring relation between a subject and an object but to the transformation process which occurs in all instances of genuine understanding. Truth refers to the self-enrichment and self-realization that occurs as a result of the play of meaning.

This process of "realization" must not, however, be understood in a Hegelian, i.e., metaphysical, sense. Metaphysical *parousia*, the final possession of the truth (Derrida's "full presence"), is not even an ideal for Gadamer, not even in the mode of nostalgia. There is absolutely no place for the metaphysical notion of "totality" (or totalization) in his thinking ("the idea of the whole is itself to be understood only relatively" [*TM*, xxiii]).

He deliberately seeks to avoid "a metaphysics of infinity in the Hegelian manner" (*TM*, 433). Instead, he resolutely insists on "the constitutional incompletion (*Unvollendbarkeit*) of experience."[46] Gadamerian self-realization is not a Hegelian *Bildung*. If there is a teleology of truth and becoming for Gadamer, it is, as Merleau-Ponty would have said, a teleology without a telos.[47] "The dialectic of experience," he writes, "has its own fulfillment not in definitive knowledge, but in that openness to experience that is encouraged by experience itself" (*TM*, 319).

I could perhaps sum this all up by saying that for Gadamer play is not just "mere" play. In contrast to Derrida's *jeu* (his "pure play"), it must, in Gadamer's case, be said: *Il y a quelque chose qui est en jeu dans le jeu; il y a un enjeu au jeu*. There is something that is at stake, at issue (*en jeu*), in the play of understanding, something, as in the Pascalian wager, that is to be won or lost, and this is nothing other than our *being* itself, the never-to-be-completed realization of our own utmost possibilities of being.[48] This is why, of course, there is no trace of Nietzschean fatalism in Gadamer's hermeneutics, a kind of nihilism that would have to be masked by a heavy dose (*pharmakon*) of Dionysian gleeful exuberance over the "innocence of becoming" (*"amor fati"*).

Unlike Derrida, who is (through no fault of his own) unable to specify what a post-metaphysical culture might look like, Gadamer can and does.[49] His *Ueberwindung der Metaphysik*, his overcoming of the tradition, does not exhaust itself in a vain and sterile (i.e., "disseminating") protest against its untenable, idealist presuppositions. This is because Gadamer finds in the tradition itself the wherewithal to overcome it productively.[50]

Chapter 9

L'ECRITURE AND PHILOSOPHICAL HERMENEUTICS

Wayne J. Froman

I Writing and *Wirkungsgeschichtliches Bewusstsein*

In *Truth and Method*, Hans-Georg Gadamer describes what happens in the course of conversation, not only with interlocutors who are present with us, but, as well, with interlocutors who have preceded us in history and who have left works, of one sort or another, that are the vehicles of conversation across the ages. What Gadamer finds in the course of that description is that our own situatedness as interpreters of these works, our own historicity, does not constitute an obstacle to our understanding of what gets handed down in these works, but rather is precisely what makes accessible the question that set our predecessor's work in motion and sustained it. The understanding that occurs in the course of conversation is an event in which we encounter that which is "question-worthy." At the same time, that which is "question-worthy" is disclosed by way of its bearing on our own historical situation.

Gadamer identifies Heidegger's recognition of the "fore-structure" of all interpretation as the breakthrough that made it possible to realize that our own historicity as interpreters is not an obstacle to understanding what gets handed down in the works of our predecessors. This fore-structure is a tripartite structure of "fore-having," "fore-sight," and "fore-conception" that is rooted in the existential structure of *Dasein*. *Dasein's* existential structure comprises *Befindlichkeit*, by virtue of which *Dasein* is always already pre-disposed toward beings (*Seiendes*), *Verstehen*, by virtue of which *Dasein* is the disclosure of those possibilities upon which it is projected, and *Rede*, by virtue of which *Dasein's* prior disposition toward beings, which involves those disclosed possibilities upon which *Dasein* is projected, is amenable to interpretation that gets expressed in words. Gadamer proposes that the fore-structure of all interpretation, which is rooted in the existential structure of *Dasein*, guides the interpretation of the work of predecessors in such a way that the dynamic of *Wirkungsgeschichtliches Bewusstsein*, "effective historical consciousness," "fuses" the horizon of the interpreter's historical situation with the horizon of the historical situation of predecessors whose work is the occasion for interpretation. The interpreter encounters the question that set the predecessor's work in motion, and that which is question-worthy, for interpreter as well as predecessor, is disclosed by way of its bearing—its effectiveness—on the historical situation of the interpreter. Possibilities constitutive of that situation are disclosed that had not previously been open, possibilities for extending dialogue with regard to that which remains always question-worthy. This disclosure attests to an inexhaustible truth that gets handed down in those works that serve as vehicles of conversation between interpreters, predecessors, and successors as well.

Of all forms of transmission from one age to another, Gadamer identifies writing as the one that "presents the hermeneutical problem in all its purity."[1] Writing, Gadamer finds, is "a kind of alienated speech" (*TM*, p. 354). That is to say that inscriptions, the written signs per se, are incapable of yielding any meaning unless they are "transformed back into speech and meaning" (*TM*, p. 355). The task of "awakening writing" is that faced by the interpreter. Because of the fact that the inscription is divorced from its original setting, the "transformation of writing back into speech and meaning" must be accomplished, Gadamer finds, without any appeal to support from the intentions of the author or the understanding of the initial audience. In this way, the interpreter—as reader—can only operate by way of the interpreter's own historical situatedness and the understanding that occurs in the reading—and that transforms the writing back into speech and meaning—is an understanding of what is question-worthy (beyond the intentions of the author or the understanding of the initial audience) in its bearing on the interpreter's historical situation. The "weakness of writing" (*TM*, pp. 354–55), the lack of support for the written inscription from the circumstances of its inscription, is, for Gadamer, precisely what makes the interpretation of writing exemplary of the dynamic of effective historical consciousness, in which, that which is question-worthy is disclosed by way of its bearing on the historical situation of the interpreter—by way of newly opened possibilities for dialogue that attest to a truth that is not exhausted in any age.

> The understanding of something written is not a reproduction of something that is past, but the sharing of a present meaning. (*TM*, p. 354)

> What [the reader] understands is always more than an alien meaning: it is always possible truth. (*TM*, p. 356)

The reading of a written text, then, is paradigmatic of the dynamic of effective historical consciousness, within which an understanding of any works that require interpretation takes place. What these works say to the interpreter, does not amount to the "true intentions" of the producers of these works, nor to a truth that would stand outside history. Herein lies what Gary Madison, in "Beyond Seriousness and Frivolity: A Gadamerian Response to Deconstruction," identifies as the "post-epistemological and post-metaphysical significance of Gadamer's enterprise." That enterprise is no longer governed by the driven seriousness of the interpreter whose measure of success is the extent to which interpretation has the final word in fixing an objective meaning of a work, or in determining precisely how far the work falls short of truth that stands outside history. It surprises Madison that Jacques Derrida does not acknowledge this much about Gadamer's work. Indeed, certain references to hermeneutics in Derrida's *Spurs/Eperons* suggest to Madison that Derrida simply misses the significance of Gadamer's work. I will return to those references shortly, but first I want to address the question as to what Derrida could find left out of account in Gadamer's description of interpretive understanding.

The answer lies in Gadamer's account of why writing "presents the hermeneutical problem in all its purity." The "self-alienation" of meaning that takes place when meaning is "written down" is what must be overcome by interpretive reading. "The sign language of writing refers back to the actual language of speech" (*TM*, p. 354). Speech—"actual language"—is contrasted with the sign language of writing. Although Gadamer would not describe spoken language as a context of signs, he does of course acknowledge that speech too is in need of interpretation. In either case, the interpretation does not lead to a meaning that lies beyond the bounds of language. But, where writing is concerned, it is only the transformation back into speech that guarantees any meaning at all. Why is that? It is because, for Gadamer, it is only spoken language that disappears in attesting to the inexhaustibility of that truth that is handed down by way of the works of predecessors. The divergence or differing between the disclosure of that which is question-worthy in its bearing on the historical situation of the interpreter, and the inexhaustible truth as such—the divergence that constitutes meaning—becomes invisible as well. This divergence or differing that Gadamer understands in terms of human finitude, is precisely what becomes an experience of the inexhaustible nature of truth that is handed down by way of the works of predecessors.

> [Effective historical consciousness] knows about the absolute openness of the meaning-event in which it shares. . . . Every assimilation of tradition is historically different: which does not mean that every one represents only an imperfect understanding of it. Rather, every one is the experience of a "view" of the object itself. (*TM*, p. 430)

I have already pointed out above that the interpretive concepts are cancelled out in the fullness of understanding because they are meant to disappear. This means that they are not just tools that we take up and then throw aside, but that they belong to the inner structure of the thing (which is meaning). What is true of every word in which thought is expressed, is true also of the interpreting word, namely that it is not, as such, objective. As the realization of the act of understanding it is the actuality of the effective-historical consciousness, and as such it is truly speculative: having no tangible being of its own and yet throwing back the image that is presented to it. (*TM*, pp. 430–31)

This disappearance of spoken language in favor of the experience of the inexhaustible nature of truth that is handed down by way of the works of predecessors, is what happens, Gadamer finds, in the course of interpretation. It "happens to us over and above our wanting and doing" (*TM*, p. xvi). In order for it to happen in the course of interpreting written texts, the writing must be transformed back into speaking. But does this event not involve the complicity of the interpreter? And in what does that complicity lie? Is it not to be found in the sublation of the divergence or differing that becomes invisible along with spoken language? Is the apparent inexhaustibleness of truth not a result of incessant sublation of this sort as a result of which all such divergence or differing is consumed in the hermeneutic experience? Is the privileging of speech not the suppression of the medium of divergence and differing *par excellence*—the sign language, as Gadamer calls it, in contrast to actual language or speech—i.e., writing? Is this not the gesture that Derrida exposes as the origin of metaphysics? This gesture is not, itself, contained within metaphysics. Hermeneutics, as understood by Gadamer, is non-metaphysical. But, what Derrida could find missing is the recognition that the non-metaphysical hermeneutical gesture takes its resources from that "sign language" that "presents the hermeneutical problem in all its purity."

Gadamer writes:

> . . .that language is capable of being written is by no means
> incidental to its nature. Rather, this capacity of being
> written down is based on the fact that speech itself shares
> in the pure ideality of the meaning that communicates itself
> in it. . . . Writing is the abstract ideality of language. (*TM*,
> p. 354)

What Derrida could find missing is the recognition that in the very repeatability of the written signifier, its "abstract ideality," the signifier differs from itself, and this differing moves throughout writing and throughout the copying of writing—the reproduction of "texts." This differing is sublated in the hermeneutical transformation of writing into speech, and this sublation is compounded by the hermeneutical gesture in which spoken language disappears in favor of an experience of the inexhaustible nature of truth. This "inexhaustibleness" appears as such only as a result of the sublation of open-ended differing, which is its inexhaustible resource.

II Frivolity and writing

Once Derrida acknowledges the differing that moves throughout writing, is he left with nothing but an "endless play of signifiers," a source, perhaps, of ongoing amusement but, in and of itself, worthless—that is to say, frivolous? Is this acknowledgment tantamount to explaining meaning away? This is what Gary Madison suggests. He quotes Derrida: meaning "is infinite implication, the indefinite referral of signifier to signifier." Let us, however, examine more closely the passage from which this is taken:

> . . .what is intolerable for structuralism is indeed the richness implied by the volume, every element of signification that cannot be spread out into the simultaneity of a form. But is it by chance that the book is, first and foremost, volume? And that the meaning of meaning (in the general sense of meaning and not in the sense of signalization) is infinite implication, the indefinite referral of signifier to signifier? And that its force is a certain pure and infinite equivocality which gives signified meaning no respite, no rest, but engages it in its own *economy* so that it always signifies again and differs?[2]

Derrida's point here is that structuralism—or better, "ultrastructuralism," which, Derrida observes, betrays the initial structuralist impetus—severs "infinite implication" from the dynamic that is its source in such a way as to enclose the "indefinite referral of signifier to signifier" within a unidimensional formal context of signifiers. "Ultrastructuralism" dismisses that dynamic as "chance," "inconsequential accident or dross." It fails to recognize what Gadamer does not acknowledge in speaking of the "abstract ideality" of writing, namely, the differing of the written signifier from itself that moves throughout writing. It is precisely by dismissing this dynamic, by identifying it exhaustively with "chance," "inconsequential accident or dross," that "ultrastructuralism" reduces meaning to, or identifies meaning with, a bare play of signifiers.

In his reading of the work of Condillac, *The Archeology of the Frivolous: Reading Condillac*,[3] Derrida observes that Condillac sought to eliminate any bare play of signifiers from philosophical discourse. He identified that play as frivolity, the lack of meaning. Condillac maintained that only by eliminating this frivolity could philosophy turn into true science. What "ultrastructuralism" dismisses as "chance," "inconsequential accident or dross," Condillac identifies as "a supervening historical evil" (*AF*, p. 124), frivolity, which "affects from the outside an essentially serious discourse" (*AF*, p. 124).

> Frivolity consists in being satisfied with tokens. It originates with the sign, or rather with the signifier which, no longer signifying, is no longer a signifier. The empty, void, friable, useless signifier. So Condillac says. (*AF*, p. 118)

> All the negativity subject to criticism [in Condillac's *An Essay on the Origin of Human Knowledge*] (bad metaphysics, bad rhetoric, bad language in general) falls under the category of the frivolous: the arrangement of hollow or unnecessary signs. (*AF*, p. 119)

Condillac sought to turn philosophy into a science by eliminating this frivolity. He first attributes it to an operation of metaphor at the origin of language and then sets out to reappropriate this operation analogically and teleologically. "Condillac's method consequently consists in indefinitely recharging signs, in saturating semiotics with semantic representation, by including all rhetoric in a metaphorics, by *connecting the signifier*" (*AF*, p. 119)—in order that there could be no bare play of signifiers, no "arrangement of hollow or unnecessary signs." But persisting in this project has as a consequence the delay or the deferral of the appearance of frivolity as such—frivolity in-itself, we might say, or pure frivolity. And by always adding "too many signs," the project has as a consequence the multiplication of the differing of the signifiers from themselves and thus a reassertion of the threat of frivolity.

The dynamic that marks "the possibility and the impossibility of frivolity" (*AF*, p. 132), marks the deferral and the reassertion of the possibility of meaning.

> The fragility, the frail structure of the frivolous *is nothing but* (the time of a) difference (of degree), the spacing that ontology, as such, simply could not be capable of. There is

a crack there. Construction *and* deconstruction are breached/broached there. The line of disintegration, which is not straight or continuous or regular—philosophy is affected by this almost by itself. Philosophy deviates from itself and gives rise to the blows that will strike it nonetheless from the outside. On this condition alone, at once internal and external, is deconstruction *possible*. (*AF*, p. 132)

The undecidability of writing—*l'écriture*—is not a matter of a bare play of signifiers, but rather an undecidability between writing as decentering, a constant deconstruction of the presumption of pure, identifiable frivolity and/or pure, identifiable meaning—a decentering that remains attached to the project of centering, and writing as an affirmation of play, that is, writing that makes of this undecidability, play.

. . . is not the desire for a center, as a function of play itself, the indestructible itself? And in the repetition or return of play, how could the phantom of the center not call to us? It is here that the hesitation between writing as decentering and writing as an affirmation of play is infinite.[4]

Derrida does not explain meaning away as a bare play of signifiers, and he does not insist upon a "pure play" among signifiers that are switched into equivalent arrangements indefinitely. To do either or to do both, would mean to fail to acknowledge the dynamic of writing—*l'écriture*.

The undecidability of writing is the issue in Derrida's discussion of the line "I have forgotten my umbrella," found in quotation marks among Nietzsche's unpublished writings.[5] Gary Madison is correct in describing Derrida's comments about a hermeneutic reading of this line as limited where different conceptions of the nature of hermeneutics are concerned. To take these into account would clearly require a more extended and more intricate discussion. But, when Derrida says that a "hermeneut ontologist" would think that this line must have some significance and that it must issue from the most personal recess of the author's thought, this is not to say that any hermeneutics takes as its ultimate goal the determination of an author's intentions. Rather, because this line resists integration within the horizon of our understanding of "die Sache" of Nietzsche's thought—what is at the heart of his thought—a hermeneutical reading of this line, by attributing it to the most personal recess of the author's thought, could regard the line as marking a limit of interpretation, an isolable instance of a limit that may be negligible given the volume of writings that are interpretable. But perhaps this line stays secret in a way that hermeneutic reading misses. Perhaps, precisely as "a piece of writing," this line differs from itself in the way that the signifiers of writing differ from themselves. It stays secret by virtue of this differing from itself that hides no secret while interminably making alternate readings possible. While hermeneutics does not acknowledge this dynamic of writing, and would now put the line aside in the course of interpreting Nietzsche's writings, Derrida finds that decoding the meanings that are possible has to proceed as far as is possible. The dynamic that marks the deferral and the reassertion of the possibility of meaning also marks the deferral and the reassertion of the possibility of frivolity. The limit of such a decoding turns into the hesitation in writing between decentering, or deconstruction of the presumption of pure meaning and/or pure frivolity—a decentering that remains attached to the project of centering, to putting at stake, to meaning—and play, that is, the turning of this undecidability itself into play. To say, as Derrida does at this point, that however far one pursues the "conscientious interpretation" of Nietzsche's work, one cannot put aside the hypothesis that Nietzsche's writings, all together, are of the type "I have forgotten my umbrella" is to say that the limit of this reading (however enormous a task the reading may be) could be the differing of writing from itself, an infinite differing that hides nothing while it also puts meaning at stake, puts meaning in play.

III   Hermeneutical application and the effects of writing

If Derrida does not explain meaning away and end up indulging in pure frivolity, is it the case that in reading and writing, Derrida severs this activity from any bearing on anything whatsoever and confines himself to virtuostic variations on architectonics in writing? This is how Gary Madison assesses Derrida's work, in contrast to Gadamer's work, where the issue of application is of paramount importance. This marks, according to Madison, the radical difference between the two.

Application, for Gadamer, means the understanding of what is question-worthy in its bearing on the historical situation of interpreters. Basically, this means a reinforcement and reaffirmation of the tradition that supports both the works of predecessors and the interpreters in their work. Application in the sense of first determining a theoretical truth that corresponds with reality and subsequently using that theoretical truth in order to submit reality to our purposes, to make the world over according to our theoretical design, is precisely the kind of application that Gadamer would replace in the various fields of the *Geisteswissenschaften.* Application, for Gadamer, is the central phase in the dynamic of effective historical consciousness, that *happens to us over and above our wanting and doing.* This is the dynamic of the tradition that supports us. And Gadamer asks: "Do we need to justify what has always supported us?" (*TM,* p. xxiv).

This which has always "supported us" is precisely what is in question in Heidegger's radical interrogation of the philosophical tradition. Gary Madison quotes Gadamer in saying that he has bypassed Heidegger's "problem of Being." This is a rather surprising statement in view of the fact that the breakthrough that makes Gadamer's development of philosophical hermeneutics possible, according to *Truth and Method,* is one that he credits to Heidegger, and that breakthrough is possible only on the basis of Heidegger's questioning concerning the meaning of Being. Where Derrida is concerned, the metaphysics of presence that has always provided meaning only by sublating, by reappropriating, and by suppressing the dynamic of writing that is its other, is disrupted. What follows, for Derrida, entails the necessity first to "catch up with the archaeological radicalness of the questions sketched by Heidegger."[6] In doing so, what is found out is that the co-appurtenance or inseparability of the meaning of man and the meaning of Being that is installed in and by the tradition of the metaphysics of presence is what is unstable, is the support or security that "is trembling today" (*MP,* p. 133).

One of the results of this "trembling" is that the entire question of the efficacy of discourse is opened up, or reopened. Derrida describes this in one of the interviews with him that were published as *Positions:*

> If what is in question in this work is a new definition of the relationship of a *determined* text or signifying chain to its exterior, to its referential effects . . . to "reality" (history, class struggle, relationships of production, etc.), then we can no longer restrict ourselves to the prior concept of a regional delimitation. What is produced in the current trembling is a reevaluation of the relationship between the general text and what was believed to be, in the form of reality (history, politics, economics, sexuality, etc.), the simple, referable exterior of language or writing, the belief that this exterior could operate from the simple position of cause or accident. What are apparently simply "regional" effects of this trembling, therefore, at the same time have a nonregional opening, destroying their own limits and tending to articulate themselves with the general scene, but in new modes, without any pretension to mastery.[7]

To say of writing that multiplies such articulations in new modes between what were once believed to be already delimited regions and the general scene—as Heidegger said of the "thinking of Being" in the well-known *Der Spiegel* interview "Only A God Can Save Us Now"—that one does not know how such articulations work, is obviously not to dismiss the issue of efficacy. Whatever remains to be determined concerning these articulations, Derrida, in any event, does not sever reading and writing from any bearing on anything whatsoever and confine himself to virtuostic variations on architectonics in writing. Writing does not take the reinforcement and reaffirmation of the inseparability of the meaning of man and the meaning of Being as installed in and by the tradition of the metaphysics of presence as the measure of its efficacy or its worth. Writing is not in the service of this *archon* that governs the standard ordering of regions of activity.

IV Conclusion

An attentive reading of Derrida's work cannot fail to find that Derrida neither reads the tradition in a manner that is driven by the attempt to find definitively objective meanings of texts, *nor* in a manner that amounts to pure frivolity, that reduces to a pure play among bare signifiers that are rearranged in equivalent configurations. To assess Derrida's work as such pure frivolity is simply to miss the dynamic of writing—*l'écriture*. Nor does Derrida's reading and writing proceed by first severing these activities from any bearings on anything. This is the case, whatever remains to be determined about the efficacy of reading and writing—an issue that is opened up or reopened by what Derrida describes as the trembling of the inseparability of the meaning of man and the meaning of Being, an inseparability put into question in Heidegger's radical interrogation of the tradition. The radicality of this opening up or reopening of the issue of efficacy disallows measuring the efficacy of reading and writing by the extent to which they reinforce and reaffirm that inseparability that is installed and established within the philosophical tradition.

If one is cognizant of the role of writing in philosophical hermeneutics as understood by Gadamer, the significance, for hermeneutics, of Derrida's work pertaining to writing—*l'écriture*—is evident. The divergence or differing of written signifiers from themselves and from other written signifiers that diverge or differ from themselves—a dynamic that is sublated by philosophical hermeneutics as understood by Gadamer—is not acknowledged in philosophical hermeneutics. If one takes this into account, a difficulty does show up in the midst of philosophical hermeneutics as understood by Gadamer. According to Gadamer, "Being that can be understood is language" (*TM*, p. 432). Writing is not "actual language." Writing per se, then, is not Being that can be understood. There is a gap between meaning that is determined by way of the hermeneutical operation and the structure of writing. Without the sublation of its dynamic by "transforming it into speech," or "actual language," writing does not provide support for Gadamer's assertion of the universality of hermeneutics. Inasmuch as writing presents the hermeneutical problem in its purest form, the gap multiplies and the consequences spread through results of interpretation by way of philosophical hermeneutics. This would seem to forestall a disappearance of interpretive language in favor of an experience of truth described by Gadamer as follows, in terms that signal a reinstatement of metaphysics by way of the hermeneutical operation: "In the use of words what is given to the senses is not presented as an individual example of a universal, but it is itself made present in what is said—just as the idea of the beautiful is present in what is beautiful" (*TM*, p. 466).

Can there be, as Gadamer suggests there always is, a prior mutual understanding between the practitioner of philosophical hermeneutics and the practitioner of writing at the limits of the philosophical tradition? Is it the case, as Gadamer asserts, that we are a conversation? At this juncture, a different question is interposed. To quote Derrida—without dismissing any of the difficulties attendant upon quoting, from writing, by Derrida, or upon accounting for the legibility of this question, or accounting for the limit of the ability to account for its legibility—"But who, we?"[8]

PART VI
HABERMAS/GADAMER

Chapter 10

ANSWERS TO CRITICAL THEORY

Graeme Nicholson

Contemporary philosophical hermeneutics and neo-Marxist critical theory both trace their origins to the Germany of the 1920s. This bestows certain common features on them, and it has ensured that the two have never been wholly ignorant of one another. But in itself this would not have been enough to bring the two into fruitful co-operation or even dialogue—such is the violent history of our century. It was after the appearance of *Truth and Method* (Gadamer, 1960)[1] that a productive encounter began to take place, largely owing to Jürgen Habermas, who held a position in philosophy at Heidelberg in the years between the book's appearance and its second edition. We see from the inaugural address Habermas gave at Frankfurt when he moved there in 1965[2] that he had thoroughly absorbed Gadamer's argument. And when he published the long essay, *On the Logic of the Social Sciences* (Habermas, 1967),[3] he launched a debate that lasted several years and that has been one of the deepest, most interesting and most important philosophical debates in recent times.

I shall sketch the two authors' contributions in historical sequence, and I shall try also to signal the **arguments** and **counter-arguments** of the two authors that run through the literature and give it its unity. As the reader will see, some of the issues recur six or seven times, or more, throughout the debate. Anyone who studies this debate in the light of the dominant issues cannot fail to see how broad its significance is. At one level, the debate is a struggle between hermeneutical thinking and the social sciences over the way to grasp our literary heritage. But this touches directly the role of universities and schools in social life. Indirectly it raises all the substantive issues of social thought that are tied to education: the place of authority, the structure of institutions, questions of family and social reproduction. At another level, the debate addresses epistemological problems, such as the role of language in our gaining access to reality, and the role of inherited frames of reference within knowledge. What lies very close to this is the set of issues that encircle the place of science and technology in modern society: how shall technology be made the instrument for all rather than for the few? The school of critical theory saw itself as bringing to the German intellectual world a rebellious and democratic element, a long overdue thrust of the Enlightenment. The school of hermeneutics saw itself as the heir of the proud German mainstream tradition of historical thinking, augmented with a further Heideggerian thrust. That these profoundly different strands of thought should have entered into a productive dialogue is a triumph of modern German intellectual life.

Though it was Habermas, in 1967, who launched the actual debate, I shall need to begin my history from Gadamer's very big and very rich magnum opus from 1960, selecting from it just the points that will become contentious in the early stages of the debate. And after I begin to introduce the arguments of Habermas, I shall attempt to appraise their relevance and their force in a series of running observations marked in the text as my own comments. In general, my conclusion will be that while it was right of Habermas to raise the social and political issues that he did, his arguments were nevertheless entirely ineffective on the issues. Gadamer's replies to critical theory have carried the day decisively.

I   Gadamer 1960

The work is decisively not a canon or doctrine of *method* for interpretation, but an inquiry into the grounds of the possibility of interpretation. It makes its start with our experience of the art work, building to a critical study of "aesthetic" consciousness. Whenever we try to isolate the pure aesthetic value of a work from its subject matter and other points of genuine interest in it, we accomplish a distanciation of the work from ourselves, an abstraction that discounts the work's own impact. We come to posit it as an interesting kind of object, and shield ourselves from the power the work may have, even over the centuries and millenia, to address us still. True, it will surely address us differently from the way it addressed earlier times, but in fact that is only a healthy indicator of our finitude. Now this argument is directed first of all against Kant's aesthetics, but widens to encompass modern art criticism and aesthetics.

Part Two offers an account of our historical consciousness that is in accord with the account of Part One. When we seek to reconstruct a past book, event, movement or theory "just the way it really was" we fall into the "aporias of historicism" by seeking to bypass the impact which that book, etc., exercises upon ourselves now, in our own situation. To make history itself, and historical things, into objects for our interested gaze is to overlook the historical process that is already at work in ourselves and in our very understanding. Our own mode of thought is a horizon we cannot eliminate; to understand something from the past is to experience the fusion of its horizon with our own; true self-understanding is to grasp our own selves and minds as exposed to history's power and history's effects. Now since the unity of the historical process is objectively constituted by the ever-renewed fusion of ever-changing horizons, it is crucial to our very being to understand ourselves out of a *tradition*. Moreover, only a false consciousness would wish to be emancipated from the *authority* exercised over us both by past works and by intermediaries. The operation of tradition in advance of all our reflection makes it inevitable, and correct, for us to have *prejudices*.

Part Three now widens the view to a general ontological theory to accord with the treatments of art and history, and it achieves this through a study of language. Language is so thoroughly the medium of all hermeneutical experience that it does not merely constitute the "objects" we interpret, but also constitutes and determines our own power to draw near to them. Language is also the medium of our current philosophizing and of all philosophizing. And if as philosophers we seek to understand it, that will be by finding words to name it, and we only find them in the thick tissue constituted by the various languages and traditions of texts that history presents us with: *logos*, *verbum*, and so on. It is vital to Gadamer to combat the illusion of a philosopher whose *rationality* would permit him to fly high above the linguistic particularities of his own time and other times. In fact, language is the very source of rationality: "The hermeneutical experience is the corrective by means of which thinking reason escapes the prison of language, and it is itself constituted linguistically" (*WM*, p. 380/ *TM*, p. 363). If our rationality is not constituted outside language but through language, this will serve, so Gadamer argues, to give foundations to the claim that truth exists in our encounter with the art work and with historical texts. It also gives warrant for the most general theory connecting *language and being*—all being that we can encounter is presented linguistically.

II   Gadamer 1966

In the article "The Universality of the Hermeneutical Problem,"[4] Gadamer gave a precis of his argument with stress upon the ontological import of his theory. The title made it perfectly clear that his was to be no mere sector theory of our interaction with cultural products, but a theory of *universal import*. All the *sciences*, too, are at issue in this theory. It is not a matter merely of academic posturing here. Gadamer's argument is not made in defence of a claim of hermeneutics to preside at the banquet of science. His point is to underline how every encounter with reality is prejudiced by the linguistic constitution of our understanding, and how the elucidation of the linguistic, and practical, motivation constituting the understanding's horizon has to be undertaken in all encounters with reality. This is the hermeneutical component of all knowing. Most centrally, such an elucidation succeeds by showing how any putative item of knowledge can be grasped as the answer to some question. "The real power of hermeneutical consciousness is our ability to see what is questionable" (*GW*, II, p. 228/ *PH*, p. 13). This is an interest of human reason itself, and this matter of universal import was only illustrated by studies devoted to art and history.

III   Habermas 1967

This piece (see note 3) has been the subject of a number of studies, including excellent works by Jack Mendelson[5] and Dieter

Misgeld.[6] Habermas has been dealing, up to page 149 of the *Beiheft*, with various initiatives to lay foundations for social science in theories of language, culminating in Chomsky's linguistics. Next, in pages 149–57, he shows that Gadamer's historically-minded philosophy of language accounts for cross-cultural understanding and translation more adequately than the views of Chomsky or Wittgenstein, principally owing to the openness implicit in the idea of a horizon. Pages 157–61 give a close and favorable reading of the theory of historicity in Gadamer (the fusion of horizons, the hermeneutical circle, and the consciousness open to the effects of history), and pages 161–67 confirm Gadamer's strengths in a running comparison with Arthur Danto. He summarizes his indebtedness to Gadamer in a remark on page 168, to the effect that it is only because we are practical agents ourselves, and able to understand ourselves in that way, that we are able to interpret anything at all from the past.[7] It is Gadamer's practical foundation for interpretation that Habermas values, and he finds this embodied in the theory that we understand something by applying it to our own circumstances, different though these circumstances may be from those affecting an author hundreds of years ago. Repeated practical application forges the bond of tradition that links generation to generation. And yet—it is exactly at this point, on page 171, that Habermas begins his polemic. For the sake of clarity, consider the following points:

(1) This polemic concerns the relationship between *tradition* and *rationality*. It is important to note that tradition is subject to rupture as much as it is to continuity, and when such ruptures are the result of free and rational thought on the part of a new generation that does not acquiesce in the old ways, we seem obliged to follow Hegel's account of rational thinking rather than Gadamer's. The latter has immersed rationality so deeply in the life of the tradition that it seems unable to explain such ruptures. So Habermas introduces a polarization here, and he builds immediately upon it to show that there are real interests of *method* and in general of *science* that turn them too, along with practical rationality, against the untroubled flow of a stable tradition. "A controlled distanciation can raise understanding from pre-scientific form to the status of a process of reflection" (*B*, p. 172, *HI*, p. 45). And this characteristic of the serious work of

historiography is important enough that it should have dis-
suaded Gadamer from rejecting methodology and closeness to
the scientific spirit (see *B*, p. 172–73, *HI*, pp. 45–46). By separating
hermeneutics from science he plays into the hands of the positiv-
ists; he needs scientific implementation, and science needs what
he has to offer.

(2) Habermas next scrutinizes Gadamer's vindication of *authority* and *prejudice* as categories of the practical roots of Gadamer's
hermeneutics (see *B*, pp. 174–77/*HI*, pp. 48–52). Gadamer wants
to see the authority of the great work and of the teacher who
explains it as a claim upon us that is rooted in knowledge and in
free recognition, never in mere force. But this general theory of
authority, says Habermas, fails to confront the sanctions that
society does use to sustain its authorities: Because of them, there
is often excellent reason to hope to be emancipated from authority. Likewise, the prejudices we acquire from our tradition are
all too often shackles upon the mind, and it has been the great
historic task of modern liberal movements to submit traditional
prejudice to justified critical scrutiny in the name of reason and
reflection. Again, here, we find Habermas insisting upon a polarization of the power of *rationality* against the apparent naturalness of tradition's ways.

(3) Now (*B*, pp. 177–80/*HI*, pp. 52–55) Habermas turns to a
further point, the relationship between *language* and *being*, first
broached in Part Three of *Truth and Method*. Gadamer's theory
implies a linguistic idealism. Language is one institution of society, but it is an idealistic fault to suppose that all the other
institutions are only present on account of language. There is the
central and imperative necessity of human labour too; its facticity
and even more its results, as in the division of labour, do not
arise out of structures that prevail in language. There is also the
matter of domination, another social fact that cannot be reduced
to linguistic structures. Because of these other two institutions,
it will always be important to recognize other technological sciences, and other modes of social analysis, beyond the scope of
mere hermeneutics.

Habermas concludes his commentary by introducing a brand
new issue: why has Gadamer shrunk from formulating a macro-
historical theory parallel to that of Christianity or Marxism? This
appears to be marginal in Habermas' critique, so, although Ga-

damer certainly states an answer to it,[8] I prefer to leave it to one side.

IV   Gadamer 1967

We shall be studying three Gadamerian texts in reply to Habermas. The first is called "Rhetoric, Hermeneutics and the Critique of Ideologies."[9] It begins by repeating the point from Gadamer 1966, that the original studies of art and history should not be mistaken for the full scope of hermeneutics, but were only illustrations of the linguistic constitution of all our relation to the world. Gadamer examines rhetoric as a kind of model for hermeneutics, both because it too possesses *universal import* and because it illustrates a species of *rationality*, one that adduces probabilities rather than deductive proofs; this is the species that shows up in the practice of text-interpretation which never claims conclusiveness and exhaustiveness. Now Gadamer will insist repeatedly, and I think correctly, that Habermas has failed to see that this species of rationality was misdescribed by rationalism and by critical theory, with their eagerness to assimilate it to the laws of reflective and axiomatic thought.

(4) This shows up where Habermas wants to assimilate hermeneutics to *science* and *method* (GW II, pp. 239–41/ HI, pp. 66–70). It is incorrect to posit a polarization between an ongoing tradition and the reflective appropriation of it. The most reflective scholar will contribute to tradition, because the activity of understanding must be seen as part of the movement of history. The same polarization is wrong when it opposes *rationality* to *authority* and *prejudice*. Psychotherapy and social reform never proceed from a totally blind neurosis, or a totally deformed community, to a perfection of lucidity and harmony: both in the sphere of the individual and on the social scale, we seek rational solutions to situations that are mixed as we find them, and when our work is done they are still mixed, although improved. Rationality moves where light and darkness are mixed.

COMMENT. Point (4) tells against point (1) both on the score of science and methodology, and on the categories of practical reason such as tradition, authority and prejudice. It seems to be well taken. Most of all, it reveals the difference between the fundamental postures of the two philosophers. Gadamer's entire strategy is a flight from dualism; Habermas' entire strategy consists in polarizing reason against the powers of tradition, and so on, that prevail in the world.

(5) Next Gadamer will treat the *universal import* of hermeneutics, putting this issue together with that of the relation between *language* and *being* that prompted the charge of linguistic idealism (*GW* II, pp. 242–43/*HI*, pp. 71–72). He stoutly asserts that we could not encounter either labour or domination if there were no language at work in articulating the phenomena for us. He rejects a dualistic separation of understood meanings from real forces. Moreover the prejudices that preform all our understanding are in part the understood deposit of relations of labour and domination.

COMMENT. Gadamer is entirely right here; Habermas has been misled, apparently, to infer from the important truth that mere linguistic change will not *overcome* exploitation and oppression the falsehood that these latter could be experienced without language. While this is completely sound as a rebuttal of point (3), there is a puzzle here, because Habermas did not consider himself refuted at this point: he went on in 1970 to defend at length the position that hermeneutical analysis of language was not germane to the uncovering of many "real" structures of the world. We shall need to watch his strategy there.

(6) Gadamer next defends his theory of *authority* at greater length (*GW* II, pp. 244–45/*HI*, pp. 73–75). Could Habermas possibly claim that there was no element of recognition that was operative in sustaining authority? If not, then Habermas would be obliged to admit that a free reflection could well lead me to continue in my recognition of an authority. The antithesis between reflection and authority cannot stand. But Gadamer points out that nothing in his theory obliges him to defend every possible self-declared "authority" at every possible cost: he sees cases of loss of authority everywhere in history.

COMMENT. Point (6) seems to me to be a good defence of the theory of authority versus point (2), yet presently we see a rejoinder that appeals, in effect, for a sociological analysis of authority rather than an analysis like Gadamer's that links it to knowledge-claims and moral recognition. This will be a welcome supplement to Gadamer, I think, but by no means a rebuttal.

V   Habermas 1970

This major study, "Hermeneutics' Claim to Universality,"[10] addresses directly the matter of *universal import* by way of a lengthy account of psychoanalysis. Now what Gadamer first meant by this claim was nothing like the claim of Plato's Gorgias that if one learned his discipline (rhetoric, in his case) one would possess ipso facto all other knowledge. Nor was Gadamer's claim that hermeneutics held primacy within the array of sciences, or took it upon itself to show them how to do their business. Rather, it was that no science could escape self-elucidation in matters of its cognitive prejudices, and that knowledge was always an answer to some question. But let us see how Habermas understands the issue. He maintains (see *HI*, pp. 129f.) that a science erected in "monologue" rather than in *Rede* (discourse), and that studies the "things" directly rather than as reflected in the mirror of speech, would not have a hermeneutical component. To explain such a science to the public might be a hermeneutical undertaking; that wouldn't make the science itself hermeneutical. "The hypothetico-deductive systems of statements in a science are not an element of discourse" (*HI*, p. 129).

COMMENT. That was a brief epistemological account. It would certainly be refuted by (a) any thesis showing the embeddedness of some part of the "system of statements" in a public or natural language; (b) any thesis showing the reducibility of some science or part of a science to some other science or part of a science that used a different "system of statements"; (c) any evidence of ambiguity or double meaning of any term employed in a science; or (d) any thesis showing that statements produced by scientists in one century might come to be reinterpreted in a later century. To the best of my knowledge, all four of these theses are now known to be true.

When he turns to his example of psychoanalysis, (*HI*, pp. 133–50), Habermas sets himself the task of showing that there is in this case a scientific practice of dealing with language (or, to be more general, symbolization) that does not proceed by interpretation. I suppose he might have argued this with the craft of typesetting, or the business of selling newspapers, for that matter, but we have his example before us. It is an unhermeneutical encounter with language and speech themselves that we are to find. When the patient produces utterance p, the therapist's scientific theory leads her or him not to award it a "hermeneutical understanding," as Habermas puts it, but to see p in a special light. It can, for instance, manifest resistance, a will not to communicate at all. Now Habermas' account is that when we diagnose resistance, or find some other such explanation for a case of systematically distorted communication, we are not interpreting—we are not being hermeneutical. He offers no further argument for this conclusion. We have to take his claim as dogged insistence on using the term "hermeneutics" in a narrow sense of his own; his expression "hermeneutical understanding" suggests it is a certain species or quality of understanding. Perhaps if we followed Dilthey, we could narrow the term to cases of empathy, and even perhaps empathy of some very special quality. But it was Gadamer that we were discussing!

COMMENT. It is clear from all Gadamer's arguments that whoever possesses an item of scientific knowledge and employs that knowledge in the encounter with phenomena is interpreting the phenomena by its aid. This knowledge, which could be the science of psychoanalysis, fuses with the rest of our projections and prejudices in our grasp of the world.

But Habermas does return to the question of *authority* at the end of the paper (*HI*, pp. 153–59). Since there are situations in which people are cowed by tyrants, bullies, and power structures of every description, one cannot always expect uninhibited communication to take place. We should not assume that the people have opened their hearts in speech; rather we should link their words to the real power structures that rule them. A political analysis will teach us to set this "speech situation" in the balance against a democratic situation in which all have an equal chance and an equal power; this would be an ideal speech situation, and constitutes our most worthy political goal.

COMMENT. All this is of mixed relevance and mixed cogency when applied to the position of Gadamer. It is far from demonstrating what, in context of the present article, it is supposed to demonstrate—that when I take due account of the constraints that prevail in a non-ideal speech situation, I am doing something other than interpreting. As with the case of neurotic resistance, this sort of measuring of words is certainly an interpretation. If, however, Habermas means to say that a political initiative to rectify the situation is more important than a mere interpretation of words, I cannot disagree with him. And if he means that some cases of what Gadamer has been calling "authority" are properly analyzed in terms of such social power and constraint, I cannot disagree either. I think, however, that Gadamer himself intended to submit authority to a moral and political criterion, too, so I believe consensus over this issue would not be far to seek.

VI   Gadamer 1971

Gadamer's "Rejoinder"[11] takes aim principally at the last Habermas piece, but responds to a wider discussion as well. It is a major philosophical essay, worthy of more attention than it has generally received (and of more than I shall give it). It fuses into a whole almost all of the themes that we have discovered in the debate, grasping them all, in one way or another, as aspects of the theme of *rationality*. First (*GW* II, pp. 251–53/*HI*, pp. 283–87) Gadamer argues that in moral and political life we seek to be guided by some form of reason, some form of knowledge, different from each and every special science, and different too from the logical form in which sciences are articulated. This *phronesis*, or practical reason, has escaped Habermas' grasp, so dominant is the expectation in critical theory of an overlap of every form of reason with the scientific model. But his *phronesis* is also what is operative in the hermeneutical enterprise (*GW* II, pp. 254ff./ *HI*, pp. 287ff.). Rejecting Habermas' account of the monological *sciences* with arguments similar to those I used in discussing Habermas 1970, Gadamer turns to the proposed analogy between psychotherapy and social praxis (*GW* II, pp. 257–60, 268– 72/*HI*, pp. 292–96, 307–12). Are we in fact able to sustain an analogy here at all? Psychiatric categories are abused when they are implemented in a political setting. The relationship holding among citizens is not at all that which holds between patient and therapist. Who can claim to be the doctor for society? Who possesses the right to interpret social resistance as neurotic defensiveness? It is a faulty analogy between "emancipation" from mental illness and "emancipation" from social evil that has bewitched Habermas here, leading him into errors he surely would have wished to avoid, above all those of the authoritarian Left. Gadamer concludes by returning to the theme of rhetoric, and the mixed form of *rationality* it shares with politics and hermeneutics (*GW* II, pp. 272ff./*HI*, pp. 312ff.). Like the politician, the rhetorician cannot aspire to articulate a final definitive expression of the Good. Only in particular circumstances can we apprehend it, and it will be fragmentary for that reason, and colored by the needs of the particular moment. So it is incumbent on the critical theorist to know that the emancipation he has before his eyes is no more an absolute than any other ideal that human beings have guided themselves by from the beginning.

VII   Gadamer 1972

The Postscript to the third edition of *Truth and Method*[12] is by no means Gadamer's effort to have *the* last word in the debate (see *GW* II, p. 478), but in a real sense it is *his* last word on it. With the greatest literary skill, he weaves answers to critical theory into the context of a much more general address to all his readers, and thus expresses his own settling of the account. A good part of it, between pages 465 and 471, is taken from the "Rejoinder" of one year earlier, and there are no new arguments added here. What is new, perhaps, is a nuance of tone, appropriate for an address to a wider audience. Gadamer is grateful to Habermas for stressing strongly the relevance of political thought and the emancipatory project. He seeks to make it clear to his readers that he too shares the hope that hermeneutics will prove to be an emancipatory discipline.

Chapter 11

MODERNITY AND HERMENEUTICS: A CRITICAL-THEORETICAL REJOINDER

Dieter Misgeld

Whoever believes that scientific rationality alone cannot be the guiding force in the transformation of contemporary developed capitalist societies into a better state will be attracted to the debate between hermeneutical philosophers and critical theorists. For both groups of philosophers and social theorists have assembled a wide set of arguments applicable to the question, whether the practices of scientific inquiry do indeed respond to the interpretive knowledge of social and political situations and structures on which most people in the pertinent societies continue to rely in order to give orientation to their actions and to work out shared understandings about their practices and actions.[1]

In this context, Hans-Georg Gadamer's work has exceptional significance. In *Truth and Method* Gadamer subjected historicist forms of philological, aesthetic and literary criticism as well as much historical research to a thorough-going critique, thus revealing that scholars studying history and the literary and artistic production of the past belong to a world of constantly interpreted and reinterpreted events and works. Any activity of research and inquiry arises from a ground of understanding and communication which reproduces itself through encounters with history and tradition not subject to regulation by research. They underlie its very possibility and provide reasons and motives for it.

In his informative detailed examination of the debate between Hans-Georg Gadamer and Jürgen Habermas, Graeme Nicholson correctly (in my view) argues that Gadamer had very good reasons for stressing the ontological import of his theory: Hermeneutics is "to be no mere sector theory of our interaction with cultural products, but a theory of universal import." "All the sciences, too, are at issue in this theory." Here Nicholson also refers to Gadamer's analysis of the "linguistic constitution of our understanding" and his ever-renewed emphasis on the *practical motivation*" of all efforts of understanding.

Thus one may say, following Nicholson, that hermeneutics has the task of breaking through all forms of alienation or separation of an understanding and interpreting subject (be they individuals and groups) from the "object" (texts, documents, artifacts, events) to be understood and interpreted. We recognize the force and cogency of interpretations only if they show us that as inquiring beings we belong to a history which encompasses us as speaking and acting subjects. It is on this background that texts, works and events have something to say to us. This is why "all the sciences are at issue" in hermeneutics as a theory of the human engagement in history (or as a theory of how human beings are engaged by history).

So far, so good. Any line of argument pursuing this aspect of Gadamer's thought and also endorsing his view that "in moral and political life we seek to be guided by some form of reason, some form of knowledge, different from each and every special science" can indeed provide hermeneutical "Answers to Critical Theory," even if only in the sense that it gives profile to a problem also recognized by critical theorists and made the cornerstone of the theory of the social sciences by Habermas.[2] Hermeneutical philosophers and critical theorists agree that the rationalization of social practice cannot be achieved merely by making use of managerial and administrative techniques derived from the social sciences or by using the methods of analysis and explanation employed in natural science and in the production of technologies. Gadamer and Habermas both claim, therefore, that an idea of reason is needed in order to address the relation between research and social practice and to identify the potential for rationality contained in social practice. The idea of reason in question has its place in those domains of social life where the results of highly specialized research enter into practical social experience and affect the political and cultural self-understanding of social groups. They both reject the view that the employment of objective methods of research as such guarantees the adequacy and correctness of findings about the lives of people in society. They are highly critical of any conception of the relation between theory (scientific inquiry) and practice, which favours the engineering of consent in society and presumes upon the capacity of social researchers, policy-makers and planners to dispense with the need for public debate and the achievement of common understandings through the course of the full articulation of possibly incompatible views. They both fear the possibility of new forms of technocratic domination, even if the grounds for their wariness hardly are the same and derive from profoundly different beliefs about the potential in modern societies for an improvement of life and for social advancement.

To this extent, hermeneutical answers to critical theory merely give profile to an area of common concern. Critical theorists must grant, however, that without Habermas's adoption of a hermeneutical stance (even prior to his discussion with Gadamer)[3] no one would have been in a position to recognize the terrain held in common by some critical theorists and some hermeneutical philosophers. And in turn hermeneutical philosophers must recognize that it is largely since the debate with Habermas that Gadamer has given full expression to the Aristotelian elements in his theory, slowly transforming hermeneutics into practical philosophy and into a theory of social reason applicable to the public issues of our times.

But what about the idea of "reason?" Do Habermas and Gadamer mean the same by it? This is unlikely. Habermas for one has made clear, in his initial review of Gadamer's *Truth and Method*,[4] that he believes reason to be able to intervene in life and to be able to achieve a rupture, as Nicholson says, with "the untroubled flow of stable tradition." Habermas then argued that Gadamer had underestimated the power of critical reflection and its capacity to break through collective illusions, especially when it is informed by general theories of the potential for rationality built into the history of modern societies.[5] At this juncture of the debate, the younger Habermas still relied on psychoanalysis as a model and example of a practice of inquiry which combined interpretive and explanatory methods, thus making plausible a process of critical reflection in which illusions are seen through and in which false projections are discarded.

Of course, as Nicholson observes, Gadamer could hardly have been expected to accept the validity of this analogy[6] between the highly specialized practice of psychotherapy—itself an instance of a healing art—and a theory which presumes to identify the suppressed potential for rationality available in the society as a whole. To speak with Nicholson: In the social domain "we seek rational solutions to situations that are mixed as we find them, and when our work is done they are still mixed, although improved. Rationality moves where light and darkness are mixed."

This, indeed, is the most basic difference between Habermas and Gadamer. Gadamer finds rationality in the existing practices of social life, insofar as the understanding of social situations which people have is not yet overwhelmed and completely distorted by methods of regulating their understanding which make common and open-minded deliberation superfluous or suppress it. There is no need, therefore, for Gadamer, to point beyond the element of social reason built into practices of deliberation as they still exist, especially as there are philosophers, such as Aristotle, from whom we can still learn what practical deliberation consists in and what kind of good can be achieved in it.

In his more recent essays on hermeneutics as practical philosophy Gadamer has developed these arguments, already foreshadowed in *Truth and Method,* with reference to the idea of *phronesis.* The practice of *phronesis* is a practice of deliberation aiming at the integration of "everything knowable by the sciences into the context of mutual agreement in which we ourselves exist."[7] Its main task is the mediation of general ideas of the good with goals of action as we know them in particular situations. Thus the primacy of application, already stressed in *Truth and Method* with respect to the understanding of texts, also holds in the case of understanding social and political situations. There is no shortage, for Gadamer, of general ideals of justice, equality and the like. But we frequently lack the concrete understandings commensurate with these ideals, which make a difference in practice.

Nicholson makes remarkably clear that Gadamer's examination of the *practice* of text-interpretation underlies his conception of practical rationality. He notes that Gadamer concludes his study of textual interpretation with the delineation of "a species of rationality" "that adduces probabilities rather than deductive proofs." It is on this background that Gadamer, in his replies to Habermas's criticisms,[8] always stresses the relevance of rhetoric for an understanding of deliberation in politics and a theory of social reason applicable to public life. The study of textual interpretation and of rhetoric as an art has implications for a theory of politics. It entails that an orientation toward mutual agreement in society cannot be rendered compatible with the belief that we can achieve a final definitive expression of the social good.

These arguments raise questions about a concept central to critical theory and to its understanding of social reason. The concept in question is the Enlightenment notion of emancipation and the belief, held by critical theorists, that in the final analysis the idea of reason refers to an organization of relations between people freed of exploitation, coercion and repressiveness. In this sense critical theorists endorse Marx's critique of Hegel and give a "historical materialist" account of the meaning of reason. At the same time they reject any reductionist interpretation of it, proclaiming the continued validity of an idea of reason which transcends the present arrangement of social relations. The idea of reason is emancipatory only insofar as it can be employed as a contrast to present realities. Therefore it may not be assimilated to them.[9]

Gadamer and Nicholson claim that this belief in the transcending power of reason entails a utopian ideal, which privileges one conception of the social good against other equally valid ones. In Nicholson's view, critical theorists have to accept that "the emancipation they envisage" is no more absolute than any other ideal. For Gadamer, reason simply means something like an attitude of reasonableness to be practiced in public affairs: It is always the case, he believes, that people and social groups have different and conflicting beliefs about the social good. All they can do, in the face of this, is to acknowledge their differences openly and to approach them in a spirit of compromise,[10] remaining mindful that there always are commonalities of understanding to which one can refer. Reason is constituted in dialogue. Dialogue consists in the give and take of conversation. It presupposes a willingness to recognize that each of us may be wrong, even with respect to some of our fundamental convictions, and that the potential for agreement lies deeper than our most strongly expressed disagreements. This is the ground of dialogue. Given these arguments, the hermeneutic philosopher detects a certain affinity between critical theory's project of social emancipation, its defense of reason as an ideal, and the Enlightenment faith in social progress as possibly analogous to the progress in knowledge achieved in the sciences.

How do critical theorists respond to these arguments? To a critical theorist such as Habermas it initially appears to be the case that Gadamer adopts a primarily defensive posture vis-a-vis modern society and the potential available in it for improving the lives of people. Gadamer also seems to deny that there indeed has been some "progress" in modern history, that it has at least become clearer, in many parts of the world, what greater freedom and justice for a majority of people could consist in. This holds, even if the historical agenda underlying these convictions also is increasingly jeopardized by profound changes in social organization consequent upon transformations in the global economy and in international politics. From the perspective of critical theory, progress always has been accompanied by regression. Systems of social domination have become more refined as well as more powerful in the twentieth century, for example, than they ever were before, while at the same time critiques of domination have become subtler and more comprehensive.[11] As a consequence of these reflections, the earlier critical theorists, such as Horkheimer and Adorno, may have been drawn into an unresolved attitude of oscillation between pessimism, on the one hand, and utopian hope, on the other.[12] Gadamer is surely right when he regards neither of these two attitudes as particularly helpful. He calmly states that what one must put first are carefully reflected insights into what is possible in a given place at a given time. This aspect of hermeneutics as practical philosophy is strongly emphasized by Nicholson.

But when it comes to major questions of social policy and the organization of life on this planet in the future, a critical theorist such as Habermas can hardly be expected to endorse Gadamer's preference for the personal attitude of good will and open-minded dialogue alone. The dispositions formative for such an attitude have their social origin in a history of erudition and cultured conversation rooted in classical and humanist learning. This history does not reflect the history of modernity in all its facets. In his initial critique of Gadamer's *Truth and Method* Habermas therefore already criticized Gadamer for giving primacy to the humanities in his understanding of the sciences; and he introduced labour (work) and power (authority) as dimensions of social life which are formed in processes of social learning just as much as an understanding of language is formed in cultured conversation.[13]

One needs to examine this criticism in terms of Habermas's entire work. It entails that an idea of dialogue can only acquire sufficient force if it *systematically* takes account of the profound changes which societies across the globe have undergone since the industrial and liberal-democratic revolutions, since the emergence of working-class movements and the period of anti-colonial revolutions. These emancipatory developments occurring in modern history are insufficiently heeded by Gadamer, less so than the emergence of scientific policy-making as a means of social control, of international power—blocs or of a global corporate economy, phenomena which both Gadamer and Habermas recognize, even if they do not describe them in the same way.

In Habermas's view, we are, for example, faced with the question whether democracy will survive under conditions of the increasing power of technocratic methods of decision-making, of the huge gap in information and knowledge existing between highly specialized groups of policy-planners and policy-makers, on the one hand, and the "general public," on the other. We are also faced with an enormous concentration of wealth and power in the hands of increasingly smaller groups of people. Systems of action in society, such as the economy, public and corporate administration, or the military, have become so specialized that they are cut off from the life-world of communication and practical deliberation, to which Gadamer alludes. This life-world itself is subverted in its structural organization by the force of these concentrated action systems, as Habermas puts it (thus turning sociological systems-theory upside down).[14] Thus the very possibility of achieving agreement in conversation to which Gadamer refers loses its social roots. The continuity of tradition, on which the communication of citizens engaging one another in public conversation and debate relies, is disrupted. Therefore critical theorists no longer need to argue that reason or the powers of critical reflection can intervene in life by breaking through the continuity of tradition. This earlier view, espoused by Habermas in the first phase of his debate with Gadamer, becomes relatively insignificant, once we acknowledge the social transformations alluded to above. Rather the question becomes how critical theory can respond to the one-sided processes of societal rationalization which find expression in economy and state.

One-sided processes of rationalization are those which have the refinement of bureaucratic-administrative management-systems and of market-structuring fiscal and other economic policies as their aim, without any regard to the need for democratic control and the growth of the capacities of people to fully participate in public processes of deliberation. Therefore critical theorists will proceed in a twofold manner in their analysis of contemporary societies and in their discussions of ideas of reason and of the social good.

First, they will analyse the history of modern societies in order to see, whether instrumental reason (as the older Frankfurt School called it) or technical methods of social control and regulation will prevail to such an extent that the potential for democratisation and for political, social and psychological liberation also built into the history of these societies will wither away.

But they are also concerned with a theory of reason which translates classical conceptions into the framework of a communications-theory of reason. Here the point is to show that language, as used in communication and under conditions of the negotiation and interpretation of the meaning of actions among equal participants in social situations, already entails a framework of intuitions and presuppositions, indicating the possibility of even fuller and less restricted communication than is presently available to us.

A communications-theory of reason pursues a *comprehensive* idea of social reason. It makes clear that this idea always entails more than the mere technical perfection of social action. It shifts the focus of debates about the rationality of action to be achieved in practice. Communicative reason (or rationality) simply represents an ideal of social action which suggests the need for a full articulation of all determinants of social action. The determinants in question include the normative features of social action (principles, norms and values) as well as its factual and historical conditions. Thus these features of social action are to be made explicit and future attitudes and courses of action to be agreed upon in group-oriented processes of reflection. It is the less powerful groups in society[15] in particular who must insist on the interventionist force of communicative reason because they frequently have little more to rely on than the force of argument and their need to make dominant beliefs problematic. They cannot acquiesce in the primacy of efficiency and controllability as criteria for "successful" social action. To be on the side of social reason entails partisanship for certain social groups as addressees for a theory, which engages them in a form of critical debate thus liberating energies for new interpretations of present institutions and practices—and for change.

The two modes of theorizing (the historical-sociological mode and the philosophical one) just referred to converge in one question: What is the potential, in contemporary developed (or advanced capitalist) societies for an increasing democratisation of their practices of deliberation? What, in other words, is the potential for the full realization of communicative reason? Gadamer does not ask this question. For him the issue is the possible loss of a potential for communicative reason already attained in the past and now threatened by the changing character of politics, the role of the "mass media" of communication, the prevalence of scientific methods of policy-making, and international politics. For him it is a question of not losing sight of the potential for communicative reason built into existing traditions and given expression in forms of philosophy and writing resistant to the Enlightenment faith in progress.

For Habermas, on the other hand, it is the Enlightenment idea of progress in knowledge, or of the mastery of life through the development of knowledge, as well as the ideals of social emancipation formulated in the democratic revolutions, carried forward by the working-class movement and now informing modern social movements such as feminism, which indicate the traditions relevant to a project of critical reflection and theorizing which has an understanding of the societal future as its aim. It is not a question of simply endorsing older Enlightenment views. The issue is whether we, in our times, can secure an understanding of emancipation which draws upon the enormous powers of rational and critical reflection unleashed in social movements and in the sciences and social sciences during the past two centuries, while *also* realizing that often these powers are turned into the opposite of critical reflection and emancipatory reasoning. It is, for example, one thing for contemporary women to discover, through feminist-inspired research into the history of women's sexuality (attitudes toward it), that for a long time women were made to believe (or came to believe) that they could or should not express their sexuality as directly as men. It is another for advertising agencies and the media to draw upon this knowledge and incorporate it into marketing strategies based on cliches of the liberated woman.

Thus the issue of emancipation needs to be articulated over against the realities of politics, society and culture in our times, while also drawing upon an understanding of it built into life and life experience in our times. The idea of emancipation refers to a history, simply to be called the history of modernity,[16] in which the pressure toward rationalization to be found in modern life has already exerted such a force that older traditions of acting, thinking and feeling have simply become unhinged. The movement of peoples across the globe, international commerce and marketing, the global media and the spread of military intervention across continents testify to this.

It is for these reasons that the notion of emancipation must retain its force: We need to ask, as social theorists and practical philosophers, whether notions of autonomy, responsibility and collectively shared and experienced solidarity can still retain the force which they had obtained in the initial phase of the formation of modern (post-feudal) societies. When we ask this question, we are already driven past the point of being able to rely on traditions of classical learning and the rhetorical discovery of the social good in common conversation and debate. Rather, one has to give renewed force to the very idea of public communication, or to the idea of a public sphere of communication. We need, in other words, conceptions of citizenship informed by a theory of reason which appeals to the competence of all societal members to participate in processes of communication. This competence is to be found in the very language people use, their ability to raise claims and refute them, to be critical of their own utterances and of those made by others.[17]

This, in short, is the idea of emancipation contemporary critical theorists wish to defend. Therefore they argue that the possibility of public communication can be supported with reference to the emergence, in modern history, of social movements which have introduced new themes and concerns, thus regularly extending the sphere of debate. And it can be further supported with reference to the Enlightenment idea that reason is incompatible with the use of force. For them this idea entails that it is part and parcel of any critical project to develop people's capacities for uncovering forms of coercion and repression not noticed in the past. All these arguments can only succeed, however, as long as one remains committed to a set of expectations and arguments also reaching us from the Enlightenment: that ideas of justice, freedom, and equality are universally valid and are to become practically real in the development of modern and recently modernizing societies. Thus, critical theorists agree with Gadamer when he says (in an interesting passage endorsing Hegel's philosophy of history) that "the principle that all are free can never again be shaken." It is the "new world-historical principle."[18] But for critical theorists, recognizing this to be the case entails more than the mere passive acceptance of a new world-historical situation. Critical theorists feel obliged to actively develop the relevant set of attitudes and convictions underlying this principle as well as the principles of equality and justice. They need to account for the emergence of these ideas in order to make them plausible. They thus examine the history of modernity as one in which the relevant public philosophies, movements and institutions arose which have given *some* practical force to these ideas. Thus it makes no sense, from their point of view, to argue that the principle of the freedom of all (a universal ideal) can no longer be ignored without examining how it has, for example, informed modern labour movements or the organization of democratic states, as well as practices of increased cultural or sexual freedom. From their point of view it then becomes uninteresting to discuss whether all this amounts to a "rupture" with tradition or to its continuous transformation.[19] Whether we want to recognize it or not, universal ideals, first announced as such in the public philosophies of the West European Enlightenment, and made part of constitutional documents (first in the United States and in revolutionary France), are now victorious around the world.

They are incorporated in a variety of constitutions, in modern forms of government, human rights legislation and international policies. Thus it can no longer be argued that the "world-historical principles" in question only are expressions of attitudes in "our" culture, i.e. of "okzidental" European and North American civilization. They are the terms which define international conflicts or with reference to which the remnants of colonialism, and of racially supremacist or sexual/patriarchal ideologies are subjected to criticism and practical refutation in many parts of the world (here one merely needs to think of the anti-Apartheid movement in South Africa). For critical theorists, an attitude of active affirmation of these principles is required, as well as the effort to give them reality in a variety of ways in different cultures and societies. Critical theorists do not assume, contrary to what some of their critics may believe, that their universalist commitments preclude respect for the integrity of different cultures and societies. Instead they believe that, let us say, the South African black population, once it achieves majority rule in a new multiracial state, will work out its own policies of "equality, justice, and freedom" (as, e.g., Zimbabwe already has). But they would also expect that universal ideals of, let us say, racial equality would indeed be adhered to and given reality in the actual legal or educational practices of this new society.

None of this entails that critical theorists have a vision of an absolute good or of an ideal society which they use as a norm and from which they derive deductively what is the right thing to do in a particular circumstance. They simply indicate a possible direction or state of social relations toward which contemporary societies can or may develop. They know, however, that this idea of a possible realization of social reason will always remain practically contested and that there *are*, indeed, competing conceptions of the social good.

But they also believe that *their* idea makes better sense than competing conceptions because it is derived from the conviction that the development of argument and reflective discourse is not merely the means toward the achievement of emancipation, but its actual realization. Thus they can allow for the open consideration of their opponents' ideas as long as their opponents accept a similar commitment to open discourse (as Gadamer obviously does). For them it follows that discourse is most successful when it is least inhibited and least constrained. But without the commitment to universal ideals of freedom, justice and equality these types of discourse and argumentation can hardly be achieved. Critical theorists do not understand why Gadamer finds it difficult to accept that ideas of justice, freedom, and equality, if they are to be universal ideals (which he does not seem to deny), cannot be made the cornerstone of a contemporary theory of social reason and be made use of in systematic interpretations of the emergence of modernity as a historical period, to which such ideas are central.

Critical theorists know, just as well as Gadamer, for example, that the pursuit of these ideals can fail. There is nothing in the notion of emancipatory reason as such which guarantees success. Nor do critical theorists believe that history will take a necessary course or that we can know the future well enough to be able to predict what it will be. Therefore they can accept compromise and the willingness to engage in the give and take of negotiation. But they will continue to insist that it is important to reflect on the potential of people to recreate the circumstances of their lives, whenever experiences of want, suffering and dependence warrant it.

Therefore the contemporary critical theorist will argue that emancipation as a social ideal is indeed to be preferred to other conceptions of the social good. For it is merely a term collecting the following set of considerations:

(1) Any idea of the social good must be open to examination in common and uncoerced deliberation and evaluation. (Here Gadamer would agree.)

(2) Once this view is accepted, the idea of uncoerced deliberation itself becomes the primary social good, superior to other social goods.

(3) Uncoerced deliberation or communication free from domination merely is a procedural ideal of emancipatory reason: It simply means that all those *actually* affected by a decision of public consequence are to be included in processes of practical deliberation and the interests of all those *potentially* affected by the relevant decisions are to be considered as well (assuming that their interests can be known or anticipated, given available knowledge and experience).[20]

(4) The ideal of unrestricted communication, the new social

ideal, is meant to be universally valid. It represents the social hope that there can be more and more space in society for the uncoerced pursuit of deliberation and communication.

(5) The ideal of communicative freedom (and justice) does not warrant the use of means to "coerce people to be free." But it entails the right to criticize beliefs which stand in the service of entrenched privileges and taken-for-granted forms of the exercise of power. It can motivate us to attempt to detect the relevant states of affairs in particular societies, under pragmatically accessible conditions, thus posing the continuous historical task of reducing the amount of coerciveness in existence in human societies, while allowing for the fact that the use of force and the existence of violence and oppression have different forms in different societies.

(6) Critical theorists do not believe that a theory of communicative reason, taken by itself, can do more than give some clearer direction to and strengthen the convictions of those already committed to the pursuit of the universalist principles in question. But they do not see an alternative to proceeding this way. An emerging world-economic system, global threats of nuclear and environmental destruction, and the *wide* acceptance in the world of *some* principles of democratic government, demand policies and agreements acceptable to all concerned, if cooperative solutions are to be found. Yet cooperative solutions are the only ones regarded as desirable by critical theorists. They are the least violent ones. Therefore culturally relativist arguments sometimes employed by Gadamer or others (Winch, Rorty) do not persuade them. For people in "other" societies (China, India, Africa) and "we" in our "North Atlantic" societies already have too much in common, both in terms of problems or of conceivable solutions, for us to be able to yield to the pleasant illusion of pluralist tolerance implicit in this relativism. The ideal of communicative reason and unconstrained discourse entails, of course, that differences can be expressed freely and that differences may be very much desirable. But regarding them as desirable requires widespread, possibly even *universal*, agreement under contemporary conditions. And there is no reason to believe, that there would not be a frequent need for rethinking agreements already made.

(7) Therefore the idea of communicative reason has something

in common with some common-sense and some philosophical convictions about the validity of science: According to these scientific inquiry is, at least at times, an instance of critical rationality. (Here Gadamer might agree as well.)[21] For it proceeds fallibistically by being oriented toward achieving revisable agreements. To the extent to which science does not develop in this spirit, critical theory becomes a critique of instrumental reason, of the transformation of science into an instrument of social control.

(8) Finally, critical theorists do not believe that any of these arguments entail a necessary commitment to utopian forms of social engineering. They want people to decide for themselves what kind of society they wish to have, and to do so on the basis of entertaining all relevant considerations, including those put forward by Gadamer. But does it not follow, then, that critical theorists, certainly since Habermas and just like Gadamer, have given expression to the hope that the spirit of dialogue and open communication can actually prevail in society? They merely have extended the frame of debate, so to speak, by giving expression to the fact that modern societies are much more subject to conflict and have been formed much more in experiences of opposition than Gadamer is willing to recognize. The history of modernity itself is the history to which critical theorists respond. Hermeneutical philosophers seem to have an ambivalent relation to it, while appearing to be much more reconciled to it than critical theorists. Tendentially at least they assimilate the future to the past. Critical theorists see no reason why we should not interpret the past in terms of the needs of the future. These needs may, after all, be quite different from those expressed in the past—as the present world is the world in which these needs already begin to take shape.

PART VII
METAPHORICAL
HERMENEUTICS

Chapter 12

GADAMER'S METAPHORICAL HERMENEUTICS

Joel Weinsheimer

Although *Truth and Method* adopts prominent metaphors in crucial situations—notably the fusion of horizons—Gadamer has little to say about metaphor as such. Unlike Derrida, he takes no apparent interest in the role of dead metaphor in philosophy; unlike Ricoeur, Gadamer does not much concern himself with living metaphor in literature either. In those few paragraphs of *Truth and Method*[1] where he does explicitly discuss metaphor, Gadamer gives it only scant mention—and then only in terms of metaphor-as-transference, conventional since Aristotle. Yet as he is about to pass on to more focal topics, Gadamer remarks, "Transference from one sphere to another has not only a logical function; rather corresponding to it is the fundamental metaphoricity of language" (*TM*, 407).

This last phrase—"the fundamental metaphoricity of language"—gives us pause because it makes such a grand claim in proportion to the attention here accorded it. Its importance becomes apparent, however, when we recall that *Truth and Method* climaxes in the conclusion that, in Gadamer's words, "Being that can be understood is language" (*TM*, 432). At the very least, this means that language is the condition of understanding anything whatever. All understanding occurs not through sympathy or even divination but through the medium of language; and thus if language is fundamentally metaphorical, as Gadamer suggests, that metaphoricity must be reflected in understanding as well. One question *Truth and Method* raises, then, is what it would mean to say that understanding itself is essentially metaphorical.

In one form, this idea is not entirely unfamiliar. Paul Ricoeur writes of a dialectic between the understanding of metaphors and that of texts. On the one hand, he says, "the understanding of metaphor is the key for . . . understanding larger texts," and on the other, "it is the understanding of the work as a whole which gives the key to metaphor."[2] I take Ricoeur to mean that metaphors are kinds of microtexts, as texts are kinds of macro-metaphors. But this is not exactly to say that understanding is itself metaphorical, for Ricoeur's formulation still suggests that metaphor, whether micro- or macrotextual, remains the object (or better, the occasion) for understanding, though not under-standing itself. Metaphor is not itself interpretation but rather the opportunity for it. As Ricoeur's early aphorism expresses it, "The symbol gives rise to thought,"[3] and yet insofar as it is a symbol it is not yet thought. So too in *The Rule of Metaphor* he writes, "Metaphor is living by virtue of the fact that it introduces the spark of imagination into a 'thinking more' at the conceptual level. The struggle to 'think more,' guided by [metaphor], is the 'soul' of interpretation."[4] Here again metaphor provides the impetus to think more, to interpret; but "interpretation," Ricoeur contends, "is the work of concepts"—of speculative, not meta-phorical, discourse (*RM*, p. 302).

Between these two modes of discourse, in Ricoeur's view, there remains an "irreducible difference" (*RM*, p. 296). Though the semantic dynamism, the liveliness, of metaphor offers the possibility for speculative discourse, nevertheless "speculative discourse has its necessity in itself" (*RM*, p. 296). It aims toward the stable, the same, the univocal—while metaphorical discourse remains suspended in a generative play of similarity and differ-ence that does not of itself terminate in a univocal concept. For just this reason, however, metaphor invites conceptual interpre-tation. It "includes a demand for elucidation to which we can respond only by approaching the semantic possibilities of this discourse with a different range of articulation, the range of speculative discourse" (*RM*, pp. 295–296). Ricoeur's thesis, then, is not that metaphor and thought are merely antithetical; rather metaphor lures thought out of its complacent inertia by challeng-ing it to think more. Thus begins the dialectical movement by which the distinction between metaphorical and speculative dis-course is *aufgehoben*.

Without denying the suggestiveness of Ricoeur's analysis, however, we can nevertheless discern that it is based on an incomplete notion of speculative discourse and, as we will see below, of metaphorical discourse as well. Metaphor, Ricoeur rightly argues, calls for interpretation, thought, conceptual elucidation. But, as Gadamer demonstrates, the same must be said of speculation as well. Like metaphor, speculation too contains a principle of growth and plurivocity. Like Ricoeur, Gadamer allies speculative discourse with the Hegelian drive toward unity: "It is true," Gadamer admits, "that the claim of systematic unity appears even less redeemable today than it did in the age of Idealism. As a result an inner affinity for spellbinding multiplicity pulls upon us . . . Nonetheless the exigence of reason for unity remains inexorable."[5] "The tradition of metaphysics and especially its last great form, the speculative dialectic of Hegel, is continually near us. The task the 'infinite relation' remains" (*TM*, p. xxiv). Yet for Gadamer, unlike Ricoeur, the synthetic impulse toward unity does not exhaust the nature of speculative discourse.

By speculative discourse we mean in part that it is not dogmatic: it does not content itself with the obvious or cling to received wisdom. The speculative person is restless, discontented with whatever is already given. He wants to know more fully and think more deeply. Not only of metaphorical thought but also of speculative thought it must be said that its reach exceeds its grasp, and for this reason the speculative statement too demands dialectical exposition. "My point," Gadamer writes, "is that the speculative statement is not a judgment restricted in the content of what it asserts, . . . a self-contained unit of meaning. . . . The speculative statement points to an entirety of truth, without being this entirety or stating it."[6] Since it does not state this entirety but yet points toward it, speculative thought contains its own impetus toward "thinking more" and need not wait for living metaphor to rouse it from moribundity. Speculation, Gadamer insists, is of itself alive to possibility.

This is not to say that speculative and metaphorical discourse are identical, but only that they do not differ in respect to their invitation to think more. Neither kind of discourse understands itself, as it were. Neither is self-interpreting, and precisely this common lack of self-transparency accounts for the fact that both require understanding and interpretation. It is no doubt true, as Ricoeur contends, that metaphor demands interpretation; but conceptual language demands it as well. It may still be the case then, as Ricoeur says, that interpretation feels the "opposite pull of two rival demands" (*RM*, p. 303). yet the pull toward the determinacy of the one cannot be associated solely with speculation while the pull toward the dynamism of the many is assigned solely to metaphor. In the speculative concept, the twin claims of the one and the many are already active.

The question thus arises whether the same is the case with metaphor. Gadamer too insists on the dynamism and fecundity which for Ricoeur define the essential character of metaphor. *Truth and Method* allies metaphor with the impulse to think more: specifically with "the freedom [of language] to form an infinite number of concepts and to penetrate what is meant ever more and more" (*TM*, p. 387). Metaphor runs ahead of conceptual language because it need not wait for the work of abstraction, the determination of a shared identity, before being able to communicate the similarity of two different things. It is possible for us to say "man is a wolf" before we have the concept of "mammal" or "rapacious." Even before we have a generic term for the common denominator, we can express the connection of disparate things by metaphorically transferring the name of the one to the other. Thus for Gadamer as for Ricoeur, metaphorical expression is prior to and the occasion for conceptual development. Yet the fact that concept formation relies on the fecundity and plurality of metaphor leads Gadamer, unlike Ricoeur, to the conclusion that there can be no dialectic between metaphorical and conceptual language because language is fundamentally metaphorical.

In this respect at least, Gadamer discerns the same universal metaphoricity of philosophical discourse that Derrida later elaborates in "White Mythology." "All the concepts which have played a part in the definition of metaphor," Derrida shows, "always have an origin and a force which are themselves 'metaphorical.' "[7] Every discourse, even discourse on metaphor, is stated within a metaphorically engendered conceptual network.[8] The metaphorical proliferation of concepts is therefore essentially uncontrollable—infinite, as Gadamer says; it runs up against no insuperable limit and finds no resting point in conceptual determination.

Phrased in this way, however, Derrida merely radicalizes and universalizes the dynamism of metaphor that Ricoeur himself stresses. Though we have already argued against Ricoeur that the speculative concept itself contains an impulse toward dissemination and not just toward determinacy, our discussion of metaphor has so far only extended his emphasis on metaphor's generative energy. We need to ask then whether there is also to be found in metaphor a contrasting, degenerative principle of entropy; and here again Derrida is of assistance.

Derrida's interest in worn out, run down, dead metaphors is not to be explained merely by reference to his focus on their role in philosophical discourse. Although his thesis is in part that metaphysics consists of effaced metaphors and that its work consists in that effacement itself, he does not conceive the work of metaphysics as an extrinsic violence: a murder of intrinsically vital, living metaphor. Rather metaphysics in his view merely collaborates with an entropic principle already immanent in tropes themselves. Although it remains the case that metaphor finds no fixed and stable point in conceptual determination, even in the definition of metaphor itself, nonetheless for Derrida the home away from home, this master metaphor, expresses the intrinsic tendency of metaphor not only toward movement but toward rest. The figure of the borrowed home, Derrida writes, signifies

> metaphor itself; it is a metaphor for metaphor:
> expropriation, being-away-from-home, but still in a home,
> away from home but in someone's home, a place of self-
> recovery, self-recognition, self-mustering, self-resemblance:
> it is outside itself—it is itself. This is philosophical
> metaphor as a detour in (or in view of) the reappropriation,
> the second coming, the self-presence. . . . The use of a
> metaphor to convey the "idea" of metaphor—this is what
> prohibits definition, but yet metaphorically assigns a
> stopping place, a limit, and fixed point: the metaphor-
> home.[9]

The metaphor of metaphor precludes arrival, as it were, and yet prescribes a destination. It implies difference, deviation, and excursion but also similarity, return, and reunion—so that a metaphor is at once essentially away from home and yet no less essentially at home there.

To Derrida's privileging of the home metaphor Ricoeur objects that it dominates philosophical discourse only to the extent that such discourse chooses to make it dominant. Yet if so, it is all the more significant that being at home is Gadamer's preferred metaphor for our situation in language. For Gadamer, language is the site of *Zugehoerigkeit*, the locus of belonging where subject and object, thought and world meet—or, more precisely, where they are already at home together prior to being split asunder by conscious reflection. "Language," he writes, "is an 'element' within which we live in a very different sense than reflection is. Language completely surrounds us like the voice of home which prior to our every thought of it breathes a familiarity from time out of mind."[10] And again, "As [language] is the one word or the unity of discourse, it is that wherein we ourselves are so completely at home that even our dwelling in the word is not at all conscious to us."[11] Since it is not conscious,

> Hegel's idea of knowledge, conceived as absolute self-transparency, has something fantastic about it if it is supposed to restore complete at-homeness in being. But could not a restoration of at-homeness come about in the sense that the process of making oneself at home in the world has never ceased to take place?. . . Is not language always the language of the homeland the process of becoming at home in the world?[12]

Being at home, however, signifies only one aspect of metaphor: its implicit tendency toward rest, stability, and univocal meaning. Of itself metaphor tends to become literal and proper. Expressions such as the "arm" or "leg" of a chair are literal as well as metaphorical to the extent that there is no more literal alternative name for chair arms and legs. Insofar as there is any proper name at all, such expressions call these things by their proper names; and in this propriety, an aspect of metaphor itself, consists its being at home. At the same time, however, metaphor is no less essentially improper since it always involves an element of alienation and difference, a divagation from the literal or—in terms of the *master* metaphor—an exodus from the homeland. Movement, this second aspect of metaphor, is already manifest in the *Poetics*, where Aristotle identifies metaphor with *epiphora*, transposition or transference. If we define the literal as what stays at home, the metaphorical, by contrast, has been transferred and finds a new home away from home. The question, then, is why occupying a borrowed home is not just being "in someone's home," as Derrida says, but coming into one's very own.

When Gadamer addresses this question, he does so in the context not of metaphor but of *Bildung* and in particular Hegel's conception of it. "Hegel," Gadamer writes.

> declares the world and language of antiquity to be especially suitable for [*Bildung*], in that this world is remote and alien enough to bring about the necessary separation of ourselves from ourselves, "but it contains at the same time all the exit points and threads of the return to oneself, for becoming acquainted with it and for finding oneself again, but oneself according to the truly universal essence of spirit."
>
> In these words of Hegel, the Gymnasium director, we recognize the classicist's prejudice that it is particularly the world of classical antiquity in which the universal nature of the spirit can be most easily found. But the basic idea is correct. To seek one's own in the alien, to become at home in it, is the basic movement of spirit, whose being is only return to itself from what is other. (*TM*, p. 14–15)

Before considering this passage in detail, we need to recall the unusual importance Gadamer ascribes to *Bildung* in *Truth and Method* as a whole. *Bildung* is, he contends, the mode of knowledge specific to the *Geisteswissenschaften*, and he argues that the human sciences of the nineteenth century owed, however unconsciously, their origin to this humanistic concept (*TM*, p. 18). Gadamer's thesis is that *Bildung*, not method, best explains the nature of hermeneutic understanding. What I propose to add to this insight is that *Bildung* also displays the structure of metaphor and that there is therefore a real sense in which we can say understanding is itself fundamentally metaphorical.

"To find one's own in the alien, to become at home in it," Gadamer writes, "is the fundamental movement of spirit, whose being is only return to itself from being otherwise" (*TM*, p. 15). In the structure of excursion and reunion defining *Bildung* we see at once the circular structure of hermeneutic understanding and also that of metaphor. Spirit consists in movement—first in its departure from its home into the strange and unfamiliar, the otherwise. If the move is complete, spirit finds a home, makes itself at home in this new place so that its new home is no longer alien. But at this point there is a reversal that is peculiar to the *Bildung* of spirit, for the elsewhere that had once seemed so foreign proves to be not only the new home of spirit but its real home. We discover that what had seemed to be home when we left it was in fact merely a way-station. The initial alienness of the other, the new home, was a mirage produced by self-alienation. The other is not merely opposed to spirit but its own hitherto unrecognized possibility.

Metaphor, I suggest, is the linguistic correlate of the *Bildung* of spirit Gadamer describes. The literal suffers what appears to be an exile into the improper when it undergoes metaphorical transference, yet the result of this transference is ideally to assimilate and integrate the two things metaphorically joined so that the literal is released from its previous confines and expanded. Its extension is broadened; it now means more than it had meant before. The previous definition and determinacy of the literal are revealed as partial and incomplete by the very success of the metaphoric transference. Through the assimilation of difference in metaphor, the literal finds in the other to which it is applied its own fuller propriety. What appeared as exile is in fact home-coming.

Spirit and metaphor, then, share the same mode of being: both exist not as a fixed essence but as *Bildung*, a movement by which something continually differs from itself and yet in that very process becomes itself more fully. Phrased in this way, *Bildung* names the way of being specific to *Dasein*, for only *Dasein* "can say to itself," in Heidegger's words, " 'Become what you are.' "[13] Human being has no definable substance. It is "constantly more than it factually is" and therefore "is what it becomes" (*BT*, pp. 185–186). Everything becomes and changes, it is true; yet *Bildung* does not mean merely linear alteration. What is peculiar to *Bildung*, the human way of being, is that *Dasein* does not simply become other when it alters but rather itself. For Heidegger, understanding refers to the fact that *Dasein* never is but always to be, and the process by which understanding develops itself (*bildet sich aus*) is interpretation (*Auslegung*). "In it," Heidegger writes, "the understanding appropriates understandingly that which is understood by it. In interpretation, understanding does not become something different. It becomes itself" (BT, p. 188). Anticipating Gadamer's fuller elaboration, Heidegger here establishes the equation of *Bildung* and understanding that underlies *Truth and Method*. As we noted above, Gadamer conceives *Bildung* as the foundation of hermeneutics. The quality of understanding specific to the human sciences consists in the fact that interpretation alters the thing understood in such a way that this alienation is at the same time a reunion. Alteration here results in self-appropriation: by integrating something other into itself, or integrating itself into something other, understanding comes more fully into its own. It appropriates its own possibilities and becomes what it is.

Beyond the connection between *Bildung* and understanding, moreover, Heidegger addresses the relationship between understanding and metaphor that is our particular interest here. In this respect too Heidegger's thought is of direct relevance to Gadamer. "For the theory of metaphor," Gadamer writes, "Kant's hint in paragraph 59 [of the *Critique of Judgment*] still seems to me the most profound: metaphor basically does not compare two contents but rather 'transfers reflection beyond the object of intuition to a completely different concept, to which perhaps an intuition can never directly correspond.' "[14] On this view, when direct intuition is impossible, understanding turns for help to metaphor. In the light of Heidegger's critique of Kant, furthermore, Kant's insight becomes even more suggestive, for *Being and Time* argues that intuition is not an alternative to but derivative from understanding. "By showing how all sight is grounded primarily in understanding," Heidegger writes, "we have deprived pure intuition of its priority" (BT, p. 18). The consequence of the derivative nature of intuition is that metaphor is not an occasional substitute for intuitive knowledge but essential to understanding itself.

Once intuition loses its priority, it becomes clear that all understanding "has the structure of something as something" (BT, p. 189).

That which is disclosed in understanding—that which is understood—is already accessible in such a way that its "as which" can be made to stand out explicitly. The "as" makes up the structure of the explicitness of something that is understood. It constitutes the interpretation. In dealing with what is environmentally ready-to-hand by interpreting it circumspectively, we "see" it *as* a table, a door, a carriage, or a bridge (*BT*, p. 189)

Even though the as-structure of understanding Heidegger here elaborates seems to have an obvious relevance to the thesis that understanding is metaphorical, his examples should cause us some hesitation. To take this thing I am now writing on *as* a table does not seem to be an instance of metaphorical understanding at all, for it is in very fact a table. Wittgenstein raises just this question: "I cannot try to see a conventional picture of a lion *as* a lion, any more than an F as that letter. (Though I may well try to see it as a gallows, for example.)"[15] It makes no sense "to say at the sight of a knife and fork 'Now I am seeing this as a knife and fork.' This expression would not be understood. . . . One doesn't *'take'* what one knows as the cutlery at a meal *for* cutlery."[16] For Wittgenstein, the question is confined exclusively to what it would make sense to *say*: what expression would be understood. Certainly he is right that we do not say "I see this as a table" but instead "this is a table," and if in his analysis of the as-structure Heidegger is explicating any word at all, it is the word *is*, not *as*. But the more important point is that Heidegger is discussing not verbal reports of interpretive seeing but rather the *as* implicit in understanding prior to its verbalization. "Any mere pre-predicative seeing of the ready-to-hand," he asserts, "is, in itself, something which already understands and interprets" (*BT*, p. 189). If the interpretation is never made verbally explicit and even if in an explicit interpretation the word *as* never appears, this absence "does not justify our denying that . . . there is any as-structure in it" (*BT*, p. 190). The hermeneutic *as* is prior to the apophantic *as* predicated in assertion: it is prepredicative, pre-linguistic.

We began our discussion of Gadamer by deriving the metaphoricity of understanding from his twin theses that language is fundamentally metaphorical and that language makes understanding possible. Clearly, Gadamer's emphasis on language owes much to Heidegger, but in this respect it is the later Heidegger of *Unterwegs zur Sprache*—not *Sein und Zeit*. Unlike *Truth and*

Method, Being and Time situates the as-structure of understanding prior to language. Yet for just this reason, it clarifies the thesis we are considering here: namely, that understanding is metaphorical. Beginning with Aristotle metaphor has been assigned to the domain of rhetoric, and for this reason we have come to conceive it as a figure of speech, an identifiable form of language to be discriminated from other, nonmetaphorical forms. *Being and Time*, however, suggests that the as-structure of understanding operates in advance of language and therefore also that the metaphoricity of understanding can be neither confirmed nor denied by the presence or absence of any particular figure of speech. Furthermore, if language is essentially metaphorical, as Gadamer contends, then his contention already calls into question the rhetorical conception of metaphor as a local and special kind of linguistic figuration. Thus the question of whether understanding is metaphorical cannot be decided by whether any metaphors are to be found in the interpretive expression of it. What I want to stress is that this conclusion holds even if, as in Gadamer's view, language is not something ancillary to understanding but its condition, for asserting the metaphoricity of language does not imply that it consists of metaphors. (I suspect that this fact explains why Gadamer pays relatively little attention to metaphor as a rhetorical device.) If it is the case that the metaphoricity of language makes understanding itself possible, the resultant interpretation will be metaphorical whether it contains any metaphors or not.

We can clarify the notion of metaphoricity without metaphor by turning to Gadamer's critique of aesthetic purism, for it is here that he relies most evidently on Heidegger's elucidation of understanding. "To do justice to art," Gadamer writes, "aesthetics must go beyond itself and abandon the 'purity' of the aesthetic" (*TM*, p. 83). Against Hamann, Gadamer argues that perception, even aesthetic perception, is not naturally or originally pure. It is rather "impure" in being always meaningful: We do not hear pure sounds but always a car in the street, a baby crying; we do not see pure colors and shapes but always a face, a knife, a wreathe of blue smoke. Perception is instinct with meaning. Perception understands, and understanding involves the construal of something *as* something. "Every construal-as articulates what is there in that it looks away from, looks at, sees together as"

(*TM*, p. 81). Gadamer's analysis of the as-structure of perceptual understanding suggests that the hermeneutic circle of alienation and reunion operates at the heart of perception. Even with respect to aesthetic perception, Gadamer observes, "mere seeing and mere hearing are dogmatic abstractions. Perception always includes meaning" (*TM*, p. 82). Nonrepresentational, nonconceptual, formalist, abstract art is therefore simply that: abstract. It is the product of abstraction, not the result of or the opportunity for more pure, more primordial perception. Perception is rather primordially impure in that it is imbued with meaning from the outset. It already understands, and this implies that perception construes or interprets something *as* something (else). Interpretation, therefore, is not something alien imposed on an artwork. Art is itself already interpretation.

The abandonment of aesthetic purism implies that art is indissolubly related to non-art. The classical term for this relationship is *mimesis*, which Gadamer allies to interpretive understanding. Art understands non-art, and all understanding involves the construal of something as something. *As* means here what it always does: both *is* and *is not*. Gadamer neither collapses art and non-art into identity nor segregates them into unrelatedness. Rather they remain connected in the irreducible tension of similarity and difference characteristic of metaphor. Art understands non-art by representing is *as*, and this understanding is therefore metaphorical regardless of whether the artwork contains metaphors. In other words, it is the relation (here, between art and non-art) that is metaphorical, not one of its terms.

If art is irreducibly related to non-art, then a picture always represents something other than itself. Nevertheless, the picture does not dissolve into identity with its original but maintains its own identity, just as the original does. Unlike the virtual image in a mirror, Gadamer argues, a picture has an actual existence; unlike a self-effacing copy, moreover, a picture not only maintains its separate identity but asserts it in independence from what it represents. Yet the independence of the picture from its original cannot be radicalized into complete autonomy, for that is only to relapse into aesthetic purism by implying that the picture does not depict anything. In picturing, therefore, there is simultaneously unity of picture and original that cannot be analyzed into their difference and a differentiation that cannot be finally synthesized into unity. Picturing establishes a metaphorical relation.

Likewise, *Truth and Method* suggests that the original undergoes a process of *Bildung* when it is depicted in an independent picture, for through just this alienation the original becomes not something else in the picture but more fully itself. The independence of the picture consists in its indispensability: it discloses something in the original that cannot be discovered except by looking at the picture. The picture "represents something which, without it, would not represent itself in this way" (*TM*, p. 124). The consequence of the indispensability of the picture is that if the original is to present itself in this way, if it is to *be* (present) in this way, it cannot do so without the picture. "This does not necessarily mean," Gadamer continues, "that it is dependent on just this representation to appear. It can also represent itself as what it is in another way" (*TM*, p. 124). That the original has alternative possibilities of self-presentation constitutes its independence from the picture; yet insofar as the original always presents itself *as something*, it is always dependent on some picture—just as the picture, if it is to represent something, is dependent on some original. This interdependence with the picture implies that the original can present itself in this way too, as this picture represents it, as well as in other ways. The original is more for the picture; it exists more fully. It now exists *as* it is represented in the picture. Representation-as enables the process of *Bildung* by establishing a metaphorical relation between art and non-art, representation and represented.

It should be emphasized that for Gadamer all pictures involve representation-as, not merely those in which the representation is itself metaphorical—for instance, Reynolds' "Mrs. Siddons as the Tragic Muse."[17] Nelson Goodman shows why "representation-as" is universal and intrinsic to all picturing when he distinguishes two senses of this phrase. In the first sense, the "as" pertains to the object depicted; in the second, to the depiction of it. These two senses are not identical, and yet both are implied in any picture.

Thus with a picture as with any other label, there are always two questions: what it represents (or describes) and the sort of representation (or description) it is. The first question asks what objects, if any, it applies to as a label; and the second asks about what among certain labels apply to it. In representing, a picture at once picks out a class of objects and belongs to a certain class or classes of pictures.[18]

Goodman does not here address a third question his analysis raises: with respect to portraiture, for example, what is the relation between labels predicated of the persons and those predicated of the portraits (themselves a kind of label)? Goodman observes that "everyday usage is careless about the distinction," yet he fails to note that this very carelessness indicates the interchange that occurs between labels of objects and labels of labels. The epithet "picturesque" is transported from the representation to the represented, though landscapes are not pictures. Correlatively, the label "sad" is transferred from the object represented to the representation of it when we call a picture of a sad subject a sad picture, though pictures have no emotions.

I mention the sad picture example because Goodman employs it not in his discussion of representation-as but in that of metaphor. Defined as "an affair between a predicate with a past and an object that yields while protesting,"[19] metaphor according to Goodman consists in a particular kind of transferred application: specifically, the application of a label with an already established denotation to an object that resists the transference and yet accedes to it as well. If metaphor consists in transferred application, the sad picture is a specially significant example because in this case the metaphor occurs not just when the term appropriate for a person is applied to a picture. Not only is the relation between representations metaphorical but between the representation and what it represents. If this same relation (between representation and represented) defines understanding, in the case of the sad picture at least we are again drawn to the conclusion that understanding is metaphorical.

Gadamer and Goodman agree not merely in locating metaphor in transference. As we noted at the outset, metaphor has been conceived as transference since Aristotle. Just as important, Goodman defines metaphor as application; and though Gadamer makes no mention of this connection, he nevertheless identifies application as the fundamental problem of hermeneutic understanding. Our consideration of Goodman thus leads us to ask whether in *Truth and Method* application links understanding to the fundamental metaphoricity of language that Gadamer claims. As Goodman remarks, not every novel application of a label is metaphorical. Applying a familiar term to a thing we have never seen before is, however unprecedented, normally an act of subsumption rather than a use of metaphor. What characterizes such routine subsumption, classification, or categorization is the lack of just the conflict and tension that distinguishes metaphor. Yet nonmetaphoric, subsumptive forms of application are those most often employed to explain the nature of understanding. On this view, we understand something when we determine the schema, law, or rule under which it falls. To understand is to apply an appropriate general rubric to the particular instance or, conversely, to subsume the particular under the general.

Even if we admit that subsumption explains what it means to understand a particular case, however, the question still remains how we understand the rule. Indeed, the subsumption view assumes that we must have already understood the rule in advance, before we can apply it, and the subsumption of yet another case under a rule already understood does not alter or further our understanding of the rule at all. Moreover, if rules can be understood only through cases, then subsumption does not explain the understanding of particular cases either, for its premise is that the particular is understood through the general, not vice versa. Application, if subsequent to understanding, does not advance it. Gadamer's conclusion is (1) that in pure subsumption there is no event, no increment of understanding, (2) that application is not to be explained by appeal to subsumption, and (3) that application, rightly conceived, is not subsequent to understanding but an element of understanding itself.[20]

If to apply is to understand, there is a dialectic between particular and general in which neither is merely antecedent or subsequent to the other. Since we need the general in order to understand the particular, the general cannot consist of the accumulation of and abstraction from particulars, as in induction. Since we need the particular in order to understand the general, particulars cannot consist of pure instances of generals, as in deduction. Neither induction nor deduction explains how concepts are formed and understanding is furthered because both are hierarchical and unidirectional: they proceed either from the "lower" particular to the "higher" general or vice versa, but not both. Thus in order to explain how understanding is altered we need a reciprocating, dialectical conception of understanding. The act of conjunction that advances understanding can still be called application so long as we do not think of application as unilateral but rather reciprocal. In application, as Gadamer thinks of it, each term is applied to the other. Each modifies and acts on the other so that they interact. Not unilateral action but only this interaction furthers understanding, for it establishes a common ground previously unthought of. The interaction that gives rise to understanding among persons of diverse times Gadamer calls *Ueberlieferung*; its correlate among persons of diverse languages is *Uebersetzung*. But most important for our purposes here is that within a single language the intersection and interaction of two spheres of a discourse Gadamer calls *Uebertragung*: metaphor. Goodman considers metaphor a type of application; Gadamer considers it, at least implicitly, the archetype. Insofar as any event of understanding in the human sciences can be conceived as the reciprocal application, the interaction, of distinct spheres of discourse which discloses their common ground, all hermeneutic understanding is in that sense metaphorical.

Max Black, an early advocate of the interaction view of metaphor, presents it in this way:

> A metaphorical statement has *two* distinct subjects—a "principal" subject and a "subsidiary" one. . . . The metaphor works by applying to the principal subject a system of "associated implications" characteristic of the subsidiary subject. . . . The metaphor selects, emphasizes, suppresses, and organizes features of the principal subject by *implying* statements about it that normally apply to the subsidiary subject."[21]

In Black's interactive view of metaphor, the subsidiary subject (in Richards' terms, the vehicle) is applied to the principal subject (the tenor), and their interaction consists most obviously in the fact that the first filters the second. If it consisted in no more than this, however, metaphor would be better characterized as unilateral action than interaction. Every adjective modifies its noun; every predicate modifies its subject. What in Black's view

196

makes a metaphor genuinely interactive, by contrast, is that the tenor modifies the vehicle as well. It is a simplification, he argues, "to speak as if the implication-system of the metaphorical expression remains unaltered by the metaphorical statement. . . . If to call a man a wolf is to put him in a special light, we must not forget that the metaphor makes the wolf seem more human than he otherwise would."[22] Because of this interaction, metaphor offers us a model of the reciprocal application that in *Truth and Method* constitutes the event of understanding.

Like metaphor, understanding involves two distinct subjects—for, as we have remarked, it construes something as something. In hermeneutics, the principal subject (to borrow Black's terminology) is the work of art or history or other representation to be understood. The second, subsidiary subject consists in the medium of representation through which the work is understood. More specifically, the medium is comprised of the prejudices, the perspective, and the horizon already implicit in the interpreter's language. This horizon is necessarily distinct from the horizon embodied in the language of the work to be understood because without this difference no understanding can occur: to copy a poem does not advance our understanding of it. Only an interpretation *in other words* can. Given the necessity for these other words, however, the problem is that only so much of the poem is revealed as the paraphrase permits. We project local prejudices, view the work from a particular perspective, and understand through a specific medium of representation that selects, emphasizes, suppresses, and organizes features of the text to be understood. Precisely this is the function of the subsidiary subject, the vehicle, of metaphor as well. The relation between a text and its interpretation, I contend, is that between tenor and vehicle.

If understanding is in this respect metaphorical, we will need to think somewhat differently about the problem of reduction. Both the interpretation and the vehicle filter the meaning of the principal subject they represent, and thus they reduce that meaning. Yet while metaphors are often enough accused of being ipso facto false or expendable, we almost never think of them as intrinsically reductive, as we do of paraphrase or interpretation generally. The foregrounding, backgrounding, and organizing effect of the metaphoric vehicle is precisely what enables a metaphor to provide an insight not otherwise achievable. So too in understanding, Gadamer suggests, the fact that the interpreter inhabits a situation and horizon distinct from that of the work and filtering it is, just as in metaphor, not the obstacle to interpretive insight but its enabling condition.[23]

As a vehicle transfers meaning to the tenor, the interpreter projects, applies, or transfers the language-world he already understands onto the text. This projection enables insight, first, in that only if the text speaks in a language intelligible to the interpreter can understanding occur. Because the work must in order to be understood find a contact point with the contemporary world of the interpreter, every interpretation (however fully appropriate to the work) will bear traces of the interpreter's present. So also "in the content of every dream," Freud remarks

> some link with a recent daytime impression . . . is to be detected. We have not hitherto been able to explain the necessity for this addition to the mixture that constitutes a dream. . . . And it is only possible to do so if we bear firmly in mind the part played by the unconscious wish and then seek for information from the psychology of the neuroses. We learn from the latter that an unconscious idea is as such quite incapable of entering the preconscious and that it can only exercise any effect there by establishing a connection with an idea which already belongs to the preconscious, by transferring its intensity onto it and by getting itself "covered" by it. Here we have the fact of "transference."[24]

Like the vehicle of a metaphor or the language-world of an interpreter, the residues of daytime impressions "cover" the unconscious wish, censor it. Yet though its connection to the contemporary impression conceals the infantile wish, only because of this connection can the unconscious idea enter the preconscious and be revealed at all.

On the other hand, the transference Freud here describes occurs not from the contemporary to the infantile but, quite the opposite, the unconscious wish transfers its intensity to the experience of the day. Not all such experiences get into dreams: only those that are selected, organized, and energized by unconscious wishes. Here we discern an effect very much like the back-pressure of the tenor on the vehicle that distinguishes Black's interaction view from unidirectional views of metaphor. In dreams, the unconscious filters and alters daytime impressions while at the same time being covered by them. This back-pressure of tenor on vehicle is crucial to *Truth and Method* as well. Since Gadamer characterizes the transfer of the interpreter's familiar world onto the text as a projection of prejudice, it is all too evident that interpretive prejudices can, and in every case do, conceal the text. Even if the text to be understood, like an archaic wish, comes to expression only under cover of such concealment, we are still left with the suspicion that Gadamer's hermeneutics explains only how the present appropriates and subsumes the past, not how it becomes appropriate to it. The application of a schema already understood to yet another instance does not further understanding at all. And worse, without reciprocal application, without transference from the past to the present as well as from present to past, Gadamer's hermeneutics will indeed seem only an explication of misunderstanding.

Yet evidence of interaction in *Truth and Method* is not hard to find. In hermeneutic experience, Gadamer writes, "both things change, our knowledge and its object" (*TM*, p. 318). Because of this dialectical interaction, interpretation cannot be conceived merely as something we do to a text, for something also "happens to us over and above our wanting and doing" (*TM*, p. xvi). In interpreting an artwork we establish contact by transferring onto it an already familiar world no doubt; yet "the intimacy with which the work of art touches us is at the same time, in enigmatic fashion a shattering and a demolition of the familiar. It is not only the 'This art thou!' disclosed in a joyous and frightening shock; it also says to us, 'Thou must alter thy life!'"[25] Thus we do not merely apply our prejudices to a text: "to understand a text always means to apply it to ourselves" (*TM*, p. 359). "In the experience of art we see a genuine experience induced by the work, which does not leave him who has it unchanged" (*TM*, p. 89). Such experiences are moments of *Bildung* in which the interpreter is altered not so much by acquiring a new piece of information as a new horizon. He learns to understand differently—most important to understand himself differently—and through that very alteration in self-understanding he becomes himself more fully. The interpreter's horizon does not remain unaltered, as if it merely subsumed the unresisting text to which it is transferred. Rather there occurs a fusion of horizons, a reciprocal transference like that which characterizes interactive metaphor.

But does metaphor result in fusion of tenor and vehicle? I. A. Richards warns us that "talk about the identification or fusion that metaphor effects is nearly always misleading and pernicious."[26] This is quite right, but it is still more misleading to talk about metaphor in terms of differentiation alone. Metaphor consists in a nondifferentiation in which difference remains operative. Let me suggest in conclusion that precisely this paradox is what Gadamer means by the fusion of horizons. On the one hand, Gadamer writes,

> Every encounter with tradition that takes place within historical consciousness involves the experience of the tension between the text and the present. The hermeneutic task consists in not covering up this tension by attempting a naive assimilation but consciously bringing it out. This is why it is part of the hermeneutic approach to project an historical horizon that is different from the horizon of the present. Historical consciousness is aware of its own otherness and hence distinguishes the horizon of tradition from its own. (*TM*, p. 273)

The historian does not assume that the text's horizon is identical with his own, that the text is transparent and automatically intelligible. Quite the contrary, he posits a distinction between past and present. The alien historical text therefore requires a corresponding self-alienation on the part of the historian who endeavors to understand it. Yet on the other hand, Gadamer adds, historical consciousness is

> itself, as we are trying to show, only something laid over a continuing tradition, and hence it immediately recombines what it has distinguished in order, in the unity of the historical horizon that it thus acquires, to become again one with itself. (*TM*, p. 273)

Logically considered, the fusion of horizons thus described is purely self-contradictory. Understanding differentiates the horizon of the past from that of the present, and yet in the same act joins them in such a way that they are indivisibly one. Both must be the case if Gadamer is to avoid the naiveté of historicism (the belief that the historian must escape his own time in order to understand the alien past) and avoid also the corresponding naiveté of prehistoricism (the belief that there is no alien past but only pure, unbroken continuity). How can the interpreter understand something other than himself and his world, and yet understand this other in a way that contributes to and enlarges his understanding of himself and his world as well? How is it possible to think difference and identity together? This is the question raised by Gadamer's explication of understanding. What I have attempted to show is that metaphor offers an answer. If we think of understanding as the establishment of a metaphorical relation, it fuses two horizons in such a way that they are both the same and different. Without mere contradiction, the hermeneutic *as* joins at one time both *is* and *is not*, and "in this *as*," Gadamer writes, "lies the whole riddle."[27]

Chapter 13

WHOSE HOME IS IT ANYWAY? A FEMINIST RESPONSE TO GADAMER'S HERMENEUTICS

Robin Schott

In his paper, "Gadamer's Metaphorical Hermeneutics," Joel Weinsheimer argues that, for Gadamer, language and understanding are fundamentally metaphorical. In developing his analysis, Weinsheimer follows the ontological direction of Gadamer's thought. Although ontology, in Gadamer's view, goes beyond the limitations of an analysis beginning with subjective consciousness, Gadamer imports into discussions of Being normative commitments drawn from social relations between subjects. In particular, Gadamer brackets questions concerning embodiment and power, and thus fails to consider how his own ontological perspective assumes as normative the history of social relations between men and women.

Weinsheimer's discussion of metaphor illustrates some of the dangers in losing sight of the concrete questions, who is speaking and what is he/she saying. For example, in seeking to define metaphor, Weinsheimer quotes Goodman, who treats metaphor as "an affair between a predicate with a past and an object that yields while protesting." Weinsheimer explicates this definition as referring to the label that is applied "to an object that resists the transference and yet accedes to it as well."[1] Goodman's reference to an "affair" in which an "object" "yields while protesting" draws on a familiar sexual myth in our culture in which "no" means "yes"—language which legitimates sexual aggression or rape. This example illustrates the danger that in bracketing self-consciousness of one's embodied identity, demeaning sexual (or racial) stereotypes may become incorporated into philosophical paradigms. This desire to transcend the body in the pursuit of truth is itself a historical product of the masculine ascetic tradition.[2] Moreover, this quest for truth that is detached from the contingencies of empirical identity leads to a "universal" understanding of language that is premissed on the exclusion of marginalized groups.

Although Gadamer's discussion of "horizon" appears to indicate a sensitivity to the situatedness of the interpreter, he does not grapple with how the concrete factors such as sex, race, or class shape interpretive perspectives. Gadamer argues that an interpreter can never be separated from the ongoing traditions in which he/she is engaged.[3] In his view, one's horizon will shape and limit one's judgments, and will spawn particular prejudices. But this pre-judgment does not undermine knowledge; rather it is the condition of human understanding. As interpreters, therefore, we should acknowledge the horizon from which we view the world as well as that of the historical period, text, or person that we are trying to understand. Because Gadamer acknowledges that the question, "What does it mean?" is linked with the question, "To whom?" many feminists have drawn on hermeneutics in developing their own critique of the universalist claims of objectivist epistemology.[4] However, Gadamer's ontological analysis undermines his project of acknowledging how history operates in human consciousness. Gadamer's concern with universality precludes raising questions about the relations of power that inform his own discourse and that are a parameter of language in general.[5]

Gadamer turns to ontology in order to avoid the "illusion of reification"[6] which views the world in terms of objects that language merely serves to name. He finds an alternative to this objectification in understanding language as a "correspondence of soul and world" that is "absolutely prior."[7] However, in seeking what is "prior" to things and to the human mind, Gadamer himself reifies language. He treats language as an objective phenomenon, rather than as a product of the interaction among people, which is both logically and factually the presupposition of language. As Marx writes, "language, like consciousness, only arises from the need, the necessity of intercourse" with other people.[8] But Gadamer's search for a relation to language that is prior to specific relations in the human community precludes seeing that one's access to language and the content of one's discourse are shaped by existing relations of power.[9] Thus, Gadamer fails to ask who historically has been entitled to participate in this tradition of ontological discourse,[10] and whether its content justifies ideologically particular interests in the historical world.

For example, Gadamer seeks to go beyond the subjective attitude towards play in order to develop an ontological understanding of play as such. He examines the linguistic usages of play, which reveal its mode of being as a to and fro without goal, to which the subjects surrender themselves.[11] Although Gadamer claims that all genuine play can be characterized in this fashion, this conceptualization itself may be entangled in assumptions about subjective identity and activity. For example, psychologists studying the play of boys and girls have noted that boys' games tend to be in larger groups than girls' games, more competitive, and longer, since boys seem to enjoy the legal disputes about rules. Girls' games, on the other hand, tend to be in more intimate groups than boys' games, more involved with turn-taking, and girls are more apt to break off a game when a quarrel breaks out than to jeopardize a relationship with other players.[12] If Gadamer defines the essential being of play as the continuation of the to and fro of the game, it would appear that girls are less able to surrender themselves to this mode of being. By defining play in terms of the game rather than the players, in order to transcend the attitude of subjectivity, Gadamer articulates an attitude towards play which typifies masculine rather than feminine psychology. In my view, Gadamer's discussion indicates the danger that ontology may project a norm of human activity, derived from one's presumed transcendence of subjective consciousness, according to which other groups are judged to be deficient. Ontology for Gadamer clearly does have normative implications, since he speaks of those who refuse to abandon themselves fully to the play. Therefore, differences in human identity (such as gender) may become inscribed normatively into interpretations of being. Perhaps Gadamer's sensitivity to the inadequacy of a subjective starting point would be more effectively addressed by seeking to understand how differences between subjects may contribute potentially different forms of self-reflection.

Like his discussion of play, Gadamer analyzes the to and fro of a "true" or "successful" dialogue, by which the subjects come under the influence of the "truth of the object."[13] He notes that if one person seeks to out-argue the other partner, to have his/her own will prevail, that individual is not falling into a true conversation where no one knows where it will lead. Gadamer's interest in understanding "true" or "successful" conversations leads him to omit a range of factors which inform our empirical conversations, such as coercion, ideology, and erotic attraction. By bracketing them from philosophical reflection, Gadamer fails to consider whether certain speakers do not need to exert their will in order for their understanding to be taken as the truth of the object, because of power they possess materially or ideologically. As Richard Bernstein notes, "A philosophical perspective such as philosophic hermeneutics can be judged not only by what it says and what comes into sharp focus but also by what is left unsaid and relegated to the fringes of its horizon. Gadamer's philosophic hermeneutics is virtually silent on the complex issues concerning domination and power."[14] In defense of Gadamer, Bernstein notes that no philosophical reflection can solve the problems of society or politics. Yet one cannot realize the hermeneutical goal of understanding interpretation, language, tradition, and community, without taking into account the social and political relations between the members of a linguistic group.

Being at home, as Weinsheimer notes, is Gadamer's preferred metaphor for understanding our fundamental relation to language. Gadamer writes, "Language completely surrounds us like the voice of home which prior to our every thought of it breathes a familiarity from time out of mind."[15] Gadamer's repeated use of the metaphor of being at home suggests that we are at home in language in a way which is more fundamental than other forms of situatedness. If language were not a primary, secure, and ongoing dwelling place, it would not be home so much as a temporary shelter.[16] But in giving primary significance to our dwelling in language, Gadamer implies that feeling, desire, and sensuality are not primary experiences. Although our emotional and physical responses become linguistically comprehended, they are not reducible to this linguistic form of knowledge. Moreover, Gadamer's metaphor of being at home brackets the way individuals may feel radically dislocated in language (e.g., I do not feel "at home" in language when it is used to undermine me as a person and as a woman, as in examples of sexual harassment). In other words, the metaphor of being at home does not account for the ways in which individuals and groups, because of relations of power, may be situated differently in existing linguistic practices.

Not only is the metaphor of being at home insufficiently concrete to understand our empirical relations to language, but being at home may not always be a desirable goal. As Biddy Martin and Chandra Talpade Mohanty point out in their essay, "Feminist Politics: What's Home Got to Do with It?" being at home may indicate blindness and complacency. They write,

> "Being home" refers to the place where one lives within
> familiar, safe, protected boundaries; "not being home" is a
> matter of realizing that home was an illusion of coherence
> and safety based on the exclusion of specific histories of
> oppression and resistance, the repression of differences
> even within oneself.[17]

As a white southern narrator indicates in her autobiography, being at home is undesirable if home is informed by the atrocities of the Ku Klux Klan in the name of protection. We must be aware of the price of our security, of the exclusions, denials, and blindness on which it is predicated.[18] In other words, what matters is not just being at home, but where home is, what takes place there, and what histories are being excluded in order to create the protection of home.

For Gadamer, as for Hegel, home is ultimately to be found in the second nature that man creates for himself.[19] Weinsheimer points out that being at home is only one aspect of metaphor and of understanding. There is also another element, that of movement, of transfer to find a new home away from home, which Gadamer articulates in his conception of being. In *Truth and Method*, Gadamer adopts Hegel's basic idea of *Bildung*, "To seek one's own in the alien, to become at home in it, is the basic movement of spirit, whose being is only return to itself from what is other. . . . Thus every individual is always engaged in the process of *Bildung* and in getting beyond his naturalness. . . ."[20] In other words, this dynamic is built on the recognition that being away from home, in someone's home, is a place of reappropriation. For Gadamer, this process of *Bildung* is the dynamic by which individuals find the world of language, customs, and institutions to be their own. It is not alienation as such, but the return to oneself which presupposes a prior alienation, which is crucial in this process.[21]

But the question is whether this dynamic of alienation and reappropriation is an adequate model for the process of human understanding, or whether it posits as normative a particular conception of human development that is linked to the history of social relations. Genevieve Lloyd, in *The Man of Reason,* suggests that this Hegelian dynamic attempts to transcend that aspect of life that is linked to particularity and material existence. She writes in regard to Hegel that,

> Self-consciousness is associated with a breaking away
> (achieved through surviving the fear of death) from
> immersion in life and its particular transient attachments.
> And self-conscious ethical life is likewise associated with a
> breaking away from the family, which—at any rate from
> the male perspective—is also associated with particularity.[22]

As Lloyd notes, both explicitly and implicitly, this sphere of particularity becomes aligned with femininity. The sphere of transcendence, which presupposes the lower form of life but nonetheless transcends it, is associated with masculinity. Lloyd's analysis suggests that there may be a social history, one concerning the relations between men and women, that informs this philosophical view of alienation and reappropriation, of leaving one's original home and finding one's true home somewhere else.[23]

Given women's historical confinement within the home and men's flight from this domain, as well as the philosophical validation of this differentiation,[24] it is puzzling that this metaphor has surfaced to explain the education of consciousness. The clue to this puzzle may be found in the ascetic, religious and philosophical tradition, which originated in classical antiquity (a historical period to which Hegel is indebted, as Gadamer notes), by which men sought spiritual immortality in order to escape the threat of change and death posed to temporal, physical existence. This desire to transcend the vicissitudes of life is evident in early Greek religious rituals such as that of "new birth." This practice was common in male initiation ceremonies in which a boy is reborn (e.g., by reenacting a birth so that a boy appears to emerge from a goat) in order to rid himself of the pollution and danger that accompany his original biological birth. The ritual of new birth is a means of sundering the boy's ties of dependency on women by socializing him into the dominant male community. Through this rite of passage, childbirth is "masculinized" and decontaminated. The attempt to rid the male initiate of the contamination of the body as a means of achieving immortality is evident in Platonic thought as well.[25] This pattern of detachment from the life-cycle and its reappropriation in purified form reappears in Hegel's and Gadamer's conception of *Bildung*. By stipulating the need for the return to oneself, which presupposes a prior alienation, detachment from one's "natural being" becomes paradigmatic in the process of achieving universality. The irony in this use of the metaphor of being at home by these philosophers is that it signifies the philosophical alienation from and reappropriation of this domain. Home becomes not the realm of everyday existence, the sustenance and nurturance which women have historically provided. Rather, "home" signifies the philosophical transcendence of particularity in the quest for universality.

Ultimately, Gadamer's attempt to move beyond the limitations of a subjective starting point remains highly problematic. In his effort to transcend Cartesian subjectivity, with its corollary in the will to dominate and objectify nature, Gadamer not only abstracts from differences between interpreters in a given culture, but he imports assumptions about universality which derive from an unacknowledged history of relations between subjects. In defense against the criticism that he has detached language from social-historical processes and action, Gadamer replies that he does not regard concrete factors of work and politics as outside the scope of hermeneutics. Instead, he means to affirm that language reflects everything that is. In this context he notes that language is a game of interpretation that we are all engaged in every day: "everybody is at the center, is "it" in this game. Thus it is always his turn to be interpreting."[26] Although Gadamer effectively argues that one can never be outside an interpretive framework, his assumption that "everybody is at the center" presupposes that all interpreters feel equally legitimated in being "it" in this game. As existential thinkers such as Sartre, de Beauvoir, and Baldwin have argued, subordinated groups (whether Jews, women, or blacks) face the danger of learning the lessons of inferiority taught by our society. Groups whose discourses, histories, and traditions are marginalized need to struggle for the self-affirmation that is both a condition and consequence of naming oneself as an interpreter. Thus, a philosophy of interpretation must go beyond Gadamer to incorporate analyses of power, of dominance and subordination, inclusion and exclusion. Such a project requires a self-consciousness about who is absent from our conversations, and a commitment to a social praxis that will empower individuals who are marginalized or subordinated to become interpreters.[27]

PART VIII
SCIENCE AND HERMENEUTICS

Chapter 14

HERMENEUTICAL PHENOMENOLOGY AND THE PHILOSOPHY OF SCIENCE

Patrick A. Heelan

I Continental and analytic philo of science compared

The two most characteristic interests of continen are (1) its preoccupation with the problem of the of knowledge, and (2) the effect of the historic world context of science on the "social constituti knowledge. Such constitution is "hermeneutical" tially involves language, natural and artifactual historical communities of interpreters.

Continental philosophy from the start sees science as an institution in a cultural, historical, and hermeneutical setting. The domain of its discourse is values, subjectivity, life worlds, history, and society, as these affect the constitution of scientific knowledge. Its notion of truth is that which pertains to history, political power, and culture. Its concern with science is to interpret its historical conditions within human society—usually in Western culture.[2] Science, from this perspective, is a human, social—and fallible—enterprise.[3] A concern of continental philosophy of science will include social failure as a possible indictment of scientific practice.

In contrast, the most characteristic interest of analytic philosophy is its concern with objectivity and truth, and its preference for the methods of formal logic.

Analytic philosophy from the start sees science as mankind's most successful truth enterprise, the fulfillment of a classical

Aristotelian—and Platonic—desire for perfect knowledge, *theoria*.[4] Analytic philosophy—before its widespread decline into relativism—had confidence in the power of abstract reason and of experimental methods to discover the objective truth that is beyond history, culture, values, subjectivity, and power.[5]

The logic and methodologies of the physical sciences are generally not a matter of dispute for continental philosophy. With respect to these questions, continental philosophers generally defer to experts who—it is assumed—are analytic philosophers of science.[6] This *surface* agreement about the "logic of science" focuses the area of dispute on the principal domain of difference, that of metaphysics—of the human knower, of the known world, and of the knowing act. In particular, the actual dispute focuses on whether science is capable of delivering a metaphysics of nature or whether science is historically and socially constituted for some other goal than metaphysics—more precisely, than a classical metaphysics.

Analytic philosophy generally defends the fundamental position that science is a knowledge of a privileged kind, not deriving from and not responsible to the projects and values of the Western cultural world or—to use Sellar's term—the Manifest Images of our culture;[7] rather, it constitutes a socially and historically independent account of reality, more reliable than any given so far. This Scientific Image of the world is truly then a classical metaphysics of nature.

Those claims come in conflict with the philosophical analysis of science as a social institution. Either society constitutes all of its institutions and has responsibility for them, or there is some privileged institution which (it is alleged) is not constituted by society and over which (it is alleged) society consequently has no responsibility or control. The latter conclusion is deeply troubling to the modern conscience remembering its recent political coming of age in which the divine right of patriarchal princes and the matriarchal Church were fought so stubbornly for the sake of human freedom—the freedom of the people to determine their own political lives and destiny. Science too must have a social constitution and, of course, a social conscience.

But how is science socially constituted? What kind of knowledge does it achieve? Continental philosophy actually finds the goal of science not in a metaphysics of nature but in society's pursuit of "technical" human interest.[8] As Apel says,

The modern natural scientist must be guided by a technical interest in the sense of this apriori dependency of the problems upon instrumental verification. In this supra-individual, quasi-objective connection, his cognitive interest differs from that of the natural philosophy of the Greeks or the Renaissance and, in turn, that of Goethe or the Romantics. And in this methodologically relevant interest, the whole of the exact natural sciences differ, above all, from the divergent practical interest and world engagement that lies at the basis of the so-called "human sciences."[9]

This paper is directed towards taking issue with this statement. Its claim that natural science is deficient relative to natural philosophy stems from the fact that within the context of Western culture and history, scientific knowledge has value and significance predominantly—though certainly not exclusively—because of the power it confers. This prevalent Western mode of appropriation of science leaves open, however, other avenues of social appropriation—even the strictly philosophical, continental style.

Continental philosophy's rejection of science as a natural philosophy is stated succinctly by Maurice Merleau-Ponty in the Preface to his *Phenomenogy of Perception*: Edmund Husserl's directive "to return to the things themselves"[10] was, he says, "from the start a rejection of science."[11] In what sense was this a rejection of science? It is principally a rejection of the presumption widespread in our culture and also among scientists that science alone is *objective* and capable of representing reality as it is unaffected by religious or racial myths, political expediency, historical forces, economic self-interest and other forms of bias and prejudice. Science is uniquely on the path of truth and privileged on that account.

Continental philosophy's strenuous rejection of these scientistic claims is motivated by its fundamental metaphysical position: reality is the life world, or just "world." This is the context of perceived nature and of social realities constituted by moral, social, political, and religious intentions; and it is the pervasive background or pre-understanding present in all human dealings with things and people. If scientific accounts are *truly objective*, then it follows that continental philosophy must regard them as not belonging by *right* to the world, but only by *utility* and *convenience*.

This, I want to point out, is a philosophical conclusion. To hold it does not mean (as some have argued) that the disciples of continental style philosophy are committed to quacks and alchemists rather than to modern medicine; like everyone else, they too prefer the medicine that works best. The question at issue is not a medical one (which heals best?) but a philosophical one (how do the entities of science—imperceptible to the unaided senses—relate to reality?). The latter question, however, cannot be addressed until the more fundamental one has been answered: Is reality to be understood classically and objectively or rather as socially constituted?

Continental philosophy usually claims that the entities of scientific theory that give to science its explanatory power have no reality because they are imperceptible to the unaided senses; it claims they are just mathematical surrogates for real objects, useful models or metaphors to manipulate the environment. Continental philosophy's attack on scientism is then an attack on the metaphysical and moral claims of rational objective knowledge such as science claims to be. Its position is: If reality is the world, then the world is presupposed by science, and science inevitably returns not to theory, but to the world for its concrete reference. Merleau-Ponty expressed rhetorically this sentiment in a much-quoted passage: Scientific objects, he says, are an "abstract and derivative sign-language, like map making [gèographie] relative to the countryside in which we already know what a forest, a prairie, a river is."[12] One may want to dispute the suggestion that science is like a map, and that forests, prairies, and rivers are scientific entities, but the judgment he expresses about science is typical of the writing of Martin Heidegger (in his later period), Hans-Georg Gadamer, Karl-Otto Apel, Jurgen Habermas, and the legions of Herbert Marcuse's and Friedrich Nietzsche's followers.[13]

Included in this group of science critics is by all accounts the later Husserl who, in *The Crisis of European Sciences and Transcendental Phenomenology*,[14] led the phenomenological attack on the entrenched objectivism of current scientistic belief and practice. A closer reading of this late work, however, shows that the critique had also a parallel and more positive aim—to look at scientific research as a human way of being-in-the-world, and from this viewpoint to make a philosophical re-evaluation of natural science.[15] The later Husserl should be counted as the leader of this secondary movement concerning *phenomenology and natural science*. This secondary movement by contrast springing from Husserl's *Crisis* gives to science a world building character. During his years at Göttingen (1901–1916), Husserl was a friend and colleague of the brilliant circle of mathematician-physicists who were to transform physics—and all science—in this century. Among them were Felix Klein, Richard Courant, Hermann Minkowski, Emmy Noether, and Hermann Weyl, but their preeminent leader was David Hilbert.[16] Hilbert, with the motto "physics is too difficult for physicists", advocated that the leadership of physics pass to mathematicians: For him, the definitive understanding of physical nature was to be provided by a universal mathematics of axiomatic theories.[17] Theory-making, axiomatic in thrust, became central to the *method* of the new physics. Such a view—let us call it the "Göttingen view"—was shared by Husserl for whom the theory of theories is, as he says, an axiomatic theory of models or manifolds (*Mannigfaltigkeiten*).

Husserl, however, made a distinction between theory-making (as the method of physics) and metaphysics (as the traditional goal of science). While he agreed with the theoretical orientation of the Göttingen School of physics, he disagreed with the underlying Cartesian or "Galilean" metaphysics that was assumed by Hilbert and his colleagues. Such science, he charged, made the mistake of attempting to replace the world with a set of mathematical models.

That the metaphysics of science enriched the perceptual world with genuine—often new—scientific phenomena, seemed evident to him.[18] Such scientific phenomena, for example, as the Euclidean character of the physical world,[19] are formed by theory (Euclidean geometry), and "realized" with the aid of scientific instruments (rulers, etc.). These technologies of construction and measurement prepare (or "corral") for scientific observation the phenomena (in this case) of physical geometry. Such phenomena are not ideal entities but perceptual phenomena that (in a sense to be discussed below) "fulfill" Euclidian theory.[20]

A new philosophy of science, Husserl intimated in the *Crisis*, can begin to address the experience of the "things themselves" of science; these are the genuine worldly phenomena of science, those which "fulfill" theory. Such phenomena enter the world

217

as socially-constituted items, laden, like all the furniture of the world, with values and history, and wearing the accoutrements of social power or impotence. Focusing attention on those phenomena lays the groundwork for a new scientific realism, continental style.[21] First among these new realists is the later Husserl. Among them also one could make a case for the Heidegger of *Being and Time*[22] and for the Merleau-Ponty of *The Visible and the Invisible*.[23] Some contemporary writers in this genre are listed among the references.[24]

Within phenomenology, then, there are two superficially opposing views about science. The first attacks the view of science as objective theory for being a peculiar historical ideology prevalent in the classical Western tradition of philosophy and culture. The second attempts to correct that mistaken ideology by showing that scientific inquiry can and should be understood as constituted by the basic situation of the human being-in-the-world. At a deeper level, these views complement one another.

They agree fundamentally about the nature of the *human subject* as a social and historical being embodied, as Merleau-Ponty said, in detachable and undetachable sensory organs,[25] about *reality* as the world, and about *knowledge*—even of "theoretical states"— as fulfilled (or, because the sense of this term is not yet clear, "fulfilled") in and through perception. In these three respects, continental philosophy differs profoundly from contemporary mainstream analytic philosophy of science.

II Hermeneutical phenomenology

Hermeneutical phenomenology shares with phenomenology a set of characteristic concerns.

Firstly, the essence of being human is defined as a practical understanding of a historical world—life world—an understanding that is worked out in and through language and other signs; human existence—that is, the experience of being a human subject—is that of being-in-the-world.[26] Secondly, I take *perception* to be that form of knowing, by a subject's practical bodily insertion in historical world situations, in which reality horizons disclose themselves to subjects as referents for language. Thirdly, there is a *hermeneutical* phenomenology concerned with language and its extensions which provide both for mystery and for historical development in the uncovering of horizons of the world. Fourthly, perception has a certain primacy for establishing world, i.e., a primacy over ordinary language.[27] By this I mean that ordinary language need not be accepted without criticism as the authority about the world; it could, and should, be corrected and enriched by attention to the phenomenological constitution of the perceptual horizons it (ordinarily) designates.

Ordinary language assumes that the criteria of theoretical scientific language have a universal and overriding privilege. In my *Space-Perception and the Philosophy of Science*, I showed that visual space often has a geometry different from scientific geometry because it often serves a different cultural function from science.

Husserl proposed a method for analysing the essence or *eidos* of a perceptual object which he called, the "*method of the variation of profiles.*"[28] This method presupposes that a perceptual essence or *eidos* can be taken to be the symmetry or invariant of an organization of perceptual profiles—a profile being some way an object can appear to a situated perceiver. Husserl was familiar with Felix Klein's *Erlanger Programme* in which a geometrical object was defined as a figural symmetry or invariant under the spatial transformation group which is both the transformation group of the coordinate reference frames (in which the object can be represented) and of its representations (within a coordinate frame). Applying Klein's model to the perceptual object, a perceptual object comes to be defined as the symmetry or invariant of one and the same transformation group which both permutes possible perceivers among themselves and possible object profiles among themselves.

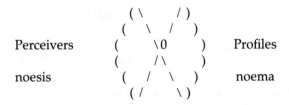

Figure 1: The perceptual object 0 is the symmetry or invariant relative to the transformation group among profiles and perceivers.

Note that the perceptual object (see figure 1) lies "in between" perceivers and profiles; it is a symmetry they both share. By this I mean that for every object transformation that leaves the perceiver untransformed, there is a correlative subject transformation that leaves the object untransformed. "Objective" and "subjective" transformations match one another, just as when one moves one's hand along a wall, one can either speak of the wall objectively, saying that parts of the wall succeed one another to the feel (the objective transformation) or one can speak of the hand subjectively, saying that it brings these parts of the wall in succession to the feel (the subjective transformation). The former objective version of the transformation (called "active" by physicists), changes the object; the latter subjective version of the transformation (called "passive" by physicists) changes the perceiver (as the object's frame of reference) *in the reciprocal way.*[29]

One and the same basic transformation group then defines the object and the subject. The subject so defined is represented by a cluster of active powers capable of recognizing, exploring, enjoying, or using the perceptual object whenever it is present and at hand. These powers may involve the use of instruments and readable technologies.[30]

Husserl's name for the objective transformation group is the *noema*; his name for the subjective transformation group is the *noesis*; each is a part of (what he called) the noetic-noematic structure. Noesis and noema share the same abstract group theoretic structure of being and action. They do not "mirror" one another passively, like picture and copy; their relationship is more like the dynamic one illustrated above by the finger touching the wall, or which Aristotle described when he said that the knower *becomes* the known by living the form of the known— the form of the known, in this case, would be the abstract transformation group.

It is clear from this account that a perceptual object is neither a sensory datum nor a formal construction out of sensory data. It is a symmetry within an established (but revisable) perceptual praxis and, consequently, already a semantic object tied in to a network of established semantical relations.

How does a scientific phenomenon come to "fulfill" its theoretical account in an act of observation? The classical tradition of physics from Galileo to Hilbert and from Newton to the Göttingen School assumed that the link between theory and observation was measurement. Measurement was supposed to be perfectible, indeed *infinitely perfectible* converging in the limit on the values which an objective and true theory would then accurately reflect. Even Husserl took this to be the case.[31] However, as Duhem, Hesse, and others have shown,[32] such an account of the link between measured phenomena and theory cannot be correct, for theory can never be uniquely determined by data.[33]

There is, however, a hermeneutical link[34] between theory and data, and this link is to be understood partly on the model of language and partly on the model of that kind of interpretation which is exemplified in artistic performance.[35] This will be taken up below.

A word about *constitution* or *object formation*: the constitution of a perceptual object O is studied from a standpoint "inside" the constituting act by the one constituting and experiencing the phenomenon—this study is a *phenomenological ("eidetic" or "experimental")* study. This role is indicated by S_x in figure 2. Husserl's phenomenological method aims to define the *eidos* of such an object O; this definition is an abstractive, objectivizing, and thematizing account.

Eidetic definitions were criticized by Heidegger because they seemed to deny the ambiguity and flexibility of what is uncovered by understanding. Such accounts—he called them, "theoretical"[36]—have to be distinguished from scientifically theoretical accounts. Scientific theory works specifically only within the

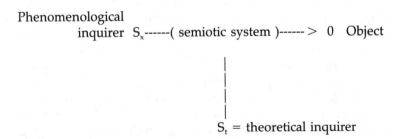

Phenomenological
      inquirer S_x ------(semiotic system)------ > 0   Object

                                   S_t = theoretical inquirer

Figure 2: The two modes of inquiry into perception, the phenomenological role S_x and the scientific theoretical-explanatory role S_t.

environment of a mathematical-experimental praxis. What this means will be discussed below.

Turning to figure 2: S_x is the phenomenological (eidetic or experimental) inquirer; S_t is the theoretical inquirer. The constituting action of S_x can be studied as a special kind of human performance from a standpoint "outside" of S_x—indicated by S_t; this would focus, for example, on the structural and semiotic conditions pertinent to the performance of the act of perception. S_x experiences the phenomenon, while S_t (as we shall see) "explains" the phenomenon. The characteristic feature of this explanation is that it produces a mathematical theory of those aspects of the object accessible to the instruments of our inquiry—technological instruments in experimental science, sensory in unaided perception. Such a theory has the characteristics of a *scientific theory*, and its *explanatory* role is a scientific one. We can compare such a theory to a "musical score," that is interpreted by S_x's performance in the medium of the instruments used—but more of this below.

What the theory refers to is indicated in figure 2 by the parenthesis "(semiotic system)," this is some underlying "score," "text," or "code" that directs the performance—S_x's performance—of the perceptual act. Such a semiotic system is envisaged not as part of an epistemological analysis (by S_x) of the performance, but as part of its ontological structure (as judged by S_t). Such performance is hermeneutical in a new and existential way, and one not too far from that which Heidegger placed at the root of all knowledge.

The semiotic system implicit in the performance directs the eidetic functions of S_x's activity in an appropriate way—actually (we surmise) according to the way a *skilled performance* like a musical interpretation is guided by its "score" without, however, being entirely defined by its "score." The score of a piece of music is not unique but depends on the social-historical-cultural context (instruments, audience, conditions of recital, etc.) for the realization of the piece of music, for a piece of music is a historical entity, different from its score and the context of its performance. It would not then be surprising to find—as we do—that perception's "score" is no more accessible to a phenomenological analysis by S_x than a musical score is to the well-practised player or singer. The (musical) score or (perceptual) "score" is not part of what is first known and then acted upon, but is rather one of the ontological conditions of possibility of the perceptual act.

Such an account is a "theory of the perceptual object," and has the character of a scientific theoretical-explanatory analysis. Its effect does not reduce the perceptual object to something *merely* there, but rather it addresses the perceptual object indirectly (through S_t) by describing a set of formal semiotic conditions for a perceptual performance terminating in such an object as perceived by S_x. How such a theory is implemented in the world in a particular medium at a particular place and time gives an existential hermeneutic *account* of perception.

The term "hermeneutics" is taken here in a new and extended sense suggested by Heidegger's transformation of phenomenological inquiry in *Being and Time*. Consider his example of the hammer.[37] The hammer reveals itself as a hammer while it is being used for hammering, but when being so used the character of being a hammer—its *eidos*—hides itself from the user within the transparency of the action executed. Just as the score hides itself in the performance, so the *eidos* of the hammer hides itself in the execution of hammering. The *eidos* nevertheless is there, as a kind of theory that "explains" the hammer in the hammering. For S_x, there is an abstractive account of the hammer's *eidos*— for Heidegger, a "theory," an *eidos*-theory. For S_t, *theory* means something different; it is any model or map of the structure internal to the instrument that makes hammering possible, e.g., the tool designer's blueprint; this enables the "musical score" of hammering to be performed.

Returning to perception: One surmises that the perceptual "score" for hammering includes neurophysiological, somatic, and environmental elements, as well as computational and other semiotic elements. Since a perceiver S_x has very limited access to the way these help "shape" the phenomenon, the standpoint of the researcher S_t is not that of the perceiver. S_x and S_t belong to different cognitive communities and they are engaged in totally different causal, hermeneutical, theoretical, and existential relationships to their respective subject matters. Neither assumes a universal transcendental viewpoint.

In every hermeneutical activity, there is a certain reciprocity, for example, between text and meaning, and between score and performance. Such reciprocity is called "the hermeneutical circle."[38] Consider S_x: On the one hand, the "score" is (existentially) prior to what is perceived, it does not permit arbitrary objects to be constituted, it exercises a certain control over the possibilities of what can be presented to S_x and recognized within any given perceptual medium for any given desired purpose. On the other hand, it is also (existentially) posterior to what is constituted, for the medium must be "tuned" to the possibilities of the "score," for only on that condition will the medium and "score" succeed in presenting to S_x an object with the anticipated perceptual content. The necessity of such "tuning" makes perception a performance and a work of artistry.

Making perceptual sense of the world is an individual and social art that involves the ability to perform transformative motions in a medium so that a common, shareable, and repeatable experience of presence or absence, of successful involvement or frustration can be realized. These intention-laden motions and environmental clues or responses are a part of language in the constitutive sense and (as I shall hold) can be studied from the viewpoint of S_t in a scientific theoretical-explanatory way. Although such abilities and resources may be sufficient for animal language, they are not, however, sufficient for human language.[39]

Spoken words and sentences—*paroles*—belonging to the home language of a human community enrich the common experience by linking present agents and speakers immersed in their current worldly involvements with exemplary epochs, spaces, personalities, and transactions adumbrated in the oral narrative resources of a culture. They bring ideal (or seemingly transcendental) normativity to the here and now, and make possible a self-perpetuating community characterized by repetitive short-term projects pursued against a background of permanent norms "given (as it were primordially)" together with the world. The world is now a set of projects "given" to humans within a traditional culture and to be fulfilled by repetition or reenactment (or—to use Piaget's terms—accomodation and assimilation). Such narratives permit the individual speaker to appropriate the norms of the group that share *orally*—as *parole*—the same home language.

Written language—*language*—brings history into being by evoking the normative differences that existed between past communities and our own. It can also bring to our attention the existence of other knowledge communities than ours with different and alien norms. Thus, from written language, hermeneutics arises as the appropriate method to study questions of the kind: With respect to world, have past—or alien—communities maintained different reality norms from ours, and if so, with what reason? In constraints on human agency (on what is morally possible, just, and worth pursuing), have people pursued different norms, and if so, with what right? In the understanding of society (whether it has a direction, what this is or should be, and who should control it), can there be different legitimate views?

Challenged as we are by synchronic and diachronic pluralisms in perception, language, science, culture, and history, I argued in *Space-Perception and the Philosophy of Science*, that such structures fit into the formal model of a lattice or quantum logic (not, as often taken, of sentences, but) of context-dependent descriptive languages.[40] This led me to call for recognition of an epistemological principle normative for human knowing: Disparate horizons and disparate languages do and should seek upper bounds in an extended quantum lattice.[41] This is one of the regulative principles suggested by a hermeneutical phenomenology of the scientific tradition.

III Elements of a hermeneutical and phenomenological philosophy of natural science

A philosopher of science in the phenomenological or hermeneutical tradition would then be guided by a new thrust different from a philosopher in the analytic tradition, both in the choice of significant problems and in the manner in which these are treated. Such a philosopher would do research into constitutional problems, human embodied subjectivity, and world (life world) as reality—problems that do not enter into the purview of analytic philosophy of science.

1. *Experimental phenomena.* In contrast with the dominant classical interest in scientific theory-making, the new thrust would center on experimental phenomena and how these come to be constituted as perceptual objects. Central to such constitution is the dual and complementary roles of experimenter (S_x) and theoretician (S_t): The theoretician tries to model mathematically

225

the readable technologies used by the experimenter to develop an institutionalized praxis for the preparation and presentation of phenomena. The two processes dialogue with each other until (provisionally at least) the last word is spoken by the experimenter when a stable phenomenon of known symmetry is capable of being produced.

Such scientific phenomena are "dressed" for the world by standardized scientific instruments used as readable technologies; these contribute to the historical and social constitution of scientific phenomena as beings in the world.[42] In this regard, what Merleau-Ponty says (in "Eye and Mind") is relevant: "our organs are no longer instruments, on the contrary, our instruments are detachable organs."[43]

2. *Scientific theory*. One often hears today that all observation whatsoever is "theory-laden." What is meant by *theory-ladenness* in this context is that whatever is observed (inside or outside of science) involves things which are not directly observed but are implied by the semantic network of the language. Such semantic connections are not of themselves scientific (i.e., explanatory-theoretical) connections, and do not constitute a theory, for they are to be found in natural language which is not a theory about the world but a description of it. A theory is rather about what underlies—"explains"—the objects of a descriptive semantic network.[44]

Are scientific phenomena *theory-laden?* What "theory-laden" means is that the same names are used of observations as of elements of scientific theory. However, scientific phenomena can be recognized within the context of a standardized praxis without the observer having to know more about the theory than the names it uses. Such phenomena are more aptly called "praxis-laden" than "theory-laden," for the theory has become embodied and hides itself in a public praxis. Such embodied theories "dress" the phenomenon and such "dressing" can become the basis for a description of the phenomenon. The experimental phenomenon is not formally theory-laden, but praxis-laden and the product of an interpretative art.[45]

Scientific theory and scientific phenomena are related within the context of a hermeneutic of sign (data) and object (phenomenon). The hermeneutic is local, historical, contextual, and realizable only within a standard institutionalized praxis.

3. *Perceptual Realism.* The thesis of the *primacy of perception* entails that theory is justified by being used to naturalize new scientific phenomena in the perceptual world.[46] Theory then is not just a technique for manipulating the environment, it is itself world-building in that it furnishes our world with new things.[47]

4. *Hermeneutical or Horizonal Realism.* Turning to the current debates in epistemology and the philosophy of science, a form of Scientific Realism is defended here which I call "Hermeneutical Realism" or, to emphasize the primacy of perception, "Horizonal Realism," or Scientific (Phenomena) Realism whenever I want to stress its opposition to the Scientific (Theory) Realism of current controversies.[48] This is opposed to the Instrumentalism of many phenomenologists and critical theorists.

5. *History of science.* The history of science is more than the history of scientific writings and discourse, including illustrations, mathematical models, or abstract theories; in addition, there is the history of the culture of laboratory instruments with special reference to *readable technologies.* For not through books, language, and pictures alone do explanatory scientific entities get their social and historical constitution as realities, but through the readable technologies by which they are "dressed" so as to become a naturalized part of the furniture of this world, laden with the ambiguity of a historical perception.

6. *Complementarity and Modern Physics.* Natural and naturalized objects of perception can equally be characterized by complementarity understood as the way some human embodiments—even non-technological ones—preclude the exercise of others, with the consequence that some kinds of phenomena can appear as "dressed" only in certain ways;[49] e.g., the geometry of a space-time object is determined by the embodiment and interests we bring to it.[50]

7. *The human knowledge community.* The community of human knowers is then comprised of irreducible complementary sub-communities, linked by linguistic and non-linguistic channels of intercommunication, and bound together—to the extent that bonds exist—by bonds of mutual trust, good will, and common goals, which mutually exclude, however, simultaneous access to common experiential horizons.[51]

8. *Scientific explanation.* Where then does this leave the account of explanation in the natural sciences? (1) In the first place,

one has to distinguish carefully between (1a) the nomological or computational aspects of explanation which deal with correlations among phenomena, and (1b) the constitutional aspect of explanation which deals with the origins of phenomena. In the vocabulary of Ricoeur, Apel, and other continental philosophers, the former alone is called "explanation" and it is taken to be the characteristic of the natural sciences. The latter is called "understanding" and this is taken to be characteristic of the human sciences.[52] It is clear that a more comprehensive account of the notion of explanation in the natural sciences employs both of these activities.

In addition, one would have to distinguish (2) between semantic and perceptual contexts—they are different, (3) between the perceptual contexts of natural world horizons (unaided by technologies) and those of naturalized world horizons in which readable technologies are used—when the last word is spoken, they are continuous and indistinguishable, and (4) among the respective communities of inquirers involved in the different phases of the inquiry, each in relation to perception with its different mode of embodiment and different hermeneutical interests—these are complementary. If the concept of explanation were to be so enlarged, it would be necessary to go beyond the semantics of mere truth-functional discourse to the practical dimension of discourse, and consequently to distinguish (5) between truth-functional sentential logic and a quantum logic of the existential contexts of discourse.[53]

Where does this leave the account of explanation in the natural sciences? It shows that if explanation is limited to (1a), i.e., to the causal, nomological, and deductive relationships among phenomena and their descriptions, then the phenomena in question cannot be natural pre-scientific phenomena as Logical Positivism and much of Logical Empiricism assumes, but naturalized scientific phenomena constituted by institutionalized processes of preparation and measurement. However, if the notion of explanation is enlarged (as it should be) to include (1b), i.e., how scientific phenomena are constituted in local media, then explanation is no longer just computational or derivational, but it is historical, social, artistic, and hermeneutical.[54]

Chapter 15

BEYOND REALISM AND IDEALISM: A RESPONSE TO PATRICK A. HEELAN

Joseph J. Kockelmans

I   Introduction

For more than two decades Patrick Heelan has been an important, albeit also a somewhat lonely, figure in the philosophy of science, whose influence continues to grow. Educated in classical philosophy as well as in phenomenology, and a student of theoretical physics for many years, Heelan has tried since 1970 to develop a consistent philosophy of science from a phenomenological point of view. His first major publication, *Quantum Mechanics and Objectivity: A Study of the Physical Philosophy of Werner Heisenberg*, was still written from the perspective of Lonergan's metaphysics, although the influence of Husserl's phenomenology is already discernable in this work, also. A few years ago Heelan drew wide attention with his very thought-provoking book, *Space-Perception and the Philosophy of Science* (1983) and a number of important articles that followed upon the publication of this second book. A quick look at the bibliographies of these two books shows immediately the road which Heelan's thought has been following for the last fifteen years. Although these publications contain much more than that, they provide us with a systematic effort to develop the foundations for a philosophy of science written from a hermeneutico-phenomenological point of view in which, in addition to ideas from Husserl and Merleau-Ponty, we also find insights first developed by Heidegger, Gadamer, and Ricoeur. The second book and the articles which followed it excel particularly because of the new conception of

the meaning of scientific perception and the idea about hermeneutic or horizonal realism.

In "On the Hermeneutic Dimensions of the Natural Sciences"
I have briefly explained my position in regard to Heelan's conception of scientific observation. In that same essay as well as in my
Address, "On the Problem of Truth in the Sciences," I have tried
to explain my position in regard to scientific realism, and why I
believe that my hermeneutical position inherently implies a "new
conception" of truth, namely a hermeneutic conception of truth
of the kind first developed by Heidegger in *Being and Time*. In
my response to Heelan's present paper, his "horizonal realism"
will be one of the issues on which I hope to focus, and so will be
his conception of truth.

It should be noted first, however, that Heelan and I agree
on many essential points; our differences flow mainly from
the different philosophical perspectives from which we make
our claims. At any rate, Heelan and I do not disagree on the
manner in which we understand modern physics in general
and quantum mechanics in particular. I share his interpretation
of quantum mechanics which rests on the Copenhagen interpretation of Bohr and Heisenberg. I also agree with his conception of the measurement processes and of the experimental
phenomena, the presence of which they provoke and signal.
I finally share his view that the relationship between experimental phenomena and theory is to be rethought along the
lines which he suggests.

Although I thus agree with Heelan in many important respects, there are nonetheless also important differences between
his and my philosophy of science. His view seems to be inspired
to a high degree by Merleau-Ponty and Husserl, whereas in
my thinking the influence of Heidegger and Gadamer is more
prominent. We stand both in a hermeneutico-phenomenological
tradition; yet we interpret the meaning of this tradition quite
differently with respect to some fundamental issues of importance. Some of these topics I hope to touch on briefly in the pages
to follow.

The difference in our conception of the meaning of the hermeneutico-phenomenological tradition, to which both of us belong,
entails that our views on some issues of minor importance will be
affected as well. This difference also can account for the different

manner in which we evaluate our present predicament. As I see it, hermeneutic phenomenologists have never taken a negative stance in regard to the sciences. They would share the view of the "analytic philosophers" who see science "as humanity's most successful truth enterprise." As a matter of fact, I have defended this opinion for many years and I had no difficulty in documenting this opinion with references to the works of the leading philosophers in this tradition. Yet all of us have always warned of the enormous implication of scientism, i.e., of a radical positivist interpretation of the meaning and function of science. We are also very concerned about the manner in which insights gained in the sciences are often applied to aspects and dimensions of our world; we are convinced that those who are engaged in this application have often acted in a very irresponsible manner. Above all, we are concerned about the fact that we are driven into a complete scientization and technologization of our entire lives. But in all of this, it is not science that is to be blamed; rather certain scientists, applied scientists, and politicians will have to take the blame for some of these developments.

But there are also other issues that must be considered here. I would not defend the view that reality *is* the life world. World is for me the totality of *meaning* in regard to the totality of all ontic entities known to us. Furthermore, although scientific entities in my view do not belong to the marketplace of the world, they nonetheless are, speaking generally, real, ontic things. In my view, they are certainly not just mathematical surrogates for real objects; and this view was held equally by Heidegger and other hermeneuticists.

Finally, I would not agree either with the three theses formulated at the very end of Part I of Heelan's present paper.

Given these differences as far as our underlying philosophical conception and our interpretation of the hermeneutico-phenenological tradition is concerned, it is obvious that Part II of Heelan's paper would become completely acceptable to me only if I were allowed to make a number of changes, some of which would touch on essential issues, others would be concerned mainly with minor details. It is impossible in this brief rejoinder to accomplish such a task. Instead I shall focus briefly on some issues which in my view go the heart of Heelan's conception of modern physics.

II Heelan's "ontology"

To make my own reflections on Heelan's position more under-standable, I shall first briefly summarize a few theses that are essential to Heelan's position.

In his view, if it is true that all forms of human knowledge are forms of interpretation, then it is legitimate to claim that perception, too, is an interpretive act. This basic thesis was de-fended in *Space-Perception and the Philosophy of Science* as well as in an article, "Perception as a Hermeneutical Act." It is explained there that visual space tends to have a Euclidean geometrical structure only when the environment is filled with objects which always have the same pattern and show us the same aspects, and when these shapes and patterns continually exhibit standard Euclidean shapes. On the other hand, our perception tends to have a hyperbolic structure when vision is not aided by such clues. In his book Heelan has tried to show that all perception, including scientific perception, is both causal and hermeneutical.

The thesis, that scientific observation is also hermeneutic in nature, was later explicitly developed further in an article, "Natu-ral Science as a Hermeneutic of Instrumentation." There Heelan argues that the perceiver and the scientific observer learn to "read" perceptual and instrumental stimuli as one learns to read a text. Thus the hermeneutical aspect of the natural sciences is located at the heart of the sciences, where one would least have expected it.

In "Hermeneutical Phenomenology and the Philosophy of Sci-ence," Heelan explains, among other things, in what sense a hermeneutico-phenomenological philosophy of science differs from scientific realism. He briefly discusses there twelve issues, some of which are of immediate importance to us here. Let me first list some of them:

1. Hermeneutic phenomenology does not focus primarily on theory but on experimental phenomena.
2. The distinction between the experimental phenomena and the events which occur in the preparation and measurement processes that produce and signal them is essential.
3. Theory is generally not prior to phenomena and phenomena are generally not prior to theory.
4. Scientific theories do not describe scientific phenomena, but

rather the existential measures of these phenomena; measured phenomena have no existence outside the processes or the virtual processes of preparation and measurement.

5. A scientific theory is not a semantic network; nor is it just a useful conceptual model with technical application; in addition, a theory must make standard processes of preparation and measurement of phenomena possible.

6. Theory can be translated into perceptual phenomena by instrumentation; these phenomena then become newly "naturalized citizens" of the perceptual world.

7. Scientific phenomena are "dressed" for the world by standardized scientific instruments used as readable technologies.

The conception of science unfolded in these seven theses implies, according to Heelan, a form of realism which he calls hermeneutic or horizonal realism. He holds this view in opposition to the instrumentalism of many phenomenologists and critical theorists. His own opinion is therefore in some sense closer to scientific realism, with which Heelan explicitly compares his own view.

He has developed the implications of this position in his book, *Space-Perception and the Philosophy of Science,* and several articles in great detail. I do not have to dwell on this here further, because the essential elements of what is needed for the discussion have now been mentioned. It is clear that Heelan maintains that in the discussion of the ontological status of science, theory plays an essential part. Secondly, he explicitly maintains the term "reality" as essential to the entire discussion about the meaning of scientific theories. And thirdly, he appears to maintain the classical conception of the correspondence theory of truth. In the sections to follow I hope to argue for the following theses: 1) The concept of reality is an epistemological concept of recent origin that should be eliminated from the ontological discussions about what-is; 2) Science nonetheless is the theory about what-is; 3) The correspondence theory of truth is to be reinterpreted from the perspective of a more primordial "revealment theory" of truth; and 4) the concept of phenomenon is to be discussed in greater detail. The second and third claims imply that in ontological reflections science cannot just be taken as a set of scientific statements logically connected with each other, but that one must focus primarily on all the activities of the group of scholars which play a part in the development and the systematic presentation of this set of statements.

III   On the notion of "reality." Beyond realism and idealism

The reason why I would not like to call the hermeneutic conception of science a form of realism is obviously not the fact that realism defends the view that there is a world, that there are natural things independent of human knowledge of them, and that science has been able to discover entities, not known in our everyday life, which truly exist, i.e., are truly present to us in our experiments as science describes them. And yet hermeneutic philosophy at the same time rejects every form of realism insofar as 1) "realism" refers to an *epistemological* position according to which the reality of the world is somehow to be proved; and 2) realism tries to explain the existence of the world by means of *causal* connections and, thus, in an ontic manner. Let me explain this briefly with a very short paraphrase of some sections of *Being and Time*.

In classical metaphysics, all understanding of meaning was one-sidedly oriented toward the mode of being that is characteristic of the entities we encounter in the world. Furthermore, these entities were taken there primarily not in the way they function in that world, but rather in the manner in which they present themselves to our theoretical reflection; thus these entities were simply identified with things, *res*. Thus "being" acquired the sense of reality (a word derived from the word *res*). Since human *Dasein* was there also considered from the same perspective, it, too, was conceived like all other things, as a real thing that is merely present to us in our theoretical reflection. In this way the concept of reality received priority over all metaphysical concepts. This priority, in turn, had several important consequences for classical metaphysics. First, the human mode of being could so no longer be understood correctly. Secondly, the problem of being was forced into an entirely wrong direction because classical metaphysics did not start from primordially given phenomena. Moreover, in the problem of reality several issues were mixed together and thus confused. 1) Those beings which supposedly transcend human "consciousness," are they indeed actually real? 2) Can we adequately prove the reality of the "external" world? 3) To what extent can the world, insofar as it is real, be known in its being-in-itself? And 4) What is the profound meaning of this being that is called here "reality"?

From an ontological point of view the last of these questions is undoubtedly the most important one. And yet it was never clearly formulated because it was always associated with the problem of the external world. That this could happen is not un-understandable. For the analysis and description of "reality" are obviously possible only if human beings have an appropriate access to "reality." Now, according to the common view of classical metaphysics, reality can be understood only by theoretical knowledge which takes place "in" consciousness. Thus, insofar as "reality" has the character of being something independent of consciousness and of something in itself, the question of the meaning of "reality" became necessarily linked with the question of how "reality" can be independent of consciousness, and whether consciousness is able to transcend itself and know the real world the way it is "in itself." Thus the possibility of an adequate ontological analysis of "reality" depended for centuries upon how far consciousness, which was supposed to transcend itself, had been clarified in its own mode of being. Yet in metaphysics' attempt to do so consciousness was arbitrarily understood as a "thinking thing," a "thinking substance," or a "*tabula rasa*," so that the radical clarification of consciousness was to be identified with the radical clarification of consciousness' knowledge.

In the problem of knowledge, traditional metaphysics since Descartes has always separated subject and object, the "thinking thing" from the "extended thing." It is not difficult to see that whoever adopts such a position must eventually in some way or other hit upon the modern epistemological problem. For whoever conceives of the world as independent of man necessarily throws man back upon himself. If one then speaks of knowledge of the world, one must interpret such knowledge as a special process taking place "within" consciousness. Anyone who maintains that the knower and the object known do not have the same mode of being and, in addition, maintains that knowledge really takes place "inside" consciousness, is confronted with the difficult, if not impossible, problem of how to relate subject and object. For only then can the problem arise of how this knowing subject is able to get out of its inner sphere into another sphere that is "external" to it, and how one is to think about the thing itself.

On the other hand, if knowing is viewed as a mode of being of an entity that is essentially oriented toward the world, *one* mode in which humans are in the world, then it does not have to be interpreted as a process in which the subject makes "representations" of "outside" things that are kept "inside" itself. And the question of how these "representations" can agree with reality then becomes a meaningless question. Moreover, the questions of whether there really is a world and whether its reality can be proven become, likewise, meaningless questions as asked by a human being whose mode of being is to be oriented toward the world. And who else but human beings could possibly ask such questions and try to answer them? The basic error of all epistemological positions lies in the fact that one starts from the supposition that human beings are originally world-less and that they, therefore, have to assure themselves somehow of the world's existence in and through philosophical reflection.

The position which I try to defend is in agreement with that of realism insofar as it does not deny in any way that there are things in the world independent of us and of our knowledge of them. Yet my position is also close to idealism insofar as it holds that meaning cannot be explained in terms of things. Yet it goes beyond both realism and idealism insofar as it understands the knowing subject not as a closed monad, but as a being whose mode of being essentially implies the orientation to the world. Thus if idealism amounts to nothing but the realization that meaning cannot be understood and explained in terms of things, and that meaning is "transcendental" with respect to all beings, then idealism offers the only possibility to posit the problem in a philosophically proper manner. If, however, idealism amounts to reducing all meaning to consciousness, a divine or a human consciousness, then idealism is just as naive as the most naive form of realism.

If we apply these general, ontological ideas to the sciences, then it will be clear why hermeneutical phenomenology here too would like to move beyond realism and idealism, while at the same time maintaining that the natural sciences are obviously sciences of *what-is*; they provide us with a *theory* of what-is. Much of what Heelan claims about theory and scientific entities can be maintained in the conception of hermeneutic philosophy that I have tried to unfold here. Yet in my opinion one can come to a truly consistent view only if one is willing to rethink our common conception of truth as correspondence. Let me try to explain this briefly. Since I have formulated my view on this issue already in another context, I shall limit myself here to a few essential observations.

IV Toward a new interpretation of the coherence theory of truth

In discussions about the problem of truth in the sciences, almost all authors hold some interpretation of the correspondence theory of truth. Yet in the opinion of many authors there is also room for the coherence and the pragmatic conceptions of truth. These latter theories, however, are not so much concerned with the nature of truth as with criteria that must be fulfilled if in a given context one is to be able to speak about truth in an unambiguous and meaningful manner.

I too hold some interpretation of the correspondence theory of truth. Yet in my view most authors who are concerned with the problem of truth in the sciences more or less "dogmatically" select a *certain* interpretation of the classical correspondence theory, without explicitly reflecting on the conditions under which this theory alone can be held meaningfully in the domain of the sciences. There are other authors who with Tarski, Field, Putnam, Stegmüller, Ellis, Boyd, and others do ask questions about the nature of truth as correspondence and about the conditions under which this notion is to be applied, but limit themselves to semantic or linguistic reflections. Since they never raised the issue on an ontological level, they ended up with theories that are epistemically and "metaphysically" underdetermined, or they saw themselves forced to accept the view that what is true is no more than a limit of reasonable belief.

In the past truth was usually defined as the adequation of intellect and thing. It was argued that the proper place of truth is the judgment, and that the essence of truth lies in the correspondence between judgment and object. Although this conception has been defended by most philosophers, and although this conception is undoubtedly correct, it is still a conception that because of its formal emptiness is affected with serious problems. One of the first questions to be raised here is how, and in what sense, judgment and thing can indeed correspond to each other. The judgment must state the thing as it is; yet it can never become identical with it. Furthermore, how is the thing to be understood here? It is clear that if one interprets the expression "the thing" to mean "the thing as it is in itself independent of our understanding of it," we shall again encounter the epistemological problem of Kant. The agreement we are looking for can furthermore not be one between a representation and a "real" thing. The agreement is rather one between the content of a claim about a thing and the thing insofar as this has been or can be discovered by us independently of our claim by means of some process of verification which is intersubjectively acceptable. Thus, to say that a statement is true really means that this statement reveals the thing as it manifests itself to us in an activity which at least logically antecedes the claim, for instance in an act of perception, or in observation and experiment.

In order for the thing to manifest itself to us it has to show itself time and again in a context of meaning. Such contexts of meaning ultimately belong to the totality of meaning of which we can now conceive. The limits which we have to impose on our judgments as well as on the contexts of meaning make it impossible for us ever to claim that in our judgments we state how things are "in themselves," i.e., comprehensively and definitively. We can claim only that our judgments state how things are as seen from some limited context of meaning. Thus every form of revealment implies for us also some form of concealment. But if every effort on our part to reveal things just as they are implies various forms of concealment, then for us truth is in principle always connected with untruth, and meaning with lack of meaning. And yet we can still maintain that our claims are true to the degree that they reveal things just as they *manifest themselves to be.*

Most philosophers who have tried to get rid of the limits of our finite knowledge have done so by means of an appeal to an absolute Being, or to some ideal order; those who refused to do so have often fallen into skepticism. Yet as I have tried to indicate, the fact that all human truth claims are claims within limited contexts of meaning does not by itself doom us to skepticism and anarchy.

We must now turn to the question of what this interpretation of the correspondence theory of truth means for a systematic discussion of the problem of truth in the sciences. Scientific claims are obviously also context-bound and these contexts always contain elements that are not absolutely necessary and whose origin often can be explained only by historical research. But this does not at all change the fact that in scientific theories, which have withstood critical scrutiny, the assumptions made were both rational and very reasonable. At any rate, all of this does not entail that there would be no longer any reason why one could not call such statements true. By calling a scientific statement true we mean to state that everyone at any time under similar assumptions and circumstances can approach the given phenomena from the same context of meaning and that he or she will find the same insights as we have come to, even though at a later time one may discover a "model" that is even better or more adequate empirically.

My interpretation of the statement that scientific claims are true, does not imply that there is some "one-to-one correspondence" between what the claim states and the things, taken independently of all claims we can make about them, the things-in-themselves, so to speak. Neither does the statement that scientific claims are true, in my interpretation, imply that the things in question are nothing but what my scientific claims state them to be. The only point that in my view is essential here is that one sees that defending the truth of scientific claims is tantamount to maintaining that things indeed manifest themselves independently of our actual claims as having the properties, characteristics, and relationships which our scientific claims assert them to have. The only point I am thus making here is that *under given conditions and under given circumstances* things do have the characteristics which scientific statements claim them to have.

These reflections finally also throw new light on the question

239

concerning the truth of scientific *theories*. As I see it, the fact that
scientific theories contain elements which are not essential and
can be explained only historically, as well as the fact that each
scientific theory, in the final analysis, is only a *possible* interpretation of the meaning of natural phenomena, do not change the
fact that scientific theories obviously are and remain theories of
what actually is, and that they legitimately can be said to be true
to the degree that they indeed do make an essential contribution
to the revealment of a certain aspect of natural things that can
be intersubjectively shared.

V Appearances or phenomena?

When he speaks about *that which* manifests itself in scientific
research Heelan usually employs the term "phenomenon." This
term is manifestly used in different ways and the differences are
usually qualified by proper adjectives. Thus he speaks about
"scientific phenomena," "perceptual phenomena," and "experimental phenomena." Sometimes the term appears to be used in
the sense in which Newton uses the term; most of the time the
term is used in the sense given to it by Husserl and particularly
Merleau-Ponty. I find this use of the term "phenomenon" somewhat confusing, particularly in view of the fact that what Newton
calls a phenomenon cannot easily be related to what Merleau-
Ponty understands by a phenomenon. To bring some of the
underlying issues to light I shall first briefly summarize Heelan's
basic position in this regard, in order then to conclude my critical
reflections with a proposal for a sharper terminology.

Heelan makes a distinction between the "experimental phenomena" and the events which, occurring within the preparation
and measurement process, produce and signal them. This distinction implies that theory is formally not descriptive of a phenomenon, but of the actual measures of that phenomenon. The
measures themselves are the signs of the "scientific phenomena."

In Heelan's view, a scientific theory is justified if it can be
"translated" by instrumentation into "perceptual phenomena,"
i.e., things that manifest themselves to us directly and without
mediation by measuring processes. These "perceptual phenom-

ena" become thereby "naturalized citizens" of the perceptual world. This means that the "scientific phenomena" become "dressed" for the perceptual world by standardized scientific instruments used as readable technologies.

On the basis of these insights Heelan can then finally state that the reference of the *mathematical theory* is the set of "readable" events, occurring within the processes of preparation and measurement, and that these events are the signs of the "scientific phenomena." The reference of the *physical theory*, on the other hand, is the set of phenomena constituted by the experimentalist within the processes of preparation and measurement, i.e. "experimental phenomena."

I would like to point out first that when a theory becomes translated by instrumentation into "perceptual phenomena," these phenomena do not thereby become "naturalized citizens" of the *perceptual* world; rather these phenomena become thereby part of the "objective" world of the relevant science. Heelan seems to have realized this problem where he explicitly allows for subcommunities in the large community of human knowers, so that some people, namely scientists, can learn to "perceive" things, which other people perceive in a different way. I find the question of precisely how insights gained in the sciences become part of the world in which all of us live, an extremely interesting and important one. Yet because of lack of time I shall refrain from commenting further on this aspect of Heelan's position, in order to focus only on his use of the term "phenomenon."

It is clear to me that if the "readable" events mentioned are indeed *signs* of the scientific phenomena, then Heelan must be holding the view that scientific phenomena do not manifest themselves to us except through these signs. But if this is so then they are not phenomena at all, neither in the ordinary sense of the term, nor in the sense of phenomenology. To avoid seeming contradiction and confusion, it will be necessary, it seems to me, to introduce a more carefully formulated terminology. I shall try to derive such a terminology from another section of *Being and Time*.

Let us call a *phenomenon* that which shows itself directly. Taken in the narrow sense, the set of phenomena is then the totality of all entities that are actually manifest to human beings without mediation through something else. Taken in the broad sense, the set of phenomena is the totality of all entities that *can* be actually manifest to human beings in the manner indicated. Let us use the term "misleading semblance" to refer to something that shows itself as something which it actually is not; it looks like something else, but in fact it is something different.

An *appearance or manifestation* is something that does not manifest itself *directly*; rather it is something that *announces* itself without showing itself directly. What appears announces itself by means of something that shows itself immediately. In this case we often speak of indications, symptoms, signs, symbols, etc. The latter expressions all refer to something that has the basic structure of appearing just indicated, even though they differ among themselves in several respects. It is important to note that appearing is possible only by reason of a phenomenon in the proper sense of the term. The fire in the woodstove (appearance) manifests itself by means of the smoke that we see coming out of the chimney (phenomenon).

A *phenomenon in the ordinary sense of the term* is an entity which manifests itself directly in every person's "ordinary" and everyday life. On the other hand, a *phenomenon in the phenomenological sense of the term* is something that as such is not explicitly manifest to people in their everyday lives, but which can be made manifest to someone provided he or she applies the proper phenomenological method. Once this method is applied properly the essential structure of the relevant entity will manifest itself directly and without further mediation.

Finally, a *phenomenon in the scientific sense of the term* would be an entity which as such does not manifest itself to human beings directly, but which can be made manifest to scientists if they apply the proper scientific methods and measuring processes. Heelan has correctly pointed out that in the domain of particle physics many "phenomena in the scientific sense of the term" have actual existence only within the measurement processes; outside these processes one can only attribute "virtual existence" to them.

Having made these distinctions it is now possible, I feel, to reformulate some of Heelan's statements more clearly. To simplify matters I shall select a concrete example and focus on the energy state of an electron:

1. "Perceptual phenomena" in the sense of Heelan are really *phenomena in the ordinary sense of the term.*

2. In physics no claim is made about the energy state of electrons outside the measurement process, the energy state of the electron-in-itself, so to speak. Yet the implicit claim is made that any electron will show itself in a given energy state provided the measurement process is repeated under specified conditions and circumstances. An electron taken in this sense is *that which* can manifest itself by means of appearances and phenomena. For the complications created by the measurement of complementary variables I must refer to Chapters 10 and 11 of Heelan's book, cited in the bibliography.

3. The electron taken within the measurement process and manifesting itself there as having a certain energy state, is not a phenomenon but rather an appearance, in view of the fact that as such it does not show itself directly; it only shows itself through certain "readable" events. Thus it is indeed an *appearance*; but *that which* announces itself in this case is a "real" electron.

4. The "readable" events occurring in the measurement processes are not phenomena in the ordinary sense of the term; for taken *as* phenomena in the ordinary sense of the term the events are merely numbers, lines, pictures, etc. It is only through the interpretation of the scientist that they become the *signs* of the variables that determine the energy state of the relevant electron. The so interpreted events are thus the signs of the appearances mentioned in the preceding paragraph, i.e., the electron as it shows itself indirectly as having a certain energy state. They themselves are thus also *appearances* which are made manifest by phenomena in the ordinary sense of the term, namely the numbers, lines, pictures, etc., taken without the interpretation of the scientists as "things" of the ordinary world in which we live.

5. What Heelan calls "scientific phenomena" are not phenomena at all, but rather *appearances of appearances*: They are entities or characteristics of entities which are made manifest by means of the measurement results which in turn are appearances made manifest by phenomena in the ordinary sense of the term. If one wishes to maintain the term "scientific phenomena," I suggest one use it for the "readable" events insofar as scientists have learned to "see" these appearances as "phenomena."

But however indirectly the electron may show itself, both the two appearances as well as the phenomena, through which it shows itself refer back to *something that is* and that under the specified conditions and circumstances manifests itself as having a determinate energy state. Scientific claims are thus ultimately about "real" entities and their characteristics which manifest themselves indirectly to be in the manner stipulated by the scientific statements; in this way scientists have true knowledge of the relevant entities and their characteristics because of the processes of measurement which as such are distinct from and independent of the claims they (later) make about them. Yet one can obviously not claim that these entities and their characteristics are actual, independent of the measuring processes. Nor can one claim that these entities could not have certain characteristics other than those which science now attributes to them.

I wish to conclude these brief reflections by stating once more explicitly that in my revised hermeneutic perspective most of what Heelan holds about scientific theories and entities as well as about the preparation and measuring processes can be maintained. The disagreement that still exists between us is related mainly to the underlying, basic ontological issues that directly pertain to questions of meaning and truth and, thus, to the manner in which both of us interpret some fundamental themes of hermeneutic phenomenology. In the preceding pages I have given an outline of my interpretation as well as some of the reasons on which this interpretation rests.

PART IX
HERMENEUTICS AND
THE TEXT

Chapter 16

THE INTERPRETATIVE TEXT

Vincent Descombes

In this paper, I propose to discuss the way in which the question of interpretation is most frequently posed in contemporary philosophy. I am first going to try to define this question, by which I mean the *quaestio disputata*, the much disputed question of interpretation; I shall then try to modify the terms of the debate. The best way for me to get into my topic is to warn you that my title must be understood in a sense which is not customary. I thought it necessary to take the liberty of using an early, perhaps archaic, meaning of the adjective *interpretative*. In contemporary French, the word *interpretatif* is no longer used, other than through recuperation of the English word *interpretative*, taken in the sense of "whatever serves interpretation." For this sense, the Oxford English Dictionary gives: "Having the character, quality or function of interpreting; serving to set forth the meaning (of something); explanatory, expository." However, the O. E. D. gives another meaning, noted as being "archaic and obsolete," which corresponds to the meaning that the adjective had in French, namely: "that which is subject to interpretation," as opposed to that which is expressly stated, explicit or formal. For example, an expressly stated order is an order that your superior communicates to you in express terms, whereas an interpretative order is an order that you must infer or surmise in the absence of any direct or explicit manifestation of his will. In those cases where there is no possibility of communicating directly with one's superior, his will then has to be interpreted, that is, it has to be determined exactly what our superior wants us to do in the case at hand, by following a line of reasoning on the different signs that we have of his will.

Consider a text and its gloss. In the current sense of the word, a gloss is held to be interpretative of the text whose gloss it is: Its function is to interpret the text. But once it was the *text* which was said to be interpretative if it called for a gloss in order to be fully understood, or utilized. By interpretative text, then, I shall mean a text which calls for or requires interpretation. The reason for this archaic usage lies in the need for a contrast between the adjective *interpretable* and something else. I am well aware that, currently, the phrase *interpretable text* would be used instead of the phrase *interpretative text*, which I am going to use here. This current usage is, moreover, perfectly well-founded, since adjectives ending in -ble (Latin -bile) are flexible enough to cover the modal scale ranging from the possible to the necessary.[1] Thus, in this case, the interpretable can be alternatively understood as: 1) that which *can* be interpreted, that which does not rule out interpretation; 2) that which *must* be interpreted, that which requires an interpretation or 3) the interpreted *as such*, the formal object of interpretation. However, it seems to me that several of the difficulties or paradoxes of contemporary philosophy stem from a failure to appreciate the difference between what *can* be interpreted and what *must* be interpreted. Now, in the adjective *interpretable*, and in adjectives ending in -able generally, the dominant meaning today is the one conveying possibility. If I speak of the interpretable text, you will initially understand by that the text that can be understood otherwise if it is read otherwise. The difference between the predicates of interpretability and interpretatively is therefore the following: In the case of the interpretable, nothing forbids us to interpret, whereas in the case of the interpretative, everything, or nearly everything, forbids us to refrain from interpretation. Clearly, to say that one *can* interpret is not yet to say that interpreting is the right thing to do. Now, my thesis will be this: The philosophical question of interpretation is not that of the interpretable text, but that of the interpretative text.

My claim has a negative part and a positive part. A few words will suffice to establish the negative part. Only then will I be able to deal with the thing itself, namely the question of the interpretative, which is much more difficult.

I The interpretable text

The philosophical question is not that of the interpretable. Questions concerning the interpretable (in the sense of that which does not rule out interpretation) are trivial. If one asks: *Does the interpretable exist?*, the answer is *yes*. *What is interpretable?* Answer: *everything is interpretable.* Not just "discourses" and "texts" are interpretable, but any arrangement of things at all, not just the Great Texts of tradition, but the fact that it rains on a specific day, or the fact that there is a black car parked across the street from my place, etc. *But why is all this interpretable?* Because it is always possible—which does not mean useful or reasonable— to suppose that what we have before our very eyes is *only* what we have before our very eyes. One can always assume that something else is being made manifest indirectly. There is no logical limit to the complexity of the hypotheses that one can invent—just human limits (fatigue, the amount of time involved in comprehension, etc.).

Now, the fact that everything *can* be interpreted does not mean that everything *must* be interpreted, in other words, that in normal circumstances, everything has to be interpreted. The fact that a text is interpretable still does not give us any reason to interpret it. Many errors derive from the fact that it is often assumed that some reason or other is needed *not* to interpret the interpretable.

Two sophisms have to be mentioned at this point, sophisms not always avoided in the recent philosophical literature. The first states: *Not interpreting is still interpreting.* The second states: *Not to interpret is to arbitrarily interrupt the work of interpretation.* The first sophism assumes that if you don't interpret something that could have been interpreted, it is because you have your reasons, good or not so good, and these reasons have led you to the decision not to interpret. But then, not interpreting still amounts to interpreting, in the sense that the absence of interpretation is the limiting case of interpretation. Of all the possible interpretations, you choose the one that says the true meaning of the text is, after all, its manifest meaning. Consider the example Derrida made famous, the fragment found in Nietzsche's papers, "I have forgotten my umbrella": According to the first sophism, one of the possible *interpretations* of this fragment is that it simply means *I have forgotten my umbrella.*

By contrast, the second sophism assumes that you have no special reason for not interpreting, but that you *should* have one. You refrain from interpreting because you think it is the right thing to do; a meaning has to be found, so, why not the manifest meaning? You put a stop to interpretation because you refuse to go any further. Here the sophism itself is close enough to an interpretation, attributing to whomever does not devote himself to the work of interpretation when he could have done so, the desire to deny the possibility of interpreting, the desire to ignore that there is still more interpretable material. Behind the absence of interpretation would therefore lie the naive belief in the natural goodness of things, the simplicity of events, the evidence of appearances, or at least the desire to preserve such a naive belief by implicitly maintaining that cases exist where it is in fact *impossible* to interpret, cases where the possibility is ruled out that what you can see is not *merely* what you can see, cases where it is clear that what you can see is what there is to see.

These arguments are sophisms because they assume that special reasons are needed to refrain from interpreting. Now, the modality inscribed in the notion of the interpretable operates in both directions: Whatever *can* be interpreted can also *not* be interpreted. Consequently, there are no general reasons for interpreting something, whatever it might be, nor are there any general reasons for not interpreting it. To say that a text does not rule out its being interpreted is also and equally to say that it does not rule out its *not* being interpreted. Therefore, the philosophical question of interpretation cannot be confined to general remarks on the nature of signs and texts. The question is not: *What is interpretable?* but rather: *What is interpretative?*

II The question of interpretation

The question of interpretation is the debate concerning the nature and goals of the activity that consists in interpreting. Here is the way I think it could be formulated in the present state of the discussion: Is *interpretation to be defined:* 1) as *deciphering meaning?* (which means deciphering a meaning which is the correct or the true meaning, a meaning that is unique); 2) as *deciphering a second meaning?* (a second meaning which is furnished by the interpreter, a meaning added to, or which is substituted for a first literal meaning); 3) as *deciphering a supplementary meaning?* (that is to say, not just the deciphering of a second meaning in addition to the first, and of a third in addition to the second, but the permanent possibility of interpreting otherwise, of a perpetual surplus of meaning, in which case it would have to be said that what one interprets—"the text"—is always "plural," that the meaning to be given to it is always multiple); or 4) as *something other than deciphering?* (namely, perhaps, inventing meaning, rather than discovering it). These different answers to the question "What is interpreting?" have been given either in turn or concurrently in recent discussions. Principally, two major controversies should be mentioned here, controversies that have given the question its current tenor: the dispute about method in the social sciences, and the dispute about the function of interpretation in the reading of texts.

It is well known that, since the end of the last century, practitioners of the social sciences have been debating whether or not the social sciences should follow some other method than that of the natural sciences. The activity that consists in understanding human conduct has been compared to the one that consists in "reading a text." Clifford Geertz, for example, writes:

> Doing ethnography is like trying to read (in the sense of "construct a reading of") a manuscript—foreign, faded, full of ellipses, but written not in conventionalized graphs of sound but in transient examples of shaped behavior.[2]

Generally speaking, it has been said that whenever the object is comparable to a text, there is room for interpretative activity. Charles Taylor expresses this point very well when he says:

> Is there a sense in which interpretation is essential to explanation in the sciences of man? . . . Interpretation, in the sense relevant to hermeneutics, is an attempt to make clear, to make sense of an object of study. This object must,

therefore, be a text, or a text-analogue, which in some way is confused, incomplete, cloudy, seemingly contradictory—in one way or another, unclear.[3]

We now come to the other controversy, which this time is directly "hermeneutic," since here we are dealing with texts in the strict sense of the word. Here I will borrow some formulations from Odo Marquard, who defines hermeneutics thus: It is "the art of extracting from a text that which cannot be found in it."[4] If this formulation seems overly irreverent, we can content ourselves with saying: It is the art of extracting from a text that which could not be found in it if we *only* had the text, nothing but the text, and no one to interpret it. But then what good are hermeneuticists? Marquard's answer is that hermeneutics is the response that has been given to the problem posed by the fact of "the civil war being waged all around the absolute text."[5] Hermeneutics was born in order to put an end to the war. As for this war, it was the result of giving a text absolute status, which means separating it from other texts. By definition, the absolute text is unlike other texts. Its content is not relative to the circumstances of its composition, nor is what is read in it relative to the circumstances of this reading. But if this is how things stand, then hermeneutics is by nature unstable, oscillating between theology and literary criticism. Theological hermeneutics seeks to discover orthodox meaning, the meaning unique to an absolute text. Literary hermeneutics seeks to show that the would-be absolute text is actually relative, or again, that in matters of reading, no orthodoxy is possible. Marquard writes:

> Hermeneutics responds to this fight to the death, this civil war being waged over the absolute text, by making hermeneutics pluralistic, that is to say, literary. It thereby invents a non-absolute text and a non-absolute reader. Consequently, hermeneutics invents something which, apart from its foreshadowing by the humanists, had not previously existed, namely the literary text and the literary reader.[6]

I think these remarks allow us to give a more concrete meaning to the different hypotheses mentioned above. We get a glimpse of the consequences of adhering to one or the other of the following possible positions: To interpret is 1) to discover a meaning; 2) to discover a second, hidden meaning; 3) to go on discovering new meanings indefinitely; 4) to invent a new use for the text other than the one that consisted in looking for one or several meanings in it.

III   The right to interpretation

The moment has come to spell out just what makes this debate pass for a philosophical, rather than a linguistic, literary, juridical or theological question. Those minds formed in the Kantian school—that is to say, *neo*-Kantian school—will believe that the answer lies in the word *right*. Indeed, they have been taught that philosophy posed the question of right, the *quaestio quid iuris*. For them, there is a philosophical problem wherever it is a question of justifying an activity. Philosophizing would then always consist in seeking out whatever would authorize us to put forward certain claims, for example, the claim to be doing science when interpreting data. If one shares this point of view, one would expect a philosophy of interpretation to conform to the following program: 1) *establishing* (and at the same time *limiting*) *our right to interpret* against those who contest it (some in the name of objectivity, others in the name of orthodoxy, etc.); 2) establishing and limiting this right through *general arguments* which will be drawn as much from *the nature of the object to be interpreted*, as from *the nature of the mind doing the interpreting;* these arguments will be furnished by what may be called either an "ontology of language" or a "theory of the sign," and by what may be called either a "phenomenology of language" or a "theory of meaning."

Of course one can ask oneself why such a program is philosophical. Is there anything especially philosophical in the treatment of "the question of right"? Is it the question that is philosophical, or the arguments?

Is the question of interpretation philosophical simply because the question is one of the *right* to interpret? Not at all. Take as an example the problem of determining who has the right to interpret the law. Who is going to respond to this problem? Should one acquire the services of a philosopher? Of course not. The law itself fixes the right to interpret it.

But then at what point does a discussion become philosophical? As we shall see, it is not enough for one to move from criticism of a particular interpretation to criticism of the right to interpret in general. In itself, a "critique of reason applied to texts" is still not philosophical. In order to get to philosophy, the solution to be given to the problem must rest on philosophical, rather than literary, juridical or theological arguments. In other words, the solution must rest on bringing out whatever is necessary in a *contingent* situation. One can therefore say that a discussion takes a philosophical turn when one has mentioned the *conditions of possibility* of something. For example, one moves from juridical science to the philosophy of right when the examination of the right to interpret leads us to speak of the very conditions of applying any law whatever in any particular situation.

I must now answer one last question in order to finish specifying what a philosophy of interpretation would be. We have just seen that it has less to do with establishing a right—with giving the activity of interpreting a "foundation"—than with attaching this contested right to the most general conditions of a certain activity. The problem posed, then, is this: *What would become impossible if we were not permitted to interpret? Of what would we be deprived?*

"Philosophical hermeneutics" is the name generally given to the argument that *interpretation is necessary in order to use language.* Within contemporary philosophical hermeneutics, two streams can be distinguished. The first is oriented towards the interpreter. This philosophy tells us that it is necessary to interpret if we want to understand a message, whether spoken or written, simple or complex, in our own or in a foreign language, etc. It tells us: *No understanding without interpretation.* The second stream puts the accent on the object to be interpreted, on the "text". This philosophy tells us: *No reading of a text without interpretation.*

In what follows, I propose to refute both of these claims. I shall try to do so by means of a philosophical argument, philosophical in the sense just specified. I will therefore invoke the conditions of possibility of an interpretation. My argument will be that interpretation would not be possible if it had to be a necessary stage in the comprehension of meaning or an essential stage in the reading of any text whatsoever. Or again, to spell out my argument in the familiar philosophical idiom: The conditions of possibility of an interpretation *in general* are such that they preclude interpretation being a condition of possibility of the comprehension of meaning *in general,* or a condition of possibility of the reading of a text *in general.* This will bring us to a final question: does the right to interpret have to be established philosophically? In other words, is there something other than interpretation whose possibility would rest upon interpretation?

IV   Interpreting and understanding

There is one point everyone seems to agree on today, which is that the interpreter's activity is exercised on a text, or on something which is analogous to a text. Reading a text is given as the definition or at least as the example *par excellence* of understanding meaning. Now, this is precisely the point that seems to me to need closer examination.

The basic condition for there being an interpretation of a given text is that the text be replaced by yet another text, one which is in certain respects its equivalent, but for which one no longer needs still another interpretation. Interpretation consists in exchanging an interpretative text for a second text which is not interpretative, and which is accepted in place of the first. I therefore believe that one can advance the following general condition: It is not possible to speak of interpretation (or of something resembling an interpretation) unless one can point to something playing the role of the interpretative text, to something playing the role of the interpreting text, and to the conditions under which the second text is accepted in exchange for the first. This basic condition holds regardless of any particular notion of interpretation that may be held.

Some think of interpretation according to the paradigm of translation. Donald Davidson, for example, explains it this way: The philosophical problem of interpretation is to explain how it is possible for us to know that Kurt said that it was raining when he uttered the words *"Es regnet."*[7] Here interpreting means interpreting Kurt's words, a task accomplished by bringing a sentence (or several sentences) in our own language into correspondence with the sentence Kurt uttered in his. Others would

255

have us understand interpretation on the model of paraphrase or explanation. To interpret the text of the statement "It's raining" would then be to offer an exegesis of this statement. At times, the correct interpretation will be: Drops of water are falling from the local heavens; at other times, it will be different.

But certain philosophers would reject characterizing interpretation as the substitution of an interpreted text for an interpretable text. These philosophers would reproach such a characterization for wanting to fix a moment of interpretation as separate from the process of establishing the interpretative text. With Nietzsche, they would readily proclaim "there are no facts, nothing but interpretations," or, with Gadamer, "all understanding is an interpretation [*Auslegung*]". But I don't want to go into whether contemporary hermeneuticists rightly call upon Nietzsche or Gadamer. Rather, I want to consider the objection in itself, remembering, however, that both of the authors just cited are thinking in the first place, and above all, of classical philology when they speak of interpretation. The situation which is therefore offered as typical is, for example, the interpretation of a pre-Socratic author. Here their objection consists in saying that one cannot really distinguish as Schleiermacher wanted to, the moment of *criticism* which establishes the text, from the *hermeneutic* moment, the moment of commentary. They would say something like this: The critic seeks to re-establish the original text, to eliminate interpolations, corruptions, errors in copying, etc. Now in order to decide on the version of the text to be retained, the critic will be anticipating possible interpretations of it. Thus, we are told, the text to be interpreted is already the result of an interpretation.

It seems to me that this objection stems from a confusion. There is no question of denying that the interpretative text can itself be the product of an interpretation. But if this is the case, it is the product of *another* interpretation, that is to say, of another substitution (for example, that of a corrected text for one that is corrupt). Better still, the fact that one interpretation should rest on another results from the very notion of the substitution of one text for another. In short, we are speaking of "text" in two different senses. If we are speaking of the text *materialiter*, that is to say, if we can see something which is materially a text, then the text providing the interpretation is just as textual as the one being submitted to interpretation. On the other hand, when we oppose text and interpretation, we reserve the name "text" for what is interpretative, and the name "interpretation" for what serves to interpret. In this second case, we are speaking *formaliter*, since what we now have before us is the formal object of interpretation, namely a text. But it follows that, in this second case, the notion of text is relative. Only from the point of view of a translation or commentary does one thing become "the text" and the other "the interpretation." Therefore, nothing precludes translating a translation, but it must be seen as another exercise in translation. Nothing stops us adding one commentary to another, one gloss to another: But we will then be dealing with another exegesis. All of these possibilities are well brought together in one of Wittgenstein's remarks:

> But an interpretation is something that is given in signs. It is *this* interpretation as opposed to a different one (running differently). So if one were to say "Any sentence still stands in need of an interpretation" that would mean: no sentence can be understood without a rider (*Zusatz*).
>
> Of course sometimes I do *interpret* signs, give signs an interpretation; but that does not happen every time I understand a sign. (If someone asks me "What time is it?", there is no inner process of laborious interpretation; I simply react to what I see and hear. If someone whips out a knife at me, I do not say "I interpret that as a threat").[8]

The supposed paradoxes of the text that is *already* an interpretation, or of the interpretation that is *still* a text are simply "dialectical appearances." These paradoxes arise as soon as one attempts to make absolute notions that are of no use unless seen as relative to one another. There is the paradox of the *Text-in-itself:* The text had to be established, and is only one possible version of what was authorized by the source manuscripts; consequently, there *are* no texts, or, what amounts to the same thing, texts are nowhere to be found, they are "always already" interpreted. And there is the paradox of *indefinite interpretation:* Interpretation has to be communicated and preserved, which it is, in the form of a text whose destiny is to become more and more obscure, until you have to start all over again, and interpret the interpretation, as well as the interpretation of the interpretation, so that one is never actually in possession of meaning. One interpretation always remains to be interpreted.

Both text and interpretation, taken in their formal senses, are only terms in an operation of substitution. As soon as one makes the notion of text absolute, one moves into the domain of text in the material sense, and here there are no more than two texts, the material text of what was the formal text (the text to be interpreted), and the material text of what was the formal text of the translation or gloss. For example, you have the text "*Es regnet*" and the text "*It's raining.*" And as long as we are not told what kind of interpretation is required—for example, into which language the text is to be translated—the two material texts remain on the same level. In one sense, what we have here is only two texts and no interpretation. In another sense, we have only possible interpretations and nothing that might pass for the Text-in-itself.

Interpretation is, initially, a substitution. But then, interpretation is only possible under the following condition: What is to be interpreted has to be distinguished from what can be taken to be its interpretation. To interpret is to risk saying that a first text A, which is enigmatic and opaque, is equivalent in meaning to a second text B, provided by the interpreter. It goes without saying that text B must be understandable. Text B must no longer be interpretative. To say the second text B must be understandable is not to rule out its being, in other respects, obscure, elliptical, or unusable. It *is* to say that it must be understandable from the point of view of the envisaged substitution, understandable, therefore, in a sense in which text A was not. If text A is interpretative due to its being badly written, illegible, then text B will be relatively well-written and legible. If the required interpretation is a translation into one's own language, then text B must be entirely written in one's language. If text A is interpretative due to its being abstract, then text B must be concrete, and so on. But if we rediscover in text B all the difficulties we had with text A, then interpretation will not have yet taken place. It is therefore impossible for *all* understanding to be interpretation. If it were, we would have to interpret the second text in order to understand it. This is precisely what hermeneutical philosophy maintains: Interpretation can never end, we can always take it further. The reading of text A given in text B must, in turn, become the object of a reading given in a third text—text C—and so on. But if this were true, then we would have to say not that interpretation can never *end*, but that it can never *begin*. If all understanding either is, or calls for, an interpretation, then what was thought to be the *understanding* of text B, given as an interpretation of text A, was then in fact itself an *interpretation* of text B. One would have in fact interpreted text B and replaced it with text C, all the while believing that one had understood text B directly. But in reading text B, what you thought you simply understood was an interpretation of text A. In other words: Thinking that you were in the process of *understanding* the interpretation of text A, that is to say, thinking that you were reading text B, you were in fact *interpreting* the interpretation of text A, that is, you were in the process of replacing text B with its own interpretation, namely, with text C. However, materially speaking, we have only two texts in front of us—on the one hand what is called "the text" or the original, and on the other, what is called "the interpretation of the text" or the translation of the original. The texts that we have in front of us are text A, which is the text to be interpreted, and the interpretation of an interpretation, namely text C. *Text B has never been produced.* What was taken to be text B (what was taken to be understanding the interpretation of text A) was in fact text C (i.e., interpreting the interpretation of text A). Text B was never produced because it *cannot* be, at least if we maintain that to understand is always to interpret. But if text B cannot be produced, it is the interpretation of text A that cannot be produced. It is therefore not possible to interpret a text. In as much as the second text is not *understood*, the first text has not been *interpreted*. If one had to maintain the hermeneutical principle whereby understanding is an interpretation, then strictly speaking there would never be any interpretation, only fruitless attempts at interpreting, only unsuccessful efforts designed to accomplish it. In order for it to be possible to interpret *certain* texts, there must be *other* texts which can be understood without having to interpret them.

V Texts

A text can be interpreted only if there exists another text which does not need to be interpreted. This is a necessary condition:

Interpretation must be understandable. But it is not a sufficient condition: In addition, the exchange has to be acceptable, the interpreting text has to be legitimately substitutable for the interpretative text. This second condition again presents us with the problem of the right to interpretation. I have tried to show that this right cannot be elicited from a general concept of the text. The notion of text-in-general is unusable: There is nothing interesting to say about it, since it is not the material text that concerns us, but rather what plays the role of the interpreted text in a translation or an exegesis.

Hermeneutics is defined as the art that lays down the rules for what is known as "the interpretation of texts." But which texts? In the definition I have just mentioned, the concept of text is not placed under any restrictions at all. The rules of general hermeneutics would therefore hold for a text-in-general. If this were how things stood, then the texts dealt with by hermeneutics would be texts in the material sense. Hermeneutics would then have as its domain every product of the processes of editing and writing. However, if one looks at the examples provided in works on hermeneutics, one notices that the "texts" that are meant are above all the ones studied in university seminars, that is, the texts taken to be classics of a given genre. At bottom, then, "texts" means the texts at issue in a particular seminar. The context provides the restriction otherwise absent from the definition of a general hermeneutics. In a seminar on Greek literature, "the texts" are the classical texts, the ones we have received from the tradition. In a seminar on modern literature, the "text" is most frequently taken from a recognized author—it will be a text by Hölderlin or Mallarmé, rather than a piece of street theatre. In a seminar on theology, people would have in mind the text of one of the canonical books. In short, there is a gap between the theory and the practice of hermeneutics. In practice, the hermeneuticist speaks of "texts" in the same way the theologian speaks of "books." In this last case, everyone understands that something has been left out: These "Books" (capital "B") are not just books thought to be absolute, they are books grasped in relation to a Canon, or a collection of authentic books, books inspired by and endowed with an authority. We move, then, from books, *ta biblia*, to *the* Book, to the Bible. But in the hermeneuticist's theory, the implicit restriction limiting the reference of "texts" to a definite collection of texts is forgotten. What happens, then, is that the hermeneuticist thinks he can present the *material* text—in other words, the text insofar as it is a *written* text—as the *formal* object of interpretation. All of hermeneutics since Dilthey uses the word *text* in a sense in which it is above all something written, as opposed to the spoken word. Hermeneutics in its entirety thinks it can establish the right to interpret on the basis of the properties characteristic of the written word. The problems of interpretation are supposed to stem from the fact that a thought has been expressed in writing. A text, any text at all, would then have to be interpreted because a thought or an experience is "objectified" in it in a form which is alien to that thought or experience. Once they have made their way into a text, life and thought are no longer accessible other than indirectly. For example, an experience takes place only once, whereas its inscription is repeatable indefinitely. A text can be copied again and again, but one cannot relive an experience, etc.

However, the preceding argument suggests to us that this would be the wrong road to take. The fact that a text is written is not, and cannot be, enough to make it interpretative. All texts are by definition written, but not all texts are interpretative—if they *all* were, then none would be. There is therefore no point in looking for the principle of a philosophy of interpretation in a general concept of the text.

We must look elsewhere. It seems to me that Gadamer puts us on the right track when he sets up an opposition between Schleiermacher's conception of hermeneutics, a conception which is still our own, and hermeneutics as it was understood before Schleiermacher.[9] Only since Schleiermacher has it become customary to speak of a *general* hermeneutics in order to designate a general doctrine of interpretation whose rules would hold good in the study of any document whatever. Previously, hermeneutics existed only in the plural. But this did not mean that meaning was plural, nor that interpretation was pluralistic. There was interpretation as it was understood by theologians, but only for the sacred texts, or *Sacra Pagina*. There was interpretation as practiced by jurists, but only on the subject of the law. And finally, there was interpretation as the humanists conceived it, but only for classical authors. The passage from these specialized hermeneutics to a general hermeneutics is supposed to constitute progress. Yet, we would be obliged to see progress in this only if there were some sense in moving from something like the religious reading of a sacred text, or the humanist reading of a classical text, to a more general sort of activity which would be reading *tout court* the text *tout court*. But what Gadamer suggests is that, by generalizing in this way, one loses the very reason one had for interpreting.

You will look in vain for a kernel common to the different hermeneutics. If it existed, such a kernel would derive from there being certain rules to follow in the reading of a text, whatever it might be. But, in fact, when we speak of interpreting a text, what we have in mind is a text drawn from a *Corpus* or a *Canon*. The word *Canon*, in the sense of an official collection of recognized books, has a religious origin, but it has since been extended to other domains. *A Canon is a collection of authentic writings.* But "authentic writing" should not be understood to mean writing whose authorship is well attested. The fundamental meaning of the word *authentic* is rather: invested with authority. An authentic writing is a text whose author speaks *authentikôs*, which means: "with authority on a certain subject." Now, what all hermeneutic practices have in common is that, in all of them, one finds the same kind of situation: In order to reach a decision, or settle a question, one first needs to consult an authority. The condition for an interpretation is the existence of a text which has authority in the domain of the matter requiring a decision or judgement. No theological hermeneutics without a collection of inspired books. No juridical hermeneutics without a legislative code in force. No philosophical hermeneutics without a list of the classics of Western metaphysics. No literary hermeneutics without a difference between the classic and the minor authors. Only the inspired books tell us what we should believe. Only the texts of metaphysics bring the meaning of being into language. Only valid laws have to be enforced. Only the classic texts offer us models of style and humanity.

It is therefore appropriate to rectify the remarks from Marquard which I cited just now. Marquard is quite right to link the fate of hermeneutics to the fact that there exists a text which is considered to be absolute. But talking about texts being "absolute" is only another way of designating the Canon of authentic texts in a certain field. Every time we agree to accept a certain canon, we give birth to a hermeneutics. There are as many hermeneutics as there are canons. There are as many conceivable definitions of interpretation as there are ways of placing aspects of one's life under the authority of a canon. This last observation gives us an answer to the question posed at the outset: How should interpretation be conceived? The answer: There is not one and only one valid definition of interpretation. The definition to be given depends on the nature of the authority enjoyed by the canonical texts at our disposal in a given domain. Nevertheless, every one of the envisaged definitions can be situated between two limits: that of the *infallible source* and that of the *unique source*. These two limits could be represented by two kinds of texts: the text of an oracle or a prophecy in the case of the infallible source, and the text of a human testimony in the case of the unique source. The closer one gets to a situation in which the text is valued absolutely, the more the interpretation resembles *consulting an oracle*. The closer the text comes to having a human— and therefore all-too-human—source, the more the interpretation resembles *examining a witness's testimony*. The texts that hermeneutics deals with are therefore *never* simply texts in the material sense: They are those texts which, because they come from a certain source, assist us in deciding something. But the genre of interpretation that we will then feel authorized to practice will be a function of this source. The two extreme cases are the sign of a sovereign will (an *oracle* or a sacred law) and the expression of a certain human experience (a simple *testimony*). The authority held by an oracle is the upper limit. There is no sense in discussing divine will: All that we may have to object to here is the theologian's interpretation of this will. The authority held by human testimony is the lower limit. A witness has no authority over what happens, nor over our life. His sovereignty can be exercised only over the content of his lived experience. Only he can say, if not what actually happened, then at least what he saw. Only he can report, if not what was actually said, then at least what he heard and thought he understood. The infallibility of the oracle is cosmic. The infallibility of the witness is phenomenological.

VI Literary criticism

It now remains for me to conclude. The question was whether a philosophical argument in favour of the right to interpretation can be found. Such an argument would have to tell us why, in certain cases, we find it quite normal to interpret the text that we happen to be invoking. Sometimes, interpreting a text is considered permissible, at other times, it is considered obligatory.

It was thought that one could give an account philosophically of this right by seeing the human condition itself as a hermeneutic situation. The right to interpretation would be the result of a particularity of human existence. Roughly, the argument states that those who want to refuse us the right of interpretation are asking the impossible of us. In order *not* to interpret, it would be necessary to stand outside history and language—it would be like asking us to choose our date of birth and our mother tongue.

Do we have to recognize that being human implies being in a hermeneutic situation? But what is a hermeneutic situation? The hermeneutic situation is one where we *must* interpret, failing which we will not be able to do something else that we either want, or have the obligation, to do. Philosophical hermeneutics tells us, it seems, that, if we do not interpret, we do not understand. But I have argued that the situation whereby something like the hermeneutic circle is put in place could not be described with the aid of only two elements, the reader and the text. We need three, because "the text" is an abbreviation for "the text drawn from a Canon of authentic texts." This kind of situation is therefore defined by a certain relation between a *reader*, a *text*, and a *canon* recognized within a particular tradition and a particular community. What kind of relation? A relation whereby the reader is mistaken if the text *seems* to be mistaken. Precisely because we are dealing with an authentic text, a text drawn from the best source, the text is authoritative. The text is always right. If someone is mistaken, it will necessarily be the reader.

There are cases in which the reader is said to be placed under an obligation to interpret. This is what we saw, for example, with the judge's obligation to interpret the law, so that it could be enforced. We find other quite remarkable examples of this in the history of allegorical reading. At the origins of this kind of reading we find the grammarians of Alexandria and the Church Fathers. Both parties justified their decision to read allegorically by invoking the sanctity of the texts that they had to read (and one hardly needs to add: the sanctity of those texts *only*, not of "texts" in general). An *allegoresis* consists in making a text say what it does not say manifestly, or, if you prefer, what it manifestly does not say. Heraclitus the rhetorician is therefore justified in his commentary on Homer: "If nothing is allegorical in this Poet's work, then there is nothing but impiety in it".[10] For his part, Origenes, in his polemic against the Gnostics, uses the following argument: You reject the authenticity of the Old Testament because its literal meaning is unacceptable, and you refuse to read it allegorically; however, you *do* recognize the authenticity of the New Testament; now, the New Testament also contains unacceptable passages, if they are taken literally. In reality, Origenes concludes, the Gnostic "cannot believe he is dealing with the words of the Saviour unless he interprets these words allegorically."[11]

Here, therefore, is the conclusion I reach: *We have a right to interpretation in a given field if, in this field, we possess a Canon of authentic texts.* This formulation calls for two remarks.

First remark: There is no unique or privileged field for the activity of interpreting—it would be a mistake to always take either a literary or a sacred text as being exemplary. In reality, it is always in order to resolve a particular point that one has to invoke the authority of a text. What we need is not a Canon having authority over all aspects of our life, but a canon which is authentic from the point of view that concerns us: It may be deciding a point of law, an historical point, an article of faith or a point about versification or style. To what extent can we agree with Gadamer's claim that there is a "universality of hermeneutics"? If we wish to speak of such a universality, it will be in a quite specific sense. It is not the hermeneutic situation that is universal.

If we always had to interpret answers, if answers were not ordinarily comprehensible *qua* answers, we would not know what an answer to a question was, and, at the same time, could not ask any questions. But it is true that an answer *can* always baffle us. The moment we consult the authoritative books, we run the risk of receiving an answer which is initially deceptive, and of being obliged to interpret it.

My second remark is a question: What happens if, in a given field, we do not possess an authentic canon? It seems to me that, in this case, a philosophical hermeneutics would have to deny the possibility of such a state of affairs, and I think it would be correct to deny that such a situation can actually obtain. In fact, it is rather here that it is right to speak of a "universality of hermeneutics."

What would a situation characterized by the absence of an authentic canon actually be like, whether in a particular field, or in all fields at once? Two types of civilization come to mind here, one very old—the civilization of those peoples without writing—and the other very modern—the civilization which comes after the end of the "absolute text," the civilization in which what Marquard calls "pluralistic hermeneutics" is flourishing.

Of course, the important factor is not the simple absence of *writings*. Peoples without writing have no canonical books, but they do have *customs*. Most often, it seems, the elders are the most authoritative interpreters of such customs; therefore people know whom to ask for the authentic formula that will allow a difficulty to be resolved. Once again, we notice that "the hermeneutic problem" is not tied to the written form of a discourse. Besides, we moderns understand what it means to interpret a custom, since we also say that, in certain cases, custom complements law (and our theologians debate amongst themselves in order to determine the exact proportion of Writing and Tradition in Revelation).

In the final analysis, therefore, the only candidate for the title of the reader deprived of any authentic canon is the "non-absolute reader" of the "non-absolute text." Strangely enough, it is at the very moment when we are no longer under any obligation to interpret that we begin to find interpretation everywhere. Where a canon of books has ceased to have any authority, we should no longer be worried about interpreting these books. However, pluralistic hermeneutics is on the increase for all texts. Given this phenomenon it seems that we must not take the statement declaring all canons invalid too seriously. We too must interpret hermeneutics, by starting out with the presupposition that interpreters have a reason for engaging in this activity. If the difference between the authentic text and all the others had merely disappeared, if all the texts of the old Canons had fused into a single inauthentic text, there would no longer be anything to interpret. Literary criticism would have to limit itself to the task that everyone condemns under the name of "positivism":

classifying documents in archives, looking for influences, etc. If the work of interpretation goes on more feverishly than ever, with *scholars* busying themselves with it on an unprecedented scale, it is hardly because the difference between the authentic and the inauthentic has disappeared. The difference is still there, but we no longer know where to draw it. All texts have to be re-read indefinitely in order to find out whether or not they can be included in the canon. The answer is always "No." Literary criticism, Marquard tells us, has its *raison d'être* in preventing an assortment of texts being brought together again and constituted as an absolute Text.

Literary criticism has to relativize the old canons and prohibit the canonization of contemporary texts. But modern literary criticism *is* literary. It deals only with texts, and wants to deal only with what is textual. It therefore refuses to accept a return from the age of the *text* to the age of *customs;* by this I mean literary criticism cannot accept a return to the principle that customs serve to complement a text's silences. Literary criticism is modern, and upholds modernity's decision to privilege texts over customs. The answer can come only from texts. The state of modern criticism therefore calls for a diagnosis of semi-lucidity: Literary criticism has succeeded in overcoming the somnambulism of "positivism" or "objectivism," that is to say, the naive belief in the possibility of resolving *all* difficulties either through a rational procedure such as a calculus, or a negotiation. Criticism today prides itself on having surpassed naive rationalism, but because criticism remains a hermeneutics—indeed, a pluralistic hermeneutics—of texts, we must conclude from this that it has sacrificed texts but not the canon in which they were united. For us moderns, there *is* still an authentic canon, since one has to engage in the task of interpretation, but this canon is empty, since none of the considered texts is recognized as authentic.

This is precisely the program of a modernist critic: to show that a text, whatever it might be, does not belong to the canon, by pointing out the impossible consequences that would have to be granted if the text were canonized. What we are left with then, in the different fields, is the empty form of a canon, the pure idea of the book, the illegible text of the law. And here we rediscover the fascinating myths of modern criticism: The book of the future which is for ever composed of blank pages, the sovereign law which is all the more imperative in that it does not tell us what we should do, and finally, Being, which, being nothing—no part—of what *is,* makes itself all the more manifest if nothing manifests it.

Chapter 17

INTERPRETING THE INTERPRETATIVE TEXT

Hugh J. Silverman

Vincent Descombes' inquiry into the interpretative text is not an ontology of the text in general, nor is it an epistemology of the text as an intelligible object. It is also not a recipe for criticizing texts, nor even a methodology for interpreting specific texts. Rather it is an attempt at formulating what is in question when a text is interpreted—the ontological and epistemological considerations underlying what is interpreted, the stages of development from what is to be interpreted to the result of that activity, and the limits or framework for the interpretation of literary, legal, theological, or philosophical writing.

The traditions out of which Descombes' formulation arises are at once hermeneutic, analytic, and deconstructive. Although these constitute the traditions out of which he operates, he designs an account which is both unique and helpful in resolving some of the confusions about what is interpreted when an interpretation goes on, and how the result that is achieved relates to the text to be interpreted. Indeed, Descombes has offered an account that clears up some difficulties in traditional hermeneutic theory and which provides an effective way to link up text theory with interpretation theory. What I propose to do in this response is to outline the main features of Descombes' formulation and then to indicate how this can be regarded both as an advance over traditional hermeneutics and as a contribution to the theory of textuality.

Descombes distinguishes four types of interpretive object or entity. These include: the interpretable, the interpretative text, the interpretation, and the interpreting text. There are a number of other operative and peripheral considerations, but for the moment, I should like to outline these four.

1. *The interpretable.* The interpretable includes everything that can be interpreted. This includes novels, sacred works, legal documents, philosophical treatises, films, dance performances, historical events, individuals' actions, the ways people dress, someone's gait as he/she walks down the street, a choice of words, a dream—indeed just about anything is interpretable. The interpretable is a very broad category which is hardly limited to writing. It includes literally anything that can be interpreted. Since this category is so broad, it would be a useful domain for a general hermeneutics, such that as in Heidegger, for instance, one might offer a hermeneutics of Being, a hermeneutics of the world, a hermeneutics of language. These are all interpretations of realms which are quite simply *interpretable*. But since this category is so broad, it fails to be interesting (or at least useful) for a theory of the text. Thus Descombes introduces his notion of the *interpretative text*.

2. *The interpretative text.* The interpretative text is written. Thus the interpretative text excludes all those interpretable things, actions, events, and sets of relations that are not writing. Descombes limits his notion of text to that which is written. Furthermore, although all texts are written, not all texts are interpretative. The interpretative texts are those texts which are brought into an interpretive process. The interpretative text is not a Text-in-itself (a *Text-an-sich*) which exists apart from any knowledge or interpretive activity. The interpretative text is a text full of possible interpretations which can be brought into play by an interpretive activity or "reading" of the text. In this respect, Descombes appeals to what he calls the "right to interpretation" that the text embodies and which is given its full status as an interpretative text. The interpretative text is the text which "demands" an interpretation. The interpretative text achieves its identity as an interpretative text by the very condition of being interpreted.

3. *The interpretation.* The interpretation is the actualization of one or more of the possible interpretations of the interpretative text. The interpretation arises from a *reading* of the interpretative text. It is the realization of the interpretative text's right to interpretation. The interpretation could be criticism or commentary,

translation or gloss. Whichever it derives from, the interpretative text involves a process of *exchange*. The interpretation is not however *that which is exchanged for something else* nor is it *the something else for which it is exchanged*. The interpretation is a kind of intermediary text. It is purely formal and not material like the interpretative text (or for that matter, like the interpreting text). The interpretation involves *understanding*. This is the hermeneutic notion of *Verstehen*. The understanding, however, does not exist apart from the production of meaning. The understanding of the interpretative text in terms of interpretation necessarily involves understanding and the understanding is an understanding in terms of meaning. Here Descombes cites four respects in which meaning can be brought into play in interpretation. There can be 1) a simple meaning, 2) a second meaning, 3) a supplementary meaning, and 4) another type of meaning— namely that which is not found in the interpretative text or better, founded in the interpretative text but rather *invented*, superimposed on, introduced apart from *what is there* in the interpretative text. The simple or single meaning, for instance, for the Nietzsche fragment: "I have forgotten my umbrella" is quite straightforwardly: that the I in question (presumedly Nietzsche) has forgotten his umbrella. This is the literal meaning that the interpretation deciphers when there is an understanding of the interpretative text. The second meaning is deciphered or furnished by the interpreter as added onto the literal meaning. This would be something like: "I have forgotten my umbrella" means: "The I in question has not taken account of the veil that covers over truth, that keeps truth from disclosing itself." (This would be something like the Heideggerian reading of Nietzsche's fragment.) Alternatively, the second meaning might be something like: The forgetting of an umbrella is forgetting what is important—for instance, one's sexuality. This might be a Freudian reading of the Nietzschean fragment. Deciphering the third meaning would be the establishment of the plurality of the text or fragment. It is open to many different interpretations. Not only the Heideggerian or Freudian readings, but also philological, literary, and other readings of this fragment are included in the understanding of the interpretative text. This multiple understanding would include Derrida's version (in *Spurs*) in which he notes that the fragment has many alternative readings. They would include for instance that the "umbrella" is not only a veil, a concealment, a covering over—as with "woman"—but that it is also the disclosure, the coming out of concealment, the remembering of what has been forgotten (the *Unverborgenheit* of the everyday, the ordinary, the ontic). At the same time, the forgetting of the umbrella is the male forgetting that woman is truth, and that the male spur, stylus, pointed instrument (used for writing, but also for dominating discourse, leaving its traces [the *Spuren*] everywhere) is the inscription of Western tradition. This understanding of the indecidability of the umbrella makes it evident that the number of interpretations can be proliferated even further—that the text is, as Roland Barthes has claimed, *plural*.

The fourth case is where something other than decipherment is at work. Here there is invention, an addition of meaning rather than an establishment of what is clearly already there. Some might want to claim that this is true of the Derridean reading just mentioned. Even more explicitly inventive would be to claim that Nietzsche was really talking about Magritte's painting "Hegel's Vacation" in which an opened umbrella is represented with a glass of water above it and clear skies all around. The claim would be that Nietzsche was describing this painting, indicating that in order to reach out for the glass of water, his imaginary hand does not notice the obstruction that the umbrella introduces. He therefore has not noticed that his umbrella is in the way, obscuring his path to clear skies ("it is not raining") and a healthy drink of water—a drink out of a glass. Alternatively, he might have been pointing out—in his interpretation of the painting—that Nietzsche, like Kierkegaard, was not fond of the Hegelian system, that he had "forgotten" the overarching system, which provides "absolute knowledge" just as an umbrella covers everything that is subsumed under it. The difficulty is that the umbrella as absolute knowledge leaves out Hegel himself and his own personal drink of water. This might all be part of Nietzsche's own interpretation—*except* for the fact that Magritte painted "Hegel's Vacation" decades after the death of Nietzsche.

The possible truth of all these meanings (literal, secondary, supplementary, and exceptional) is an implication of the understanding of them. Reading a text in a particular way, with a particular interpretation (and understanding particular meanings) does not guarantee the truth or falsity of the interpretation itself, nor even of the meaning(s) themselves. Even the understanding itself might be misguided. But what is important here is the "possible truth" imbedded in the interpretation and in the understanding of meanings.

4. *The interpreting text*. The interpreting text is the fourth category of the consideration that Descombes offers in his paper. The interpreting text is not the interpretable (that range of whatever can be interpreted), nor the interpretative text (writing which has a right to and which demands interpretation), nor the interpretation (the understanding of meaning[s] when reading the interpretative text). Descombes calls the interpretation a text—such that if the interpretative text is text *A*, and the interpretation is text *B*, then the interpreting text is text *C*. Text *B* is not a material text at all. Text *B*—the interpretation—is however a stage in the interpretive process such that it constitutes itself as a kind of text. However its status is not material like the interpretative text (which is to be interpreted) or the interpreting text (which is substituted for the interpretative text in the interpretive process). What is important about the interpreting text is that it should not itself require interpretation. If the interpreting text does not diminish the difficulties that were in the interpretative text, then the virtues of the interpreting text as a substitute or exchange for the interpretative text are diminished. This does not exclude the possibility of (and even the need for) interpreting texts to become *themselves* interpretative texts, requiring additional interpreting texts to substitute for them. It is, however, a prescription of the interpreting text that it not introduce more problems than were already present in the interpretative text. There are many instances, however, in which the interpreting text does indeed become an interpretative text. Ficino's *Commentary on Plato's Symposium*, Lucretius' *De Natura Rerum* (as an account of Epicurus' philosophy), or Nietzsche's *Birth of Tragedy* and Derrida's *Spurs: Nietzsche's Styles* are but a few examples.

To summarize, then, Descombes' account of the interpreting text is that of a text which is exchanged for the interpretative text. However the exchange is done by materializing an interpretation. The interpretative text is drawn from the field of interpretables. The interpretables include many things which are not texts.

Restricting the domain to that of texts, however, Descombes points out that any particular interpretative text participates in a canon. He argues that there are three functions: the text, the reader, and the canon. The reader is the one who knows the sort of interpreting activity relevant to the text. The canon follows from what Descombes (following Marquard) calls the "absolute text." The "absolute text" is that interpretative text which serves as the authority for a whole tradition: the Bible, Plato and Kant, Dante, Shakespeare, Racine, Molière, and Corneille, Goethe, and so forth. These are the interpretative texts which are authoritative. They are not in any way in doubt. They establish the canon, they formulate what counts as the tradition; they are either infallible (as in oracles), or unique (as in a testimony or witness). Whatever is written (or understood) after them is derived from their authority, defined as either infallible or unique. Interpretative texts, which are offered in exchange for these absolute texts, stand in relation to the authenticity, authority, and authoritativeness of these absolute texts.

There are, however, limit conditions to the canonical texts, whose value is absolute. These are cases which antedate the canonical text, e.g., peoples without writing, prior to the Bible, prior to Plato, even prior to Dante and Beowolf. Descombes resolves this easily by appealing to some sort of *custom* that itself establishes the authority of whatever texts might be appealed to as authoritative. But the more imposing problem is the case of the *modernist* text, which is offered up as in direct contradiction to tradition, and which refuses the oracular and testimonial character of absolute texts. What gives the modernist text its authority if it is not to be part of the canon? Descombes claims that these post-"absolute texts" occupy a class—namely a canon—whose membership is limited to *one instance*. Thus, the modernist text— the innovative, tradition-breaking text, the text which inaugurates a new tradition—becomes itself authoritative by virtue of its novelty and newness. Its authorization, authoritativeness, authority, and authenticity are all conditions of these individual interpretative texts—not of any authorial statement or point of view.

Traditional hermeneutics—which takes on a variety of shapes, from Schleiermacher and Dilthey to Heidegger and Gadamer to Ricoeur—is founded on a notion that there are canonical works.

The Bible, Plato, and Freud, for example, are to be interpreted through the artfulness of the interpreter. Hermeneutics involves the understanding (*Verstehen*) of their meaning (Schleiermacher) in terms of the *Zeitgeist* and *Weltanschauung* of their author (Dilthey). Even Ricoeur, who appeals to texts, rather than *works* (i.e., the created objects of an author) still speaks of a nostalgia for the author. By treating the interpretative text in relation to a canon and the canon as introducing its own authoritativeness, Descombes avoids even the semblance of an appeal to the author or creator, divine or human.

He does not, however, leave out the consideration of *meaning*. Heidegger's examination of the meaning of Being as an act of hermeneutic inquiry was concerned with what meaning interpretation could render. Gadamer and Ricoeur are also committed to the exploration of the polysemous quality of works (later: texts) but then so too was Hugh of St. Victor in his fourfold method of interpretation which Dante made famous in his *Letter to Can Grande della Scalla* at the beginning of the fourteenth century. This elaboration of meaning(s) as what is understood in various ways—the four alternative types of meaning that Descombes offers—is then part of the hermeneutical canon. Descombes only reformulates the conditions of supplementarity (elaborated at length in Derrida's multiple writings). But then Derridean deconstruction is hardly hermeneutic in character and hence Descombes' incorporation of the Derridean logic of supplementarity adds to the syncretic character of his account.

What is especially valuable in Descombes' account of the interpretative text is that he avoids those claims that are indeed a misreading of Barthes and Derrida; that "everything is a text" or "the whole world is a text." Descombes makes it clear that there are many things which are interpretable—in this he agrees with the semiotics of Barthes, Eco and others—but Descombes limits texts to writing and, furthermore, not all writing is interpretative.

That the interpretation becomes a text-of-sorts (along with the interpretative text and the interpreting text) establishes the independent yet relative character of interpretation. The interpretation may not be realized as an interpreting text. It may only be a series of understandings or meanings. Once reformulated and exchanged for the interpretative text, the interpretation takes on the character of an interpreting text (and hence makes itself available for further interpreting texts that might substitute for it).

In all three instances (the interpretative text, the interpretation, and the interpreting text), *types of text* are at issue. It is the interpretation which establishes the textuality of the interpretative text. This is important, for it indicates in a fairly precise way what the limits and features of textuality (though Descombes does not call it that) would be in his general account. If textuality is the meaning-structure of the text (as I have called it), then it is not implausible to consider Descombes' fourfold typology of meaning-understandings as his version of what will constitute the textuality of what he calls the interpretative text. The textuality of a text is not its right to interpretation, for it is the interpretative text that would have such rights. The textuality of the text does, however, both result from and establish the need for a right to interpretation—just as humans living and seeking to survive establish their right to life. A text can establish itself in a variety of ways. Its right to interpretation is hardly a right to any particular interpretation—though a particular understanding might determine it in such a way. An interpretative text is interpretative in a wide variety of ways—in interpretation, in its textuality and textualities, it formulates the dominance and limits, centrality and supplementarity, decidability and indecidability of its interpretativity.

NOTES

Chapter 1   Gadamer on Gadamer

1 See Hans-Georg Gadamer, *Platos dialectische Ethik: Phaenomenalogische Interpretationen zum Philebos*, in *Gessamelte Werke, Band* 5 (Tübingen: J. C. B. Mohr, 1985 [First publication, 1931]). This work is not available in English.

Chapter 2   Plato as Impulse and Obstacle in Gadamer's Development of a Hermeneutical Theory

1 Hans-Georg Gadamer, *Wahrheit und Methode (Truth and Method*, Tübingen, 1965). Hereafter *WM*. Translations are my own. I will also refer to Gadamer's *Dialogue and Dialectic* (New Haven: Yale University Press, 1980), hereafter *DD*, and *The Idea of the Good in Platonic-Aristotelian Philosophy* (New Haven: Yale University Press, 1986), hereafter *IGPAP*, both of which are my translations to begin with.

2. Given that encomia of love were standard, Phaedrus is fascinated by the sophistic craft Lysias demonstrates in condemning love (Phaedrus, 277c) and with that the stage is set for the dialogue. To win Phaedrus for dialectic, Socrates simply uses it to outplay Lysias at his own game, making love first look bad and then good. But plainly this is not the serious use to which dialectic ought to be put. Indeed, it is said expressly that both Socrates' speeches are given in play *(paidai pepaisthai)* (265d), and neither is to be taken seriously.

3 This argument, that original truth as "being in the open" devolves to correctness, is Heidegger's. See *Vom Wesen dur Wahrheit* (Frankfurt: Klostermann, 1954) on *aletheia* and "Richtigkeit." In Part 4 of this often revised work, Heidegger has turned freedom into "letting be." Gadamer also takes over the reversal of agent and patient here when

he treats Plato's *pathos tōn logōn,* the passive experience of hearing what things spoken reveal to us. See below.

4 It takes a printer's eye to see the reality of letters.

5 Gadamer's example is "This man is called Socrates" (*WM,* 389). I have taken Gregory Nagy's because it is richer and it elucidates the Greek idea of naming. See Gregory Nagy, *The Best of the Achaens* (Baltimore: Johns Hopkins University Press, 1979), pp. 69 ff.

6 Those who cite Plato's writings, among them Aristotle (see *IGPAP,* 144), are either consciously or unconsciously misreading him.

7 What is spoken is not prior to what is written because it is somehow closer to the presence of something to be designated. This was never Gadamer's argument, for the word, as we have seen, does not designate something already present at all. Rather the spoken word is primary because the sense of what is, of the reality itself, is first displayed in sound. The relevation of sense, this *pathos tōn logōn,* has an acoustical, not optical, structure even when it occurs internally in the mind. He who sees has a reality arrayed before him from which he can even look away if he chooses (*WM,* 438); but he who hears is, as Hölderlin makes clear, surrounded by tone and rhythm and caught up in them. In this regard Gadamer refers to our *Einbezogenheit,* our being drawn up into what is said, and also, in playing on the German for hearing, *Hören,* to our *Zugehörigkeit* or belonging to it. Implied in heard speech is a reversal of agency that writing for all its "ideality" (*WM,* 372) does not make evident: We do not speak, rather speech speaks to us. In listening we are spoken to. Thus before he writes, Shakespeare hears what the word "peace" says to him.

Chapter 3   A Response to Christopher Smith

1 The text abbreviations employed within this paper are as follows. Unless otherwise stated, numerals refer to page numbers.

TM   Hans-Georg Gadamer, *Truth and Method,* trans., ed. G. Barden and J. Cumming (New York: Seabury Press, 1975).

DD   Hans-Georg Gadamer, *Dialogue and Dialectics,* trans. P. Christopher Smith (New Haven: Yale University Press, 1980).

BT   Martin Heidegger, *Being and Time,* Sections 31–34, trans. Kurt Mueller-Vollmer, in *Hermeneutics Reader,* ed. Kurt Mueller-Vollmer (Oxford: Basil Blackwell, 1986), pp. 214–240.

HUH   Wolfhart Pannenberg "Hermeneutic and Universal History," trans. Kehm, in Pannenberg, *Basic Questions in Theology* (SCM Press, 1970), pp. 96–136.

TPS   Wolfhart Pannenberg, *Theology and the Philosophy of Science* (Darten, Longman and Todd, 1976), pp. 156–224.

2 P. Christopher Smith, "Plato as Impulse and Obstacle in the Development of Gadamer's Hermeneutics." This volume, p. 23.

3 Ibid. p. 37.

4 J. Habermas, *The Philosophical Discourse of Modernity*, trans. F. Lawrence (New York: Polity Press, 1988), p. 154.

5 Christopher Smith, "Plato as Impulse and Obstacle." This volume, p. 26.

6 Ibid. p. 29.

7 Ibid. p. 35.

8 Ibid. p. 34.

9 J. Richardson, *Existential Epistemology: A Heideggarian Critique of the Cartesian Project* (Oxford: Clarendon Press, 1986), p. 37.

10 K. Mueller-Vollmer, *Hermeneutics Reader* (New York: Continuum Press, 1985), p. 35.

11 Richardson, *Existential Epistemology*, p. 31.

12 Christopher Smith, "Plato as Impulse and Obstacle." This volume, p. 33.

13 The influence of Heidegger's concept of truth (*aletheia*) as a simultaneous disclosure and concealment upon Gadamer is nowhere more obvious than here.

14 J. Weinsheimer, *Gadamer's Hermeneutics: A Reading of Truth and Method* (New Haven: Yale University Press, 1985), pp. 4–62.

15 Gadamer's replies to Pannenberg focus mainly on the latter's remarks about the Hegelian component in his hermeneutics. He does not appear to take up Pannenberg's challenge over statements. See the following by Gadamer: *TM*, pp. xvi, 499; "On the Scope and Function of Hermeneutical Reflection," in *Philosophical Hermeneutics*, ed. D. Linge (Berkeley: University of California, 1977), p. 67; and *Rhetorik, Hermeneutik und Ideologiekritik*, trans. J. Habermas and N. Luhmann (Frankfurt: Suhrkamp, 1980), pp. 57–82.

16 Does Pannenberg's argument imply that "statements in and of themselves can totally reveal and make explicit the hidden horizon of a text being interpreted"? Such a criticism suggests that Pannenberg's actual use of the term "full" and "explicit" implies a total thematization or objectification of a text's horizon. However, Pannenberg's argument does not at all suggest such totalization. Firstly, any "Totalization" would fall foul of precisely the assumption that Weinsheimer exposes in Gadamer's position, namely that objectifying (scientific) propositional discourses can indeed totalize their own horizons of meaning, an assumption which, as we have seen, cannot be granted.

Secondly, "full" and "explicit" in Pannenberg's argument do not imply "complete" or "total" but ample, embrasive, and adequate. This follows from the fact that Pannenberg clearly accepts Gadamer's insight into the infinite horizons of unspoken meaning which are lit up by the said (see *HIH*, 126). Given that acceptance, his position cannot infer totalization as our critic might insist. The central point, however, remains (and this is surely Pannenberg's intended meaning), namely, that without thematizing a text's horizon not even that unsaid proportion of a text's horizon would come into view. The purpose of making what inevitably must remain a partial proportion of a text's horizon explicit is precisely to infer, or to cause to resonate in the mind, that part of a horizon which remains implicit. Without that initial making explicit, the implicit proportion would not be able to be brought into consciousness as implicit in the first place. It is the latter insight that constitutes the real thrust of Pannenberg's position. Its value is its ability to attribute to propositional discourse the dialectical or speculative nature which Gadamer reserves exclusively for conversational discourse: hence, the argument put above that the statement within a given discourse not only is lit up by but also lights up the horizon of meanings which circumscribe that discourse.

Chapter 4 Dialogue, Text, Narrative: Confronting Gadamer and Ricoeur

1 Hans-Georg Gadamer, "Hermeneutics as Practical Philosophy," in *Reason in the Age of Science*, trans. Frederick G. Lawrence (Cambridge: the MIT Press, 1986), pp. 105–08. Henceforth *RAS*.

2 Hans-Georg Gadamer, "The Problem of Historical Consciousness" in *Interpretive Social Science: A Reader*, ed. Paul Rabinow and William M. Sullivan (Berkeley: The University of California Press, 1979), p. 127.

3 Hans-Georg Gadamer, *Truth and Method*, trans., ed. G. Barden and J. Cumming (New York: Seabury Press, 1975), p. 158:

> Our starting point is the proposition that to understand means primarily for two people to understand one another. Understanding is primarily agreement or harmony with another person. Men generally understand each other directly, i.e. they are in dialogue until they reach agreement. Understanding, then, is always understanding about something.

4 Gadamer, "The Problem of Historical Consciousness," p. 127.

5 Gadamer, *Truth and Method*, pp. 125–34.

6 Paul Ricoeur, "The Task of Hermeneutics," in *Hermeneutics and the Human Sciences*, trans. and ed. John B. Thompson (Cambridge: Cambridge University Press, 1981), pp. 43–62. Henceforth *HHS*. See also "On Interpretation," in *Philosophy in France Today*, ed. Alan Montefiore (Cambridge: Cambridge University Press, 1983), pp. 175–97.

7 Paul Ricoeur, "Existence and Hermeneutics," in *The Conflict of Interpretations*, ed. Don Ihde (Evanston: Northwestern University Press, 1974), pp. 15–16:

> I see this general hermeneutics as a contribution to the grand philosophy of language which we lack today. We have at our disposal today a symbolic logic, a science of exegesis, an anthropology, and a psychoanalysis; and, for the first time perhaps, we are capable of encompassing as a single question the integration of human discourse. The progress of these dissimilar disciplines has at once made manifest and worsened the dislocation of this discourse. The unity of human speech is the problem today.

8 This point is extensively argued in *Time and Narrative, vol III* (Chicago: University of Chicago Press, 1988). A short summary of this position is found in "Narrative and Hermeneutics," in *Essays on Aesthetics: Perspectives on the Work of Monroe C. Beardsley*, ed. John Fisher (Philadelphia: Temple University Press, 1983). Ricoeur states there (p. 149) that "time becomes human time to the extent that it is articulated in a narrative way, and narratives make sense to the extent that they become conditions of temporal existence."

9 Paul Ricoeur, "Hermeneutics and the Critique of Ideology," in *HHS*, p. 92: ". . . the appearance of semiological models in the field of the text convinces us that all explanation is not naturalistic or causal. The semiological models . . . are borrowed from the domain of language itself."

10 Paul Ricoeur, "What is a Text?" in *HHS*, pp. 145–64. See also "The Task of Hermeneutics."

11 Ricoeur, "What is a Text?" p. 158: ". . . the interpretation of a text culminates in the self-understanding of a subject." This point is also treated in "The Hermeneutical Function of Distanciation," in *HHS*, pp. 133–44.

12 Paul Ricoeur, "Phenomenology and Hermeneutics," in *HHS*, pp. 101–28. See also "On Interpretation."

13 Paul Ricoeur, "The Question of the Subject: The Challenge of Semiology," in *The Conflict of Interpretations*, pp. 263–66. See also "On Interpretation," p. 187: "I should like to characterize this philosophical tradition by three features: it stands in the line of reflexive philoso-

phy; it remains within the sphere of Husserlian phenomenology; it strives to be a hermeneutical variation of this phenomenology."

14 See Ricoeur "Appropriation," in *HHS* pp. 182–93.

15 See Gadamer, "What is Practice?" in *RAS*, p. 72: ". . . the twentieth century is the first to be determined anew in a decisive fashion by technology, with the onset of the transfer of technical expertise from the mastery of the forces of nature to social life."

16 See Gadamer, "Science and Philosophy," in *RAS*, pp. 11–12.

17 Ibid., especially pp. 11–15.

18 Hans-Georg Gadamer, "Amicus Plato Magis Amicus Veritas," in *Dialogue and Dialectic: Eight Hermeneutical Studies on Plato*, trans. P. Christopher Smith (New Haven: Yale University Press, 1980), p. 198.

19 See Gadamer, *Truth and Method*, pp. 278–89. Also, "Hermeneutics as Practical Philosophy," in *RAS*, pp. 88–112.

20 See, for example, Gadamer, "On the Natural Inclination Toward Philosophy," in *RAS*, especially pp. 147–48.

21 See Gadamer, "Hermeneutics as Practical Philosophy."

22 See Gadamer, *Truth and Method*, p. 319:

> . . . for experience itself can never be a science. It is in absolute antithesis to knowledge and to that kind of instruction that follows from general theoretical or technical knowledge. The truth of experience always contains an orientation toward new experience . . . The dialectic of experience has its own fulfillment not in definitive knowledge, but in that openness to experience that is encouraged by experience itself.

23 See Ricoeur, "Phenomenology and Hermeneutics," in *HHS*, p. 117: "Hermeneutics . . . begins when, not content to belong to a transmitted tradition, we interrupt the relation of belonging in order to signify it."

24 Paul Ricoeur, *Interpretation Theory: Discourse and the Surplus of Meaning* (Fort Worth: Texas Christian University Press, 1976), p. 32.

25 Ricoeur, "Hermeneutics and the Critique of Ideology," in *HHS*, p. 91.

26 Ricoeur, "Phenomenology and Hermeneutics," in *HHS*, p. 117.

27 See Gadamer, *Truth and Method*, pp. 58–63.

28 Ibid., pp. 321–25.

29 See Ricoeur, "The Hermeneutical Function of Distanciation," *HHS*, p. 141. "In oral discourse . . . reference is determined by the ability to point to a reality common to the interlocutors. If we cannot point to the thing about which we speak, at least we can situate it in relation to the unique spatio-temporal network which is shared by the interlocutors."

30 Ibid., p. 133.

31 See Gadamer, *Truth and Method*, pp. 378–87.

32 See Ricoeur, "What is a Text?" *HHS*, pp. 146–47.

33 See Ricoeur, "Metaphor and the Problem of Hermeneutics," in *HHS*, p. 169: "It is easy to show that all texts are discourses, since they stem from the smallest unit, the sentence."

34 See Ricoeur "Appropriation."

35 For a short summary of Ricoeur's notion of emplotment, see "Narrative and Hermeneutics." (fn.8). A more extended discussion occurs in *Time and Narrative*, vol. I, trans. Kathleen McLaughlin and David Pellauer (Chicago: University of Chicago Press, 1984), pp. 31–51.

36 Ricoeur, "Narrative and Hermeneutics," p. 155.

37 See Ricoeur, *Time and Narrative*, vol. I, p. 53: "It is the task of hermeneutics . . . to reconstruct the set of operations by which a work lifts itself above the opaque depths of living, acting, and suffering."

38 Ibid., pp. 52–76.

39 Ibid., p. 77.

40 Ibid., p. 40.

41 See Ricoeur, "The Hermeneutical Function of Distanciation," *HHS*, p. 138: "Man individuates himself in producing individual works."

42 Ibid., p. 136: "To impose a form upon material, to submit production to genres, to produce an individual: these are so many ways of treating language as a material to be worked upon and formed. Discourse thereby becomes an object of praxis and a techne."

43 See Ricoeur, "Metaphor and the Problem of Hermeneutics," *HHS*, p. 175.

44 See Ricoeur, *Time and Narrative*, vol. III, p. 246.

45 See Ricoeur, "Appropriation."

46 Ibid., p. 90

47 See Gadamer, *Truth and Method*, p. 419.

48 See Hans-Georg Gadamer, "Concerning Empty and Ful-Filled Time," in *Southern Journal of Philosophy*, vol. 8 (Winter 1970), p. 348: "The experience of time which is here transpiring is that of becoming something else—not as something which has changed on a constant substratum, but rather in the immediacy of having become something else."

49 See Gadamer, "The Continuity of History and the Existential Moment," *Philosophy Today*, no. 16 (Fall 1972), pp. 230–40.

50 Ibid., p. 235.

51 Ibid., p. 236.

52 See Gadamer, "Concerning Empty and Ful-Filled Time," pp. 349–50.

53 Ibid., p. 350.

54 Ibid., p. 351.

55 Ibid., pp. 352–53.

56 See Ricoeur, "Appropriation," p. 185.
57 See *Time and Narrative*, vol. III, pp. 12–22.
58 Ibid., p. 21.
59 Ibid., pp. 23–96.
60 Ibid., pp. 99–126.
61 Ibid., pp. 125–26.
62 Ibid., p. 128.
63 Ricoeur's readings of these texts constitute most of *Time and Narrative*, vol. II (Chicago: University of Chicago Press, 1985).
64 Ricoeur, *Time and Narrative*, vol. III, p. 138.
65 Ibid., p. 181.
66 Ibid., p. 190.
67 Ibid., p. 192.
68 Ibid., pp. 198–99.
69 Gadamer, "Concerning Empty and Ful-Filled Time," p. 346.
70 Ibid., p. 349.
71 Ibid.
72 Paul Ricoeur, *Freud and Philosophy: An Essay on Interpretation* (New Haven: Yale University Press, 1970), p. 46.
73 See Hans-Georg Gadamer, "Practical Philosophy as a Model of the Human Sciences," *Research in Phenomenology*, vol. IX (1979), pp. 74–75.
74 Hans-Georg Gadamer, "Hermeneutics and Social Science," *Cultural Hermeneutics*, no. 2 (1975), p. 316.

Chapter 5   The Dialectical Unity of Hermeneutics: On Ricoeur and Gadamer

The following abbreviations are used in the text and notes. Where necessary I have modified the English translations of both Ricoeur and Gadamer.

HD   Hans-Georg Gadamer, *Hegel's Dialectic*, trans. P. Christopher Smith (New Haven: Yale University Press, 1976).

HHS   Paul Ricoeur, *Hermeneutics and the Human Sciences*, trans. John B. Thompson (New York: Cambridge University Press, 1981).

INT   Paul Ricoeur, *Interpretation Theory: Discourse and the Surplus of Meaning* (Fort Worth: Texas Christian University Press, 1976).

MV   Paul Ricoeur, *The Rule of Metaphor*, trans. Robert Czerny with Kathleen McLaughlin and John Costello, SJ (Toronto: University of Toronto Press, 1977).

PPR   Paul Ricoeur, *The Philosophy of Paul Ricoeur*, eds. Charles Reagan and David Stewart (Boston: Beacon Press, 1978).

TM   Hans Georg Gadamer, *Truth and Method*, second revised edition, trans. revised by Joel Weinsheimer and Donald G. Marshall (New York: Crossroad, 1989).

1 My paper originated out of a sort of double quarrel with that of Aylesworth. I do not believe that Ricoeur's notion of meaning implies the sort of teleological closure that Aylesworth ascribes to him. In particular, if one examines Ricoeur's "The Hermeneutical Function of Distanciation," and "Appropriation," one sees that appropriation, the event character of understanding, always complements distanciation, which defines the Ricoeurean notions of meaning and text (cf. especially *HHS*, p. 185). It seems to me that distanciation and appropriation are essentially inseparable for Ricoeur. Yet, Aylesworth provides sufficient textual evidence to support his position. Ricoeur's description of the text as "a kind of atemporal object" seems to imply "eventless" understanding and closure (*IT*, p. 91). Perhaps this dispute over Ricoeur cannot be resolved. I agree with Aylesworth that Gadamer does not possess the "metaphysical" type of teleology in which the end or concept stands outside the process of time (cf. *TM*, pp. 459, 465–66). Aylesworth's paper, however, implies that Gadamer's hermeneutics is free from all teleology. In contrast, I try to show that in Gadamer a "naive" teleology functions, as he says on page 453 of *Truth and Method* (cf also *TM*, p. 350). One can see what Gadamer means by "naive" teleology by following his use of the words *"Vollendung"* and *"Perfektion."*

2 Most of the ideas presented in Section 1 were first developed in my "Dialectic and Iterabililty: The Confrontation between Paul Ricoeur and Jacques Derrida," *Philosophy Today*, 32:3 (1988), pp. 181–194.

3 Cf. Paul Ricoeur, *Time and Narrative*, vol. I, trans. Kathleen McLaughlin and David Pellauer (Chicago: University of Chicago Press, 1984), pp. 48, 66; Paul Ricoeur, "On Interpretation," in *Philosophy in France Today*, ed. Alan Montefiore (New York: Cambridge University Press, 1983), p. 177.

4 Cf. Ricoeur, *Time and Narrative*, vol. I, pp. 38–42, 66–70; Ricoeur, "On Interpretation," p. 179.

5 Paul Ricoeur, "The Function of Fiction," *Man and World*, vol. XII (1979), p. 123.

6 Paul Ricoeur, "The Metaphorical Process as Cognition, Imagination and Feeling," in *Philosophical Perspectives on Metaphor*, ed. Mark Johnson (Minneapolis: University of Minnesota Press, 1981), pp. 228–47.

7 Ricoeur has at times noted the similarities between Hegel and Husserl. Cf. Paul Ricoeur, *Fallible Man*, trans. Charles Kelby (Chicago: Henry Regnery, 1965), pp. 37–56, in particular pp. 45–46; Hegel and

Husserl on Intersubjectivity," in *Reason, Action and Experience,* ed. Helmut Kohlenberger (Hamburg: Meiner, 1979), pp. 13–29.

8 Cf. Ricoeur, *Fallible Man,* pp. 26–71; Paul Ricoeur, "A Study of Husserl's *Cartesian Meditations,* I–IV," in *Husserl,* trs., Edward G. Ballard and Lester E. Embree (Evanston: Northwestern University Press), pp. 96–100; Ricoeur, "Husserl and the Sense of History," in *Husserl,* p. 145; Paul Ricoeur, *Freud and Philosophy,* tr., Denis Savage (New Haven: Yale University Press, 1970), pp. 424–524. [I must thank Martin C. Dillon for reminding me of this detailed and important discussion of ideality and teleology in *Freud and Philosophy.*]

9 On Ideas in the Kantian Sense, see Edmund Husserl, *Ideas, First Book,* tr., Fred Kersten (The Hague: Martinus Nijhoff, 1982), pp. 90–2, 197–99, 342–43.

10 For Ricoeur, philosophy or speculation rigorously takes up the impossible task of conceptual determination of meaning. See Ricoeur, *The Rule of Metaphor,* "Eighth Study."

11 Cf. Hans-Georg Gadamer, "Amicurs Plato Magis Amica Veritas," in *Dialogue and Dialectic,* tr., P. Christopher Smith (New Haven, CT: Yale University Press, 1980), pp. 210–11.

12 To achieve a sort of perfection in this paper, it would be necessary to analyze two aspects of Gadamer's work. First, the concatenation of *Anwesenheit, Darstellung,* and *Gegenwärtigkeit* demands an analysis aiming at the unity of these three terms. Because this unity lies in temporality, Aylesworth's paper provides an important first step in such an analysis. Second, Gadamer's suggestive comments about the idea of the beautiful in the final section of *Truth and Method* demand a careful rereading of Part I of *Truth and Method* and Gadamer's article, "The Relevance of the Beautiful" (in *The Relevance of the Beautiful and other Essays,* ed., Robert Bernasconi [New York: Cambridge University Press, 1986], pp. 1–56). Unfortunately, space and time forbid this completion.

Chapter 6   Reading the Text

1 Vincent Leitch provides an excellent account of the history and scope of contemporary literary criticism in his *Deconstructive Criticism, An Advanced Introduction* (New York: Columbia University Press, 1983).

2 See for example Christopher Norris's "Methodological postscript: deconstruction versus interpretation?" in his *The Deconstructive Turn* (London: Methuen, 1983), pp. 163–73; and also the Appendix to *Deconstructive Criticism,* pp. 259–63.

3 Roland Barthes, "The Death of the Author" and "From Work to Text" in *Image—Music—Text,* trans. Stephen Health, New York: Hill and Wang, 1977). Hereafter DA and WT respectively.

4 In *The Pleasure of the Text* Barthes indicates another way of under-standing this non-personal reader. Guided by Nietzsche's assertion that we have no right to ask *who* it is who interprets, the reader appears as "fiction:" "A certain pleasure is derived from a way of imagining oneself as *individual,* of inventing a final, rarest fiction: the fictive identity. This fiction is no longer the illusion of unity; on the contrary, it is the theater of society in which we stage our plural: our pleasure is *individual*—but not personal." *The Pleasure of the Text,* trans. Richard Miller (New York: Hill and Wang, 1975), p. 62.

5 In "From Work to Text" Barthes briefly notes how the history of music parallels the history of the text. At one time playing and listening combined in one activity, but then separates. There is a succession, first the performer, "the interpreter to whom the bour-geois public . . . delegated its playing," then the passive amateur, "who listens to music without being able to play." Today, post-serial music has radically altered the role of the interpreter/listener (WT 163).

6 See Hans-Georg Gadamer, *Wahrheit und Methode* (Tübingen: J.C.B. Mohr, 1960), pp. 97–161. English translation: *Truth and Method,* trans. and ed. Garrett Barden and J. Cumming (New York: The Seabury Press, 1975), pp. 91–150. Hereafter *WM* and *TM* respectively.

7 Hans-Georg Gadamer, *Philosophical Apprenticeships,* trans. Robert R. Sullivan (Cambridge: The MIT Press, 1985), pp. 189–90.

8. Hans-Georg Gadamer, "Text und Interpretation" in *Text und Inter-pretation,* ed. Philippe Forget (Muchen: Wilhelm Fink, 1984), p. 30. Hereafter *TI.*

9 For Gadamer, language is essentially "speculative." Explicitly ac-knowledging the roots of this conception in Hegel, Gadamer main-tains that a speculative relation is comparable to a mirror image in which the reflected image—what appears—is tied dramatically to what is reflected. Strictly speaking mirroring is not copying. Ac-cording to Gadamer, someone speaks speculatively "when his words do not copy [*abbilden*] beings but express a relationship to the whole of being and let it come to language." (*WM* 445, *TM* 426) Language is speculative, in other words, as the event of speech. For a more thorough treatment of this topic see Kathleen Wright, "Gadamer: The Speculative Structure of Language" in *Hermeneutics and Modern Philosophy,* ed. Brice Wachterhauser (Albany: SUNY Press, 1986), pp. 193–218.

10 Gadamer, "Philosophy and Literature," trans. Anthony J. Steinbock, Man and World, Vol. 18 (1985): 247.

11 One needs to be reminded here of Gadamer's discussion of the logic of question and answer in *Truth and Method.* A text becomes an object of interpretation when it asks a question of the interpreter. The sense

of the text emerges in acquiring the horizon of the question for which the text itself is a possible answer. Interpretation is thus a matter of responding to questions raised by what is spoken of in the text. It is in this sense that one is never free to merely discuss the statements of a text. The dialectic of question and answer always precedes the dialectic of interpretation (*WM* 447, *TM* 429).

12 Gadamer takes this term from Austin. In *How to Do Things With Words,* Austin distinguishes between performative and constative utterances. Constative utterances describe a state of affairs and are true or false. Performative utterances perform the action to which they refer and are neither true nor false. See Jonathan Culler, *On Deconstruction, Theory and Criticism after Structuralism* (Ithaca: Cornell University Press, 1982), pp. 112ff, for a discussion of this distinction as it relates to deconstruction.

13 Gadamer is explicitly referring here to the Derridian critique of hermeneutics. A brief exchange between Gadamer and Derrida occurred at a conference at the Goethe Institute in Paris in 1981. The papers from that conference are printed in TI. For a commentary on that exchange see my "Two Faces of Socrates" in *Dialogue and Deconstruction* (New York: SUNY Press, 1989).

14 See *WM* 278, *TM* 261.

15 "Philosophy and Literature," 253.

Chapter 7 Rereading Gadamer: A Response to James Risser

1 Martin Heidegger, *Being and Time,* trans. John Macquarrie and Edward Robinson (New York: Harper & Row, 1962), p. 73.

2 Edmund Husserl, *Zur Phenomenologie des inneren Zeitbewusstseins* (The Hague: Martinus Nijhoff, 1966).

3 Hans-Georg Gadamer, *Truth and Method,* trans., ed. G. Barrett and J. Cumming (New York: Seabury Press, 1975), p. 261. Henceforth *TM*.

4 To make this comparison more complete, reference should also be made to the work of Michel Foucault. It is the author's belief, however, that such a comparison would substantially undermine any attempt to find similarities between poststructuralism, understood as a unified set of theories, and hermeneutics. The differences between poststructuralist theories are no more evident than when one compares Derrida and Barthes to Foucault. To simplify the discussion, then, I shall deal only with the poststructuralism of Barthes and Derrida.

5 Jacques Derrida, *Of Grammatology,* trans. Gayatri Spivak (Baltimore:

The Johns Hopkins University Press, 1974), p. 61–62. Cited henceforth in the text as *OG*.

6 Roland Barthes, *Le Plasir du Texte* (Paris: Seuil, 1973), pp. 97–98. Cited henceforth in the text as *PT*.

7 Friedrich Nietzsche, *Aus dem Nachlass der Achtzigerjahre* (Munich: Carl Hanser, 1980), p. 487: "Man darf nicht fragen: 'wer interpretiert denn?' sondern das Interpretieren selbst, als eine Form des Willens zur Macht, hat Dasein (aber nicht als ein 'Sein,' sondern als ein Prozess, ein Werden) als ein Affekt." Cited henceforth in the text as *AN*.

8 Terry Eagleton, *Literary Theory: An Introduction* (Oxford: Basil Blackwell, 1983), p. 139. Cited henceforth in the text as *LT*.

9 Gadamer, *Truth and Method*, pp. 239, 319, 325.

10 Martin Heidegger, *Poetry, Language, Thought*, trans. Albert Hofstadter (New York: Harper & Row, 1971), p. 71.

11 Jacques Derrida, *Positions* (Paris: Minuit, 1972), p. 86.

12 Jacques Derrida, *La Carte Postale: De Socrate à Freud et au-delà* (Paris: Aubier Frammarion, 1980), p. 8.

13 Jacques Derrida, *La Dissemination* (Paris: Seuil, 1972), p. 71.

14 Jean Greisch, *Hermeneutique et Grammatologie* (Paris: Editions du Centre National de la Recherche Scientifique, 1977), p. 193. Cited henceforth in the text as *HG*.

Chapter 8   Beyond Seriousness and Frivolity: A Gadamerian Response to Deconstruction

1 See my book, *Understanding, A Phenomenological-Pragmatic Analysis* (Westport: Greenwood Press, 1982), as well as "Merleau-Ponty and the Counter-Tradition," Appendix I to my study, *The Phenomenology of Merleau-Ponty* (Athens: Ohio University Press, 1981).

2 Richard Bernstein accurately describes the playfulness characteristic of postmodern thought when he says: "What characterizes so much of what is sometimes called post-modernity is a new playful spirit of negativity, deconstruction, suspicion, unmasking. Satire, ridicule, jokes and punning become the rhetorical devices for undermining "puritanical seriousness." This esprit pervades the writings of Rorty, Feyerabend, and Derrida". *Philosophical Profiles* (Philadelphia: University of Pennsylvania Press, 1986), p. 59.

3 See Jacques Derrida, *Positions*, trans. Alan Bass (Chicago: The University of Chicago Press, 1981), pp. 12, 14. Cited henceforth in the text as *Pos*.

4 Hans-Georg Gadamer, "Deconstruction and Deconstrauction," talk given at McMaster University, November 14, 1985.

5 For "Bottomless Chessboard" see Jacques Derrida, "Difference," in *Speech and Phenomena*, trans. David Allison (Evanston: Northwestern University Press, 1973), p. 154. Cited henceforth in the text as *Dif*.

6 And yet Derrida says that he recognizes the need for ethical reflections: ". . . je crois qu'une théorie de l'éthique, de la spécificité des actes éthiques, des intentions éthiques, des lois morales, etc., est indispensable, qu'elle est à constituter" ("Table ronde: Philosophie et Communication," in *La Communication, Actes du XXe congrés de l'Association des Sociétés de philosophie de langue francaise, Montreal 1971* [Montreal: Editions Montmorency, 1973], vol. II, p. 426).

7 In much the same way that my paper, "Eine Kritik an Hirschs Begriff der 'Richtigkeit'," in Hans-Georg Gadamer and G. Boehm, eds., *Seminar: Die Hermeneutik und die Wissenschaften* (Frankfurt: Suhrkamp Verlag, 1978), was a Gadamerian response to E. D. Hirsch.

8 Bernstein, *Philosophical Profiles*, p. 61.

9 Jacques Derrida, *Dissemination*, trans. B. Johnson (Chicago: The University of Chicago Press, 1981), p. 54. Cited henceforth as *Dis*.

10 I think the following words of Rorty in praise of Derrida amount in fact to a devastating criticism of him: "Lack of seriousness, in the sense in which I just attributed it to Derrida, is simply this refusal to take the standard rules seriously, conjoined with the refusal to give a clear answer to the question, "Is the old game played differently, or rather a new game?" Richard Rorty, *Consequences of Pragmatism* (Minneapolis: University of Minnesota Press, 1982), p. 98.

11 Hans-Georg Gadamer, "Le défi hermeneutique," *Revue internationale de philosophie*, no. 151 (1984), p. 334.

12 See for instance Hans-Georg Gadamer, *Truth and Method*, trans. ed. G. Barrett and J. Cumming (New York: Seabury Press, 1975), p. 460. Cited henceforth as *TM*. See also Gadamer's discussion of Dilthey in his essay "The Problem of Historical Consciousness," in P. Rabinow, and W. M. Sullivan, eds., *Interpretive Social Science: A Reader* (Berkeley: University of California Press, 1979).

13 Jacques Derrida, *Spurs/Eperons*, trans. Barbara Harlow (Chicago: The University of Chicago Press, 1979), p. 106. Cited henceforth as *S/E*.

14 See *S/E*, p. 130 where Derrida speaks of the assumption of the "hermeneute ontologiste" that a text "doit vouloir dire quelque chose" and "doit venir du plus intime de la pensée de l'auteur."

15 The three themes of interpretation, language, and application are most forcefully linked together on pp. 274–75 of *Truth and Method*.

16 Deconstruction, Irene Harvey tells us, is not a theory; rather, "it can be called, tentatively of course, a 'textual strategy' and more precisely a 'practice' instead of a theory." "Hermeneutics and Deconstruction: Ricoeur and Derrida," a paper presented at the Penn State Conference on Interpretation Theory, April 5, 1984. I wish to thank Profes-

sor Harvey for graciously providing me with a copy of her manuscript. A summary of some of the points she makes in this paper can be found in Richard Palmer, "The Scope of Hermeneutics and the Problem of Critique and the Crisis of Modernity," in *Texte* (University of Toronto), vol. 3 (1984).

17 ". . . the enterprise of deconstruction always in a certain way falls prey to its own work." Jacques Derrida, *Of Grammatology*, trans. G. Spivak (Baltimore: The Johns Hopkins University Press, 1976), p. 24. Cited henceforth as *G*.

18 The work of hermeneutics, Gadamer says, "is not to develop a procedure of understanding, but to clarify the conditions in which understanding takes place. But these conditions are not of the nature of a 'procedure' or a method, which the interpreter must of himself bring to bear on the text." (*TM*, 263).

19 Richard Palmer is, in my opinion, absolutely right when he portrays hermeneutics as itself including a deconstructive movement. He speaks for instance of "the importance of seeing the unfolding of the hermeneutical problematic in terms of the philosophical critique of the metaphysics of modernity," and says:

> The demands of the critique of modernity generate the need for the hermeneutical strategy of deconstruction. In this context, deconstruction appears not as some incommensurable strategy that emerges from the blue but as the latest stage in the development of hermeneutics. . . . The relation of deconstruction to hermeneutics is, I think, more like that of child and parent, parasite and host, member and tradition to which that member relates. . . . Derrida offers us in deconstruction what is intrinsically a hermeneutical approach . . . deconstruction is essentially a hermeneutical strategy." "The Scope of Hermeneutics," pp. 233–34.

20 Jacques Derrida, *Writing and Difference*, trans. Alan Bass (Chicago: The University of Chicago Press, 1978), p. 292. Cited in the text as *WD*.

21 Jacques Derrida, "Bonnes volontés de puissance: Une reponse à Hans-Georg Gadamer," *Revue internationale de philosophie* (1984), p. 337.

22 "The play of differences supposes, in effect, syntheses and referrals which forbid at any moment, or in any sense, that a simple element be present in and of itself, referring only to itself. Whether in the order of spoken or written discourse, no element can function as a sign without referring to another element which itself is not simply present. This interweaving (*Enchainement*) results in each 'element'— phoneme or grapheme—being constituted on the basis of the trace

within it of the other elements of the chain or system. This interweaving, this textile, is the text produced only in the transformation of another text. Nothing, neither among the elements nor within the system, is anywhere ever simply present or absent. There are only, everywhere, differences and traces of traces." *Positions*, p. 26. See also "Difference", pp. 142–43.

23 See Ferdinand de Saussure, *Course in General Linguistics*, trans. W. Barkin (New York: Philosophical Library, 1959), p. 120.

24 "Différance is . . . the production, if it can still be put this way, of these differences, of the diacriticity that the linguistics generated by Saussure, and all the structural sciences modelled upon it, have recalled is the condition for any signification and any structure." *Positions*, p. 9.

25 "The concept of differance . . . develops the most legitimate principled exegencies of 'structuralism.' " *Positions*, p. 28. See also "Differance," pp. 140–41. The structuralist origins of deconstruction are attested to by Derrida's remarks on p. 146 of "Difference."

26 The logic of Derrida's position leads him to maintain that there is not even such a "thing" as a text. Speaking of "what used to be called a text," he says "a 'text' . . . is henceforth no longer a finished corpus of writing, some content enclosed in a book or its margins, but a differential network, a fabric of traces referring endlessly to something other than itself, to other differential traces." Derrida, "Living On," in Harold Bloom et al., *Deconstruction and Criticism* (New York: Continuum Press, 1984), pp. 83–84.

27 Reading "cannot legitimately transgress the text toward something other than it, toward a referent (a reality that is metaphysical, historical, psychobiographical, etc.) or toward a signified outside the text whose content could take place, could have taken place outside of language." *Of Grammatology*, p. 158.

28 "Reading is freed from the horizon of the meaning or truth of being. . . . Whereupon the question of style is immediately unloosed [*se dechaine*] as a question of writing. The question posed by the spurring-operation is more powerful than any content, thesis, or meaning." *Spurs/Eperons*, p. 107.

29 Rorty, *Consequences of Pragmatism*, p. 94.

30 Ibid., p. 152.

31 For a succinct account of Peirce's semiotic and for references to the following Peirce quotations, see my *Understanding*, pp. 20–22.

32 For a good account of Peirce's theory of signs which emphasizes the difference between his "semiotic" (which incorporates the elements of habit and action) and Saussurian or structuralist "semiology" (which takes into account nothing more than the diacritical play of

signifiers) see Milton Singer, *Man's Glassy Essence: Explorations in Semiotic Anthropology* (Bloomington: Indiana University Press, 1984).

33 I fully expect that Derrida would protest this assertion. In answer to Paul Ricoeur who said to him *"si on fait une théorie de l'écriture, il fait faire une théorie de la lecture. Vous ne pouvez pas faire une theorie abstraite de l'écriture, vous ne pouvez faire qu'une théorie du couple éciture-lecture . . . c'est dans la lecture que s'achève l'écriture,"* Derrida responded *". . . je pense tout à fait comme vous qu'une théorie de l'écriture est insepérable d'une théorie de la lecture."* (*"Table ronde,"* in *La Communication*, vol. II, pp. 413–14). I simply do not see Derrida taking his own assertion seriously; to do so he would have to take seriously the hermeneutical notion of application, with all that entails, in regard, notably, to the question of "decidability." Derrida's "reader" simply is not *"un individu singulier et irremplaçable"* (see *ibid.*, p. 407), which is what, as a matter of phenomenological fact, all readers are.

34 For what is in effect a Gadamerian or hermeneutical response to deconstruction which seeks to emphasize the importance of context, see Stanley Fish, "Normal Circumstances and Other Special Cases," in *Is There a Text in This Class? The Authority of Interpretive Communities* (Cambridge: Harvard University Press, 1980). Fish writes:

> In the view I put forward, determinacy and decidability are always available, not, however, because of the constraints imposed by the language or the world—that is, by entities independent of context—but because of the constraints built into the context or contexts in which we find ourselves operating. . . . [L]anguage does not have a shape independent of context, but since language is only encountered in contexts and never in the abstract it always has a shape, although it is not always the same one. The problem with this formulation is that for many people determinacy is inseperable from stability; the reason that we can specify the meaning of a text is because a text and its meanings never change. What I am suggesting is that change is continually occurring but that its consequence is never the absence of the norms, standards, and certainties we desire, because they will be features of any situation we happen to be in (*Is There a Text*, pp. 268–69).

The matter could be put the other way around by saying that where there is no "context," that is where we do not already have some kind of preunderstanding (in Gadamer's sense of the term) in terms of which we can approach that which is to be understood ("prejudices" which are constitutive of our personal-cultural being at any given time), then what we are confronted with in a text is indeed nothing but a collection of signifiers which refer to nothing other than themselves and thus which mean, can mean, for us, nothing at all. This sort of situation is rare, for normally we are not lacking in some kind of preunderstanding of even the very foreign and remote. But it does happen. This is precisely why the meaning of Mayan "writing" remains completely undecidable (that we even have to do with "signifiers" here is itself a "prejudice"—dare I say a "grammatological" one?). As the teacher tour-guide in Italo Calvino's *Mr. Palomar* says of a Columbian relief-frieze to a group of school-children, contradicting the interpretation offered by a self-appointed expert: "*No se sabe lo qui quiere decir*' "; We *don't* know what it means."

35 Regarding the "proper" see also Derrida, "Ousia and Gramme," in Derrida, *Margins of Philosophy*, trans. A. Bass (Chicago: The University of Chicago Press, 1982), p. 64, no. 39. Mario Valdes of the Centre for Comparative Literature is putting it mildly when he says: "the process of appropriation through which the reader engages the text remains to be considered by Derrida." ("Paul Ricoeur's Hermeneutics as a Basis for Literary Criticism," *Revue de l'Université d'Ottawa/ Ottawa Quarterly*, vol. 55, no. 4 (Oct–Dec., 1985), p. 126.

36 See for instance my article, "Ricoeur and the Hermeneutics of the Subject," forthcoming in *The Philosophy of Paul Ricoeur* ed. Lewis E. Hahn (The Library of Living Philosophers).

37 Derrida's critique of totality and enclosure is, as he himself says, "primarily not one which opens an inexhaustible wealth of meaning on the transcendence of a semantic excess." *Positions*, p. 46.

38 "Inasmuch as the tradition is newly experienced in language, something comes into being and exists from now on that had not existed before." *Truth and Method*, p. 419.

39 See Bernstein, "What is the Difference that Makes a Difference? Gadamer, Habermas, and Rorty," in *Philosophical Profiles*.

40 As Lévi-Strauss once said to Ricoeur in the course of a famous discussion: "*dans ma perspective, le sens n'est jamais un phénomène premier: le sens est toujours réductible. Autrement dit, derrière tout sens il y a un non-sens, et le contraire n'est pas vrai.*" "Réponses à quelques questions," *Esprit* vol. XXXI (Nov. 1963), pp. 36–37.

41 "The linguistic world in which we live is not a barrier that prevents knowledge of being in itself, but fundamentally embraces everything in which our insight can be enlarged and deepened." *Truth and Method*, p. 405.

42 I am not using the word "experience" in a metaphysical, i.e., Derridean, sense. (See for instance *G*, p. 60.)

43 ". . . from the first texts I published, I have attempted to systematize a deconstructive critique precisely against . . . history determined in the last analysis as the history of meaning. . . ." *Positions*, p. 49. For

Derrida, to think of history as the history of meaning is hopelessly
metaphysical. See *ibid.*, p. 56.

44. Johan Huizinga, *Homo Ludens* (Boston: Beacon Press, 1955), p. 19.

45 We are, it is evident, in disagreement with the interpretation offered
by Richard Detsch which presents Gadamer's use of "play" as an
attempt "to banish subjectivity." See his article, "A Non-subjectivist
Concept of Play—Gadamer and Heidegger versus Rilke and Nietzsche," *Philosophy Today*, vol. 29 (Summer 1985), p. 159.

46 Gadamer, "Le défi herméneutique," p. 336.

47 See Madison, *The Phenomenology of Merleau-Ponty*, pp. 252, 263.

48 In the Derridean *"jeu de différance,"* on the other hand, there are no
winners and no losers; everyone is a winner and everyone is a loser:
"we must admit a game where whoever loses wins and where one
wins and loses each time." *Differance*, p. 151. A kind of perpetual
zero-sum game, in effect, a genuine merry-go-round.

49 It would be the task of another paper to spell out in detail the specifics
of the Gadamerian alternative to "metaphysics." The reader will
understand, I hope, that no attempt can be made to do so here.

50 Gadamer's "retrieval" thus contrasts with Heidegger's *"Wiederho-
lung,"* in that it does not seek to overcome the tradition by going back
beyond the tradition to a mythical age of metaphysical innocence in
the pre-Socratics so as to effect a totally new beginning. He is not
reduced, therefore, to saying that "only a god can save us now."
"What man needs," he says instead, "is not only a persistent asking
of ultimate questions, but the sense of what is feasible, what is
possible, what is correct, here and now." (*TM*, xxv). It is his practical
concern with the "here and now" which sets Gadamer apart (in
different ways) from both Heidegger (whose "problem of Being" is
one which, as he says, he has by-passed [see "The Problem of
Historical Consciousness," p. 106]) and Derrida. A good example
of Gadamer's creative, appropriative, rereading of tradition is his
recently published study, *The Idea of the Good in Platonic and Aristotelian Philosophy*, trans. P. Christopher Smith (New Haven: Yale University Press, 1986).

Chapter 9 *L'Ecriture* and Philosophical Hermeneutics

1 Hans-Georg Gadamer, *Truth and Method*, trans., ed. G. Barden and
J. Cumming (New York: Seabury Press, 1975), p. 354. Henceforth
cited in the text as *TM*.

2 Jacques Derrida, "Force and Signification," in *Writing and Difference*,

trans. A. Bass (Chicago: The University of Chicago Press, 1978), p. 25.

3 Jacques Derrida, *The Archeology of the Frivolous: Reading Condillac*, trans. J. P. Leavey Jr. (Pittsburgh: Duquesne University Press). Henceforth cited in the text as *AF*.

4 Jacques Derrida, "Ellipses," in *Writing and Difference*, trans. A. Bass (Chicago: The University of Chicago Press, 1978), p. 297.

5 Jacques Derrida, *Spurs: Nietzsche's Styles/Eperons: Les Styles de Nietzsche*, French-English version, trans. B. Harlow (Chicago: The University of Chicago Press, 1979), 122/123–142/143.

6 Jacques Derrida, "The Ends of Man," in *Margins of Philosophy*, trans. A. Bass (Chicago: The University of Chicago Press, 1982), p. 128. Henceforth cited in the text as *MP*.

7 Jacques Derrida, *Positions*, trans. A. Bass (Chicago: The University of Chicago Press, 1981), pp. 90–91.

8 See, for example, this question remaining at the end in "The Ends of Man," p. 136.

Chapter 10   Answers to Critical Theory

1 *Wahrheit und Methode* (Tubingen: Mohr Siebeck, 1960). English translation *Truth and Method*, trans., ed. G. Barrett and J. Cumming (New York: Seabury Press, 1975). Henceforth, *WM* and *TM*.

2 *"Erkenntnis und Interesse"*, in *Technik und Wissenschaft als "Ideologie"* (Frankfurt: Suhrkamp, 1968).

3 The title was *Zur Logik der Sozialwissenschaften* when it first appeared as *Beiheft 5* of the *Philosophische Rundschau* (Tubingen, 1967) and when it was published in a separate edition by Suhrkamp. An extract of about ten pages, beginning from the bottom of p. 172 of the *Beiheft*, henceforth *B*, appears in the volume *Hermeneutik und Ideologiekritik*, Habermas et al., eds. (Frankfurt: Suhrkamp, 1971), henceforth *HI*, under the title "Zu Gadamer's *Wahrheit und Methode,*" and the bulk of the section treating of Gadamer appears as "Review of Gadamer's Truth and Method" in McCarthy, T. and F. Dallmayr, eds., *Understanding and Social Inquiry* (South Bend: Notre Dame, 1977). My page references will be to the *Beiheft*, first, then, after a stroke, to *HI* thus: (*B*, p. 172/*HI*, p. 45).

4 "Die Universalität des Hermeneutischen Problems," first published in the *Philosophisches Jahrbuch* 73 (1966) and in Gadamer's *Kleine Schriften* I, pp. 101–112 (Tubingen: Mohr Siebeck, 1967). It is reprinted in his *Gesammelte Werke* II, pp. 219–231 (Tübingen: Mohr Siebeck, 1986), cited here as *GW* II, and published in English translation in Gadamer, *Philosophical Hermeneutics*, trans., ed. D. Linge (Berkeley: University of California Press, 1976), cited as *PH*.

5 Jack Mendelson, "The Habermas-Gadamer Debate," *New German Critique*, no. 18 (1979), pp. 44–75.
6 Dieter Misgeld, "Critical Theory and Hermeneutics: The Debate Between Habermas and Gadamer," in J. O.'Neill, ed., *On Critical Theory* (New York: Seabury Press, 1976), pp. 164–183; and "Science, Hermeneutics and the Utopian Content of the Liberal-Democratic Tradition," *New German Critique*, no. 21 (1981), pp. 123–44.
7 *"Ich sehe Gadamers eigenliche Leistung in dem Nachweis, dass hermeneutisches Verstehen transzendental notwendig auf die Artikulerung eines handlungsorientierenden Selbstverständnisses bezogen ist."*
8 Gadamer, 1967: *GW* II, p. 240/*HI*, p. 68.
9 With subtitle in German, "Metakritische Erörterungen zu *Wahrheit und Methode*." It appears both in *GW* II and in *HI* and I shall give page references to both. An extremely free English translation is contained in *Philosophical Hermeneutics* under the title "On the Scope and Function of Hermeneutical Reflection," but since it departs widely from the original, it will not be cited here.
10 "Der Universalitätsanspruch der Hermeneutik" appeared in *Hermeneutik und Dialektik* I, ed. R. Bubner, K. Cramer and R. Wiehl (Tubingen: Mohr Siebeck, 1970) and has been reprinted in *HI*, whose pages I cite.
11 "Replik" appeared first as the concluding contribution to *HI* and is also reprinted in *GW* II.
12 *GW* II, pp. 449–78.

Chapter 11 Modernity and Hermeneutics: A Critical-Theoretical Rejoinder

1 The group of critical theorists I have in mind here have been influenced mostly by Jurgen Habermas's work. Classical critical theory, from approximately 1935 to Adorno's *Aesthetische Theorie*, first published in 1970, was not open to a reception of hermeneutical considerations at all, nor to ideas derived from Husserl's theory of the life world. It was Habermas who included both within the scope of critical theory, thus also rethinking the latter.
2 The entire history of critical social theory, originating in Frankfurt in the late 1920s, has been deeply formed by its attitude critical of theories or philosophies of science (or methodologies in the social sciences) which entail a radical objectification of social states of affairs. Habermas gave additional force to this critique by linking it with hermeneutical and language-theoretical considerations and by developing forms of critical social science which build on the self-understanding of social actors, but also draw on objective knowledge

about them. For an extensive documentation of the history of the Frankfurt School and its position on this issue, see H. Wiggerhaus, *Die Frankfurter Schule Geschichte, Theoretische Entwicklung, Politische Bedeutung* (München: Carl Hanser, 1986).

3 Cf. J. Habermas, *Technology and Science as Ideology* (Boston: Beacon Press, 1970), especially pp. 50–80. Here the implications of a translation of the results of scientific inquiry into the horizon of the practically interpreted life world are considered by Habermas. He conceives of the process in hermeneutical terms.

4 I refer the reader to the literature listed in G. Nicholson's essay and to the stages of the debate discerned by him.

5 Habermas's reconstructions of the emergence of modern formal law and of public moral conceptions anchored in universal principles aim at such theories. See J. Habermas, *Communication and the Evolution of Society*, trans. T. McCarthy. (Boston: Beacon Press, 1979), especially the introduction. These essays have been written in partial fulfillment of the programme announced by Habermas in *Zur Logik der Sozialwissenschaften* (Frankfurt: Suhrkamp, 1985), pp. 271–310, the text in which he reviewed Gadamer's *Wahrheit und Methode* as contributing to the foundations of social inquiry and social science.

6 In his introduction to *Theory and Practice* (London: Heinemann, 1974), pp. 16–40, Habermas grants that Gadamer was right when he objected to the analogy. As a consequence he acknowledges that there is a certain separateness of theory from social practice. This is the basis of his critique of Leninist conceptions of the relation between theory and practice (cf. pp. 32–40 of the same text).

7 Hans-Georg Gadamer, *Reason in the Age of Science*, (Boston: The MIT Press, 1984), p. 137. His theory of practical deliberation (the rationality of practice) derived from Aristotle is developed on pp. 69–138. Cf. also the collection of essays in vol. II of his *Gesammelte Werke* (Tübingen: Siebeck, J.C.B. Mohr), especially the essays written after the publication of *Wahrheit und Methode*, pp. 219–329. R. J. Bernstein has given the most careful exposition of Gadamer's recent views in *Beyond Objectivism and Relativism: Science, Hermeneutics and Praxis* (Philadelphia: University of Pennsylvania Press, 1983), pp. 144–75.

8 See the literature listed by Nicholson, as well as the two texts mentioned in note 7, above.

9 This conception of reason has been most vigorously defended by Herbert Marcuse. See his *Reason and Revolution* (New York: Oxford University Press, 1941). But it also lies at the heart of Adorno's subtle dialectical reflections, most systematically pursued in T. W. Adorno, *Negative Dialektik* (Frankfurt: Suhrkamp, 1966).

10 Compromise is a notion discussed by Gadamer in a variety of ways. In his view, the necessity for compromise in public life derives from

the impossibility of knowing what is best for all independently from engaging in practical deliberation. He therefore limits the tasks of politics to the preservation of conditions conducive to the pursuit of deliberation.

11 See M. Horkheimer and T. Adorno "The Culture Industry: Enlightenment as Mass Deception," in *Dialectic of Enlightenment* (New York: Herder and Herder 1972), pp. 120–67, for a representative analysis of the new forms of domination. See also H. Marcuse, *One Dimensional Man* (Boston: Beacon Press, 1964).

12 See the critical analysis of pre-Habermasian critical theory in S. Benhabib, *Critique, Norm, and Utopia: A Study of the Foundations of Critical Theory* (New York: Columbia University Press, 1986), pp. 147–223.

13 In his critical interpretation of Gadamer, Habermas argues that language is merely one dimension of society, and that the organisation of power and labour are the other two most consequential ones. For Habermas, Gadamer seems to turn language into an absolute, thus making it independent of other social activities. He thus restates elements of Marx's critique of Hegel against Gadamer. For Habermas, Gadamer's theory does not provide the means to analyze how both power and labor impinge upon language and what can be communicated in it. There are structural limitations to discourse and communication, which do not show in language. This is not to say that phenomena of power and work cannot be discussed in and with language, as Gadamer and Nicholson erroneously assume. For my purposes, I abstract from the specifics of the debate, and refer to the overall tendencies toward divergent theories of language, in both Gadamer's and Habermas's case. Gadamer's philosophy of language rests on the experience of cultured and erudite philosophical conversation; Habermas's theory builds on experiences of argument, debate, and public confrontation.

14 See Habermas's fascinating critique of T. Parsons and N. Luhmann in *Theorie des Kommunikativen Handelns*, vol. 2 (Frankfurt: Suhrkamp 1981), pp. 295–44. And my critical discussion: D. Misgeld, "Critical Hermeneutics versus Neoparsonianism?" *New German Critique* no. 35 (Summer 1985), pp. 55–82.

15 Critical theorists following Habermas will regard sections of the middle class as primary agents of social change rather than the industrial working class. The latter is too committed to the dominant values of the industrial system of developed capitalist societies to be able to act as a critical agent opposing consumerist values, for example. But sections of the middle classes, especially sections of the helping professions (from teachers to social workers) may be in a position to articulate universalist demands of justice and participation in opposition to the commodity-intensive form of production

(and its private appropriation) dominant in these societies. The same may hold for women, groups of young people, the old, or students. In these times, one can only count on a plurality of oppositional groupings, sometimes engaging in common activity as in the peace or ecological movements. The case of the international women's movement is closest to classical working-class movements.

16 Cf. J. Habermas, *Der philosophische Diskurs der Moderne* (Frankfurt: Suhrkamp 1985).

17 I am referring to Habermas's theories of language and argument, most fully developed in *Theory of Communicative Action*, vol. II (Boston: Beacon Press, 1984), pp. 1–101, and 273–338.

18 Gadamer also says: "Has not history since then been a matter of just this, that the historical conduct of man has to translate the principle of freedom into reality?" See his "Hegel's Philosophy and Its After Effects Until Today," in *Reason in the Age of Science*, p. 80.

19 Gadamer, *Reason in the Age of Science*, p. 135.

20 Cf. Habermas's theory of an advocacy model of practical discourse. Advocacy in practical discourse gives expression to generalizable, but surpressed interests. Cf. his *Legitimation Crisis* (Boston: Beacon Press, 1975), pp. 111–16.

21 Habermas's most recent discussion of the relation between scientific inquiry and philosophy as a theory of reason is contained in *Moralbewußtsein und Kommunikatives Handeln* (Frankfurt: Suhrkamp 1983), pp. 9–28. Gadamer uses the term "critical rationality" approvingly in *Reason in the Age of Science*, p. 136. The same standards of critical rationality apply to the methodical procedures of all the sciences, he says, even if they differ in terms of their interests, etc.

Chapter 12 Gadamer's Metaphorical Hermeneutics

1 Hans-Georg Gadamer, *Truth and Method*, trans., ed. G. Barden and J. Cumming (New York: Seabury Press, 1975), pp. 388–91. Henceforth cited as *TM*. I have in a few places altered this translation to bring it into accord with the fourth German edition.

2 Paul Ricoeur, "Metaphor and the Main Problem of Hermeneutics," *New Literary History*, 6 (1974), 100.

3 See the title of the final chapter of Paul Ricoeur, *The Symbolism of Evil* (Boston: Beacon Press, 1957).

4 Paul Ricoeur, *The Rule of Metaphor*, trans. Robert Czerny et al. (Toronto: University of Toronto Press, 1977), p. 303. Henceforth cited as *RM*.

5 Hans-Georg Gadamer, *Reason in the Age of Science*, trans. Frederick G. Lawrence (Cambridge: MIT Press, 1981), p. 19.

6 Hans-Georg Gadamer, *Hegel's Dialectic: Five Hermeneutical Studies*, trans. P. Christopher Smith (New Haven: Yale University Press, 1967), p. 96.

7 Jacques Derrida, "White Mythology: Metaphor in the Text of Philosophy," *New Literary History*, 6 (1974), 54.

8 I borrow here from Ricoeur's summary in *The Rule of Metaphor*, p. 287.

9 Derrida, "White Mythology," p. 55.

10 Gadamer, *Hegel's Dialectic*, p. 97.

11 Hans-Georg Gadamer *Kleine Schriften 4: Variationen* (Tubingen: J.C.B. Mohr [Paul Siebeck], 1977), p. 83. My translation.

12 Hans-Georg Gadamer, *Philosphical Hermeneutics*, trans. and ed. David E. Linge (Berkeley: University of California Press, 1976), pp. 238–39.

13 Martin Heidegger, *Being and Time*, trans. John Macquarrie and Edward Robinson (New York: Harper and Row, 1962), p. 186. Henceforth cited as *BT*.

14 Gadamer, "Anschauung und Anschaulichkeit," *Neue Heft für Philosophie*, 18/19 (1980), 13. My translation.

15 Ludwig Wittgenstein, *Philosophical Investigations*, trans. G. E. M. Anscombe (New York: Macmillan, 1953), p. 206.

16 Ibid., p. 195.

17 I have discussed this painting at length in "Mrs. Siddons, the Tragic Muse, and the Problem of As," *Journal of Aesthetics and Art Criticism*, no. 36 (1978), pp. 317–29.

18 Nelson Goodman, *Languages of Art: An Approach to a Theory of Symbols* (Indianapolis: Bobbs-Merrill, 1968), p. 31.

19 Ibid., p. 69.

20 See *TM*, pp. 278–89.

21 Max Black, "Metaphor," reprinted in *Philosophy Looks at the Arts: Contemporary Readings in Aesthetics*, ed. Joseph Margolis (New York: Scribner's Press, 1962).

22 Ibid., p. 232.

23 See *TM*, pp. 258–67.

24 Sigmund Freud, *The Interpretation of Dreams*, trans and ed. James Strachey (New York: Avon, 1965), p. 601.

25 Gadamer, *Philosophical Hermeneutics*, p. 104.

26 Cited in Black, "Metaphor," p. 229n.

27 Hans-Georg Gadamer, *Kleine Schriften 2: Interpretationen*, second ed. (Tubingen: J. C. B. Mohr [Paul Siebeck], 1979), p. 22. My translation.

Chapter 13 Whose Home Is It Anyway? A Feminist Response to Gadamer's Hermeneutics

1 Joel Weinsheimer, "Gadamer's Metaphorical Hermeneutics," this volume, p. 194.

2 See Part I of my book, *Cognition and Eros: A Critique of the Kantian Paradigm* (Boston: Beacon Press, 1988).

3 Hans-Georg Gadamer, "On the Scope and Function of Hermeneutical Reflection," in *Philosophical Hermeneutics*, trans. and ed. David E. Linge (Berkeley: University of California Press, 1976), p. 28.

4 For example, see Catherine MacKinnon, "Feminism, Marxism, Method, and the State," in *The Signs Reader: Women, Gender, and Scholarship*, ed. Elizabeth Abel and Emily K. Abel (Chicago: University of Chicago Press, 1983), p. 250.

5 It is Gadamer's ontological turn which fundamentally distinguishes his discussion of horizon from Nietzsche's more radical perspectivism. Thus, Nietzsche thematizes the question of power in a way which is foreclosed in Gadamer's thought.

6 Hans-Georg Gadamer, "The Nature of Things and the Language of Things," in *Philosophical Hermeneutics*, p. 78.

7 Ibid., p. 78.

8 Karl Marx, *The German Ideology* ed. C. J. Arthur (New York: International Publishers, 1970), p. 51.

9 Tom Bottomore et al., eds., *A Dictionary of Marxist Thought* (Cambridge: Harvard University Press, 1983), pp. 281–282.

10 For example, Sartre notes that in an anti-Semitic society, Jews do not have the privilege of metaphysical concerns. Jean-Paul Sartre, *Anti-Semite and Jew*, trans. George J. Becker (New York: Schocken Books, 1948), p. 133.

11 Hans-Georg Gadamer, *Truth and Method*, trans. and ed. G. Barden and J. Cumming (New York: Seabury Press, 1975), p. 93.

12 Carol Gilligan, *In a Different Voice: Psychological Theory and Women's Development* (Cambridge: Harvard University Press, 1982), pp. 9–10.

13 Gadamer, *Truth and Method*, p. 341.

14 Richard Bernstein, *Beyond Objectivism and Relativism* (Philadelphia: University of Pennsylvania Press, 1983), p. 156.

15 Gadamer, *Hegel's Dialectic*, p. 97, quoted in Weinsheimer, p. 186.

16 See the lead story in Mary Gordon's collection, *Temporary Shelter* (New York: Random House, 1987).

17 Biddy Martin and Chandra Talpade Mohanty, "Feminist Politics: What's Home Got to Do with It?," in *Feminist Studies; Critical Studies*, ed. Teresa de Lauretis (Bloomington: Indiana University Press, 1986). p. 196.

18 Ibid., p. 206.

19 My use of the masculine is intentional here, since I argue that this view of being at home is built on a masculine ascetic tradition which seeks a flight from the uncertainties of sexuality and death, associated with women, in order to attain the certainty of universal truths.

20 Gadamer, *Truth and Method*, p. 15.

21 Ibid., p. 15.
22 Genevieve Lloyd, *The Man of Reason: "Male" and "Female" in Western Philosophy* (Minneapolis: University of Minnesota Press, 1984), p. 92.
23 Feminist psychologists might also add that this conception of *Bildung* expresses the feature of masculine psychological development by which separation from the mother and from love relations in general become the fundamental goal of identity formation, and attachment to others becomes viewed as threatening. By contrast feminine psychological development is bound up with relations, and separation is experienced as threatening. See Gilligan's discussion, *In a Different Voice*, pp. 7 ff.
24 See, for example, Jean Bethke Elshtain, *Public Man, Private Woman: Woman in Social and Political Thought* (Princeton: Princeton University Press, 1984), and Susan Moller Okin, *Women in Western Political Thought* (Princeton: Princeton University Press, 1979). The identification of women with the home is also expressed in literature. Virginia Woolf, in *To the Lighthouse*, (San Diego: Harcourt, Brace, Jovanovich, 1964), expresses her ambivalence about this role in the character of Mrs. Ramsey, who is the source of life in the home (while her husband, a philosopher, dreams of reaching the letter R in his achievements), and yet is the antithesis of the woman artist.
25 See the discussion in my book, *Cognition and Eros: A Critique of the Kantian Paradigm*, pp. 31 ff.
26 Gadamer, "On the Scope and Function of Hermeneutical Reflection," p. 32.
27 Bernstein also argues that an immanent critique of Gadamer's hermeneutics leads to questions and practical tasks that take us beyond hermeneutics. *Beyond Objectivism and Relativism*, p. 161.

Chapter 14 Hermeneutical Phenomenology and the Philosophy of Science

This paper was originally written for the Research Conference on Continental and Anglo-American Philosophy: A New Relationship, organized by Stephen Toulmin and Paul Ricoeur at the University of Chicago (1984). I thank Stephen Toulmin, Hugh Silverman, Joseph Kockelmans and Lajla Lund for their comments on the paper; these have helped greatly in the revision of the original text.
1 See the bibliography for a listing of some of the more important works in this tradition. For an overview of contemporary German work on the philosophy of science, see Rudiger Bubner, *Modern German Philosophy* (London and New York: Cambridge University Press, 1981), pp. 69–154.

2 Cf. the works of J. Ellul, M. Foucault, H. Marcuse, and others.
3 A view going back before psychoanalysis to Nietzsche and picked up later by many, such as G. Bachelard, M. Heidegger, H. Marcuse, and others.
4 (Aristotelian) *Theoria* is a disinterested form of general knowledge often taken as the ideal of science; it is not, however, constituted by human life but it is (according to the classical authors) a sharing of the exemplary ideas of the Demiurge. Heidegger, in *Being and Time*, trans. J. Macquarrie and E. Robinson (New York: Harper and Row, 1962), sees modern science as the heir to classical metaphysics, the metaphysics (as he says) of the merely "present at hand." Also, see Gadamer's comments in *Truth and Method*, trans., ed. G. Barden and J. Cummings (New York: Seabury Press, 1975), p. 413; Joseph Kockelmans *Heidegger and Science* (Pittsburgh and Washington, D.C. CARP and University Presses of America, 1985), henceforth *HS;* and Kockelmans, "On the Hermeneutic Dimensions of Natural Science," in *Etudes Phenomenologiques*, no. 3 (1986), pp. 33–81.
5 Cf. *The Structure of Scientific Theories*, ed. Fred Suppe (Urbana: University of Illinois Press, 1974), henceforth *ST*, for an excellent overview of the analytic tradition of the philosophy of science.
6 Such are the background assumptions, say of Apel, Gadamer, Bernstein, Habermas, and Heidegger.
7 Wilfred Sellars, "Philosophy and the Scientific Image of Man," in *Science, Perception, and Reality* (London: Routledge and Kegan Paul, 1963), pp. 1–40.
8 Cf. Jurgen Habermas, *Knowledge and Human Interests*, trans. J. J. Shapiro (Boston: Beacon Press, 1971); Karl-Otto Apel, *Towards a Transformation of Philosophy*, henceforth *TP*, trans. G. Adey and D. Frisby (London and Boston: Routledge and Kegan Paul, 1980) (Apel misreads Peirce in this respect); Hans-Georg Gadamer, *Reason in the Age of Science* (Cambridge: MIT Press, 1981) and *Truth and Method*, pp. 409–11. See Kockelmans, *HS*, chapter 5 for an excellent review of Heidegger's thought on the *mathesis* of the natural sciences.
9 Apel, *TP*, p. 49.
10 Edmund Husserl, *The Crisis of European Sciences and Transcendental Phenomenology*, trans. D. Carr (Evanston: Northwestern University Press), p. 252. Henceforth *Crisis*. See also Patrick Heelan "Husserl's Later Philosophy of Science," *Philosophy of Science*, vol. 54 (1987), pp. 368–90. Henceforth *HLPS*.
11 Maurice Merleau-Ponty, *Phenomenology of Perception*, trans. Colin Smith (London: Routledge and Kegan Paul, 1962), p. viii. Henceforth *Phenomenology*.
12 Ibid., p. ix, my free translation.
13 See for example, *Truth and Method*, pp. 409–11, and the works refer-

enced below. See also K. R. Pavlovic, "Science and Autonomy," *Man and World*, 14 (1981), pp. 127–40, and Lorenzo Simpson "Science, Language, and Experience: Reflections on the Nature of Self-Understanding," *Man and World*, 16 (1983), pp. 25–42.

14 Husserl, *Crisis*, also prefigured in Husserl, *Ideen zu einer reinen Phaenomenologie und phaenomenologische Philosophie, Band II: Phaenomenologische Untersuchungen zu Konstitution*, ed. M. Biemel. *Husserliana*, vol. 4 (The Hague: Nijhoff, 1952). Henceforth *Ideen*.

15 Cf. Francis J. Zucker, "Phenomenological evidence and the "Idea" of physics," in *Phenomenology Dialogues and Bridges*, Ronald Bruzina and Bruce Wilshire, eds. (Albany, SUNY Press, 1982).

16 Heelan, *HLPS*.

17 Cf. Constance Reid, *David Hilbert* (New York: Springer-Verlag, 1970).

18 Husserl, *Crisis*.

19 Husserl, "Origins of Geometry," pp. 353–78 in *Crisis*.

20 Quotation marks usually signify that there is something problematical about the usual meaning of the term and include a promise to deal with the problem below—or later.

21 Despite its different vocabulary, the thrust of this latter movement has much in common with a variety of contemporary Anglo-American movements (or counter-movements) that have all tended to undermine the traditional belief in the objectivity of science, and to give support instead to the view that science is a function of human life, social values, and historical-cultural-technological environment. See, for example, Stephen Toulmin, *Philosophy of Science* (New York: Harper, 1960) and *Human Understanding*, vol. 1 (Oxford: Clarendon Press, 1972); also the historical work of T. S. Kuhn, G. Holton, L. Fleck, and L. Laudan; the sociological studies of such as B. Barnes, D. Bloor, B. Latour, M. Mulkay, S. Shapin, and S. Woolgar (see Karin Knoor-Cetina, "Social and Scientific Method or What do we make of the Distinction Between the Natural and Social Sciences?" *Philosophy of Social Science* 11 (1981), pp. 335–60; and the critique of logical empiricism by Ju. Compton, P. Feyerabend, M. Grene, N. R. Hanson, M. Hesse, M. Polanyi, R. Rorty, S. Toulmin, G. Von Wright, and M. Wartofsky. For a summary see Fred Suppe, *ST*.

22 Heidegger, *Being and Time*. For a study of the implications of Heidegger's early views for a philosophy of natural science, see Hans Seigfried, "Scientific realism and phenomenology," *Zeitschrift für Philosophische Forschung*, 24 (1980), pp. 395–404; Theodore Kiesel, "On the dimensions of a phenomenology of science in Husserl and the young Doctor Heidegger," *Jour. Brit. Soc. Phenom.*, 4 (1973), pp. 217–34; and Joseph Kockelmans, *HS*.

23 Maurice Merleau-Ponty, "Eye and Mind," in *The Primacy of Perception* (Evanston: Northwestern University Press, 1964), and *The Visible and*

the Invisible, trans. A. Lingis (Evanston: Northwestern University Press, 1968); Paul Ricoeur, *Hermeneutics and the Human Sciences*, trans. J. B. Thompson (Cambridge: Cambridge University Press, 1981), henceforth *HHS*. See also, for example, the works of Compton, Dreyfus, Ihde, Kiesel, and Zucker, to mention a few, who share this project.

24 Among writers currently working in the genre of a phenomenological philosophy of natural science are, to mention just a few, John J. Compton, Robert Crease, Hubert Dreyfus, Marjorie Grene, Gary Gutting, David Hemmendinger, Don Ihde, Theodore Kiesel, Joseph Kockelmans, Wolfe Mays, Joseph Rouse, Hans Seigfried, Elizabeth Stroeker, and Francis Zucker. Not all of these would agree with the positions here enunciated, but I believe all would appreciate their relevance to the basic problematic of a phenomenological philosophy of science. Among those who notably fail to exploit aggressively the positive implications of the insight that the standpoint of science cannot be objective and universal is, for example, Gadamer, in *Truth and Method*, pp. 409–11; also K. R. Pavlovic, "Science and autonomy," *Man and World*, 14 (1981), pp. 127–40, and Lorenzo Simpson, "Science, Language and Experience: Reflections on the Nature of Self-Understanding," *Man and World*, 16, 1983, pp. 25–42.

25 "Eye and Mind," p. 178.

26 *Truth and Method*, pp. 397–431.

27 Patrick Heelan, *Space-Perception and the Philosophy of Science* (Berkeley: University of California Press, 1983). Henceforth *Space-Perception*.

28 See Husserl, *Ideen* and *Crisis*. A perceptual essence is for Husserl the invariant (noematic) law among the set of profiles (perspectives) through which a perceptual object reveals itself to a perceiver, who explores it actively (noetically) with his or her body. See also Heelan, "Husserl's Later Philosophy of Science," *Philosophy of Science*, vol. 54 (1987), pp. 368–90, for an interpretation of these as related to the representations of active and passive transformation groups. For the notions of essence and specific essence, see *Ideen*.

29 See Eugene Wigner, *Reflections and Symmetries* (Bloomington: Indiana University Press, 1967).

30 The constituting role of scientific technologies has generally been overlooked wherever science has been accepted, as it has been by most writers in the phenomenological tradition, as a culmination of the classical tradition. See Kocklemans, *HS*, Section 22 for the critique of technology that follows from this position. Heidegger, in *The Question Concerning Technology and Other Essays*, trans. W. Lovitt (New York: Harper Colophon, 1977), begins with a critique of modern science and modern technology and eventually ends with something like the kind of resolution which lies at the basis of this paper.

31 See Heelan, *HLPS.*

32 Pierre Duhem, *Aim and Structure of Physical Theory* (Princeton: Princeton University Press, 1954), and Mary Hesse, *Revolutions and Reconstructions in the Philosophy of Science* (Bloomington: Indiana University Press, 1980), on the underdetermination of theory by data.

33 I make a terminological distinction between "datum" and "phenomenon"; a datum is to a phenomenon as a profile is to a perceptual object; thus, data, e.g., a set of measured values of O, provide the profiles of the phenomenon O that is being measured.

34 The nature of this mediation is suggested by the view of the early Heidegger that all human knowledge is existentially hermeneutical. See *Being and Time*, in which existential hermeneutics is introduced. Methodological hermeneutics is the traditional discipline which concerns itself with the meaning of signs. Once the signs are successfully interpreted, however, they become transparent, and do not occupy a place in the objective perceptual field. It is in fact characteristic of a successful hermeneutic that the signs disappear from the objective field; it may sometimes be the case that the signs were never presented or understood as a system antecedent to being used interpretatively. Once a sign system is used successfully, it may be difficult to recover anew, or perhaps uncover for the first time the objective system of signs that is being used; the difficulty of the linguistic studies suggest this. Existential hermeneutics is the name for the ontological character of human understanding. I have proposed to give an account of this as structured by a relationship between objects meant and the underlying codes to which they are related. See John Bleicher, *Contemporary Hermeneutics: Hermeneutics as Method, Philosophy and Critique* (Boston: Routledge and Kegan Paul, 1980), for a general overview, and Ricoeur, *HHS*; also, for the last point, see "Natural science as a hermeneutic of instrumentation," *Philosophy of Science*, 50 (1983), pp. 181–204.

35 See Heelan, "Perception as a Hermeneutical Act," *Review of Metaphysics*, 37 (1983), pp. 61–75, and "A Heideggarian Meditation on Science and Art," in *Hermeneutic Phenomenology*, ed. J. Kockelmans (Washington, D.C.: University Press of America and CARP, 1988).

36 The Heideggarian notion of theory, as found, say, in Heidegger, *The Question Concerning Technology*, trans. W. Lovitt (New York: Harper Colophon, 1977), and the later works, is well articulated by Kockelmans in *HS* and "On the Hermeneutic Dimensions of Natural Science."

37 Heidegger, *Being and Time*, p. 98.

38 Ibid., pp. 188–95; also *Truth and Method*.

39 For Gadamer's view on the role of language in the making of a human world, see *Truth and Method*, pp. 397–447.

40 Heelan, *Space-Perception*, Chapters 10 and 13.
41 Heidegger, *Being and Time*, pp. 188–95.
42 See Heelan, *Space-Perception*, Chapter 15. The "dressing" analogy is not to be pushed too far; there is no "naked" entity, just as there is no "naked" perceptual essence. A particular "dressing" is a particular set of perceptual profiles constituting a particular perceptual essence for the scientific entity.
43 Merleau-Ponty, "Eye and Mind," p. 178.
44 Cf. Pierce on "Thirdness"; that something—a sign—is taken to stand for something—an object—by an interpretant—the act of interpretation by a community of interpreters. See C. S. Peirce, *The Collected Papers of Charles Sanders Peirce*, vol. 2, eds. Charles Hartshorne and Paul Weiss (Cambridge: Harvard University Press), 1.300–1.353, especially 1.338; also 2.228–2.308; for the interpretative character of perception and science, see 5.182–5.184.
45 See, for example the discussion in *ST*, pp. 124–190. Also see Heelan, *Space-Perception* and "Experiment and Theory: Constitution and Reality" in *The Journal of Philosophy*, 85 (1988), pp. 515–24.
46 Many, such as Hanson and Churchland, make an analogous claim that science transforms the way we perceive the world. The argument they present is based solely on the kinematical aspects of the prescientific and scientific theories, and so the choice between the frames they offer to describe the sun is no more than a matter of convention, not revolutionary and with nothing to do with complementarity. However, there is a truly scientific difference between sun-centered and earth-centered theories because these are related to different laws of dynamics. To find a valid argument one would choose to compare Aristotle (and the old dynamics) with Newton (and the new dynamics), instead of Kepler and Tycho Brahe, for in the latter case the evidence was merely kinematical. See N. Russell Hanson, *Patterns of Discovery* (New York: Cambridge University Press, 1961), pp. 6f.; and Paul Churchland, *Scientific Realism and the Plasticity of Mind* (Cambridge: Cambridge University Press, 1979), pp. 30–35, for their treatment of this question.
47 Heelan, *Space Perception*, Chapter 11; this is also a position held by Peirce, see Peirce, *Collected Papers*, vol. 1, 5.189–5.2212.
48 See Patrick Heelan, "Natural Science is a Hermeneutic of Instrumentation," "Perception as a Hermeneutical Act" and *Space-Perception*, Chapter 8.
49 Cf. Merleau-Ponty, *The Visible and the Invisible*, e.g., pp. 90–91, 94–95. It is interesting and significant that the term "complementarity" used by Merleau-Ponty and Apel is used with the conscious suggestion that such a sense could resolve the more than fifty year old enigma of what is called "complementarity" in quantum mechanics.

This suggestion I believe is correct, and I have shown elsewhere how the peculiar logic of quantum mechanics, quantum logic, can be understood as the general logic of contextual embodied discourse within language. See *Space-Perception*, Chapters 10, 11, and 13.

50 Heelan, *Space-Perception*, Part I.

51 Gadamer, *Truth and Method*, pp. 397–447, and Ricoeur, *HHS*.

52 Ricoeur, *HHS*, pp. 145–64.

53 Note how this analysis contrasts with the common assumption of continental philosophers such as Apel, Habermas, the early Merleau-Ponty, and by analytic philosophers such as Sellars, Rorty, Churchland, that problems in the philosophy of science center on the replacement of the semantics of natural perception (say, of heat-as-felt), rather than on the complementarity of such frameworks stemming from the embodied and hermeneutical character of acts of perceiving.

54 See Heelan, *Space-Perception*, Chapter 10.

Chapter 16   The Interpretative Text

1 As Fowler tells us: "The suffix *-able* is a living one, and may be appended to any transitive verb to make an adjective with the same sense *able*, or *liable*, or *allowed*, or *worthy*, or *requiring*, or *bound*, to be—ed." *Modern English Usage* (Oxford: Oxford University Press, 1965), p. 2.

2 Clifford Geertz, *The Interpretation of Cultures* (New York: Basic Books, 1973), p. 10.

3 Charles Taylor, "Interpretation and the Sciences of Man," *The Review of Metaphysics*, 25 (1971).

4 Odo Marquard, *Abschied vom Prinzipiellen* (Stuttgart: Reklam, 1981), p. 117.

5 Ibid., p. 127.

6 Ibid., p. 130.

7 Donald Davidson, "Radical Interpretation," in *Truth and Interpretation* (Oxford: Oxford University Press, 1984), p. 125.

8 Ludwig Wittgenstein, *Philosophische Grammatik* (Oxford: Basil Blackwell, 1969), p. 47.

9 See Hans-Georg Gadamer "Hermeneutik" in *Historisches Worterbuch der Philosophie*, vol. III, ed. J. Ritter (Stuttgart, Basel, 1974), pp. 1061–1073.

10 Quoted by F. Buffière, *Les mythes d'Homère et la pensée greque* (Paris, Les Belles-Lettres, 1956), p. 21.

11 Quoted by J. Pepin, *Les deux approches du christianisme*, (Paris: Minuit, 1961), p. 47.

BIBLIOGRAPHY

GADAMER AND HERMENEUTICS

Hélène Volat-Shapiro

TEXTS BY HANS-GEORG GADAMER
(available in English listed according to dates of original German publication)

Editor's Note: original German titles are included for corresponding books only. All of Gadamer's published writings are to be collected together in the *Gesammelte Werke*, published by J. C. B. Mohr (Paul Siebeck) in Tübingen. Ten volumes of the *Gesammelte Werke* have been projected. The first six (1. *Hermeneutik I (Wahrheit und Methode)*; 2. *Hermeneutik II*; 3. *Neuere Philosophie I*; 4. *Neuere Philosophie II*; 5. *Griechische Philosophie I*; 6. *Griechische Philosophie II*) have already appeared. The seventh *Griechische Philosophie III* is scheduled for publication in 1990. Volumes 8 and 9 are to be entitled *Ästhetik und Poetik* and the tenth volume *Nachträge und Verzeichnisse*.

1934
"Plato and the Poets." In *Dialogue and Dialectic: Eight Hermeneutical Studies on Plato*. Trans. P. Christopher Smith. New Haven: Yale University Press, 1980, pp. 39–92.

1942
"Plato's Educational State." In *Dialogue and Dialectic*, pp. 73–92.

1954
"The Festive Character of Theater." In *The Relevance of the Beautiful and Other Essays*. Trans. Nicholas Walker. Ed. with an introduction by Robert Bernasconi. Cambridge: Cambridge University Press, 1986, pp. 57–65.

1960

Truth and Method. Trans. and ed. Garrett Barden and John Cumming. New York: Continuum, 1975 and 1979.
Wahrheit und Methode: Grundzüge einer philosophischen Hermeneutik. Tübingen: Mohr, 1960.
"Heidegger's Later Philosophy." In *Philosophical Hermeneutics*, Trans. and ed. David E. Linge. Berkeley: University of California Press, 1976. pp. 213–28.
"The Nature of Things and the Language of Things." In *Philosophical Hermeneutics*, pp. 69–81.

1961

"Composition and Interpretation." In *The Relevance of the Beautiful*, pp. 66–73.

1962

"Dialectic and Sophism in Plato's Seventh Letter." In *Dialogue and Dialectic*, pp. 92–123.
"The Philosophical Foundations of the Twentieth Century." In *Philosophical Hermeneutics*, pp. 107–29.
"On the Problem of Self-Understanding." In *Philosophical Hermeneutics*, pp. 44–58.

1963

"The Phenomenological Movement." In *Philosophical Hermeneutics*, pp. 130–81.

1964

"Aesthetics and Hermeneutics." In *Philosophical Hermeneutics*, pp. 95–104.
"Image and Gesture." In *The Relevance of the Beautiful*, pp. 74–82.
"Martin Heidegger and Marburg Theology." In *Philosophical Hermeneutics*, pp. 198–212.

1965

"The Speechless Image." In *The Relevance of the Beautiful*, pp. 83–91.

1966

"Art and Imitation." In *The Relevance of the Beautiful*, pp. 92–104.
"Heidegger and the Language of Metaphysics." In *Philosophical Hermeneutics*, pp. 229–40.
"Man and Language." In *Philosophical Hermeneutics*, pp. 59–68.
"Notes on Planning for the Future." *Daedalus* (Spring 1966), pp. 572–89.
"The Universality of the Hermeneutical Problem." In *Philosophical Hermeneutics*, pp. 3–17.
"On the Scope and Function of Hermeneutical Reflection." In *Philosophical Hermeneutics*, pp. 18–43.

1968

"Amicus Plato Magis Amica Veritas." In *Dialogue and Dialectic*, pp. 194–218.
"Plato's Unwritten Dialectic." In *Dialogue and Dialectic*, pp. 124–55.

1969

Truth and Historicity/ Verité et historicité. Ed. Hans-Georg Gadamer. The Hague: Nijhoff, 1972. Entretiens in Heidelberg (September 12–16, 1969). Text in English, French and German.
"The Science of the Life-World." In *Philosophical Hermeneutics*, pp. 182–97.

1970

"The Power of Reason." *Man and World*, 3 (Fall 1970), pp. 5–15.
"Concerning Empty and Ful-Filled Time." *Southern Journal of Philosophy*, 8 (Winter 1970), pp. 341–53.

1971

Hegel's Dialectic: Five Hermeneutical Studies. Trans. P. Christopher Smith. New Haven: Yale University Press, 1982.
Hegels Dialektik: fünf hermeneutische Studien. Tübingen: J.C.B. Mohr, 1971.
"On the Contribution of Poetry to the Search for Truth." In *The Relevance of the Beautiful*, pp. 105–15.

1972

"The Continuity of History and the Existential Moment." *Philosophy Today*, 16 (Fall 1972), pp. 230–40.
"Logos and Ergon in Plato's *Lysis*." In *Dialogue and Dialectic*, pp. 1–20.
"Poetry and Mimesis." In *The Relevance of the Beautiful*, pp. 116–22.
"Semantics and Hermeneutics." In *Philosophical Hermeneutics*, pp. 82–94.

1973

"On Man's Natural Inclination Toward Philosophy." *Universitas*, vol. 15, no. 1 (1973), pp. 31–40.
"The Play of Art." In *The Relevance of the Beautiful*, pp. 123–30.
"The Proofs of Immortality in Plato's *Phaedo*." In *Dialogue and Dialectic*, pp. 21–38.

1974

"Idea and Reality in Plato's *Timaeus*." In *Dialogue and Dialectic*, pp. 156–93.

1975

"Hermeneutics and Social Science." In *Cultural Hermeneutics*, 2 (Fall 1975), pp. 307–16.
"The Inverted World." In *The Review of Metaphysics*, 28 (March 1975), pp. 401–22.
"The Problem of Historical Consciousness." *Graduate Philosophy Journal*, 5 (Fall 1975), pp. 8–52.
"Responses to *Theory and Practice*." *Cultural Hermeneutics*, 2 (Fall 1975), p. 357.
"Summation" (Symposium on "Hermeneutics and Social Science"). *Cultural Hermeneutics*, 2 (Fall 1975), pp. 329–30.

1976

Philosophical Hermeneutics. Trans. and ed. David E. Linge. Berkeley: University of California Press, 1976.
Reason in the Age of Science. Trans. Frederick G. Lawrence. Cambridge: MIT Press, 1981. *Vernunft im Zeitalter der Wissenschaft*. Frankfurt: Suhrkamp, 1976.

1977

Philosophical Apprenticeship. Trans. Robert R. Sullivan. Cambridge: MIT Press, 1985. (Studies in Contemporary German Thought).
Philosophische Lehrjahre. Frankfurt: Klosterman, 1977.
"Philosophy and Poetry." In *The Relevance of the Beautiful,* pp. 131–39.
"The Relevance of the Beautiful." In *The Relevance of the Beautiful,* pp. 3–53.
Die Aktualität des Schönen. Stuttgart: Reclam, 1977.
"Theory, Technology, Practice: The Task of the Science of Man." Trans. H. Brotz. *Social Research,* vol. 44, no. 3 (Autumn 1977), pp. 529–61.
"The Western View of the Inner Experience of Time and the Limits of Thought." In *Time and the Philosophers,* Paris: UNESCO, 1977. pp. 33–48.

1978

"Aesthetic and Religious Experience." *Nederlands Theologisch Tijdschrift,* vol. 32 (1978), pp. 218–30.
"Correspondence Concerning *Wahrheit und Methode*" (Correspondence between Leo Strauss and Hans-Georg Gadamer). *The Independent Journal of Philosophy,* 2 (1978), pp. 5–12.
"Plato and Heidegger." In *The Question of Being.* Ed. Mervyn Sprung. University Park: Penn State University Press, 1978. pp. 45–54.

1979

"Historical Transformations of Reason." In *Rationality Today,* Ed. Theodore F. Geraets. Ottawa: University of Ottawa Press, 1979. pp. 3–14.
"Heidegger's Paths." *Philosophic Exchange,* 2 (Summer 1979), pp. 80–91.
"The Heritage of Hegel." In *Reason in the Age of Science,* pp. 38–68.
Das Erbe Hegels: Zwei Reden aus Anlass des Hegel-Preises. Frankfurt: Suhrkamp, 1979.

1980

Dialogue and Dialectic: Eight Hermeneutical Studies on Plato. Trans. P. Christopher Smith. New Haven: Yale University Press, 1980.
"The Eminent Text and its Truth." Trans. Geoffrey Waite. *Bulletin of the Midwest Modern Language Association,* vol. 13 (1980), pp. 3–10.
"Intuition and Vividness." Trans. Dan Tate. In *The Relevance of the Beautiful,* pp. 155–70.
"Religious and Poetical Speaking." In *Myth, Symbol, and Reality,* Ed.

Alan Olson. Notre Dame: University of Notre Dame Press, 1980. pp. 86–98.

1981

"A Classic Text—A Hermeneutic Challenge." Trans. Frederick G. Lawrence. *Revue de l'Université d'Ottawa*, 1981, pp. 637–42.
"The Religious Dimension in Heidegger." In *Transcendence and the Sacred*, Ed. Alan Olsson. Notre Dame: University of Notre Dame Press, 1981. pp. 193–207.
"Heidegger and the History of Philosophy." *The Monist*, 64 (October 1981), pp. 434–44.
"Science and the Public." Trans. M. Clarkson. *Universitas*, vol. 23, no. 3 (1981), pp. 161–68.

1982

Hegel's Dialectic: Five Hermeneutical Studies. Trans. with an Introduction by P. Christopher Smith. New Haven: Yale University Press, 1982.
Lectures on Philosophical Hermeneutics. Pretoria: Universiteit van Pretoria, 1982.
"Being, Spirit, God." Trans. S. Davis. In *Heidegger Memorial Lectures*, Ed. Werner Marx. Pittsburgh: Duquesne University Press, 1982. pp. 55–74.
"The Conflict of Interpretations" by Paul Ricoeur and Hans-Georg Gadamer. In *Phenomenology: Dialogues and Bridges*. Ed. Ronald Bruzina and Bruce Wilshire. Albany: SUNY Press, 1982. *Selected Studies in Phenomenology and Existential Philosophy* 8, pp. 299–320.
"Culture and Words—from the Point of View of Philosophy." *Universitas*, vol. 24 (1982), pp. 179–88.
"On the Problematic Character of Aesthetic Consciousness." *Graduate Faculty Philosophy Journal*, 9 (Winter 1982), pp. 31–40.

1983

"The Drama of Zarathustra." Trans. Z. Adamczewski. In *The Great Year of Zarathustra (1981–1981)*, Ed. D. Goicoechea. Lanham, Pa.: University Press of America, 1983. pp. 339–69. Also in *Nietzsche's New Seas: Explorations in Philosophy, Aesthetics, and Politics*, Ed. Michael Allen Gillespie and Tracy B. Strong. Chicago: University of Chicago Press, 1988. pp. 220–31.
"History of Science and Practical Philosophy." In *Contemporary German*

Philosophy, vol. 3, University Park: Penn state University Press, 1983. pp. 307–13.

1984

"Articulating Transcendence." In *The Beginning and the Beyond: Papers from the Gadamer and Voegelin Conferences: Supplementary Issue of Lonergan Workshop*, vol. 4, Ed. Frederick G. Lawrence. Chicago: Scholars Press, 1984. pp. 1–12.

"Gadamer on Strauss: An Interview." *Interpretation*, vol. 12, no. 1 (1984), pp. 1–13.

"The Hermeneutics of Suspicion." *Man and World*, 17 (1984), pp. 313–24. Also in *Hermeneutics: Questions and Prospects*, Eds. Gary Shapiro and Alan Sica. Amherst: University of Massachusetts Press, 1984. pp. 54–65.

"Text and Interpretation." Trans. Dennis J. Schmidt and Richard Palmer. In *Dialogue and Deconstruction: The Gadamer-Derrida Encounter*, Eds. Diane P. Michelfelder and Richard E. Palmer. Albany: SUNY Press, 1989. pp. 21–51.

"Reply to Jacques Derrida." Trans. Diane Michelfelder and Richard Palmer. In *Dialogue and Deconstruction*, pp. 55–57.

1985

"Letter to Dallmayr." Trans. Richard Palmer and Diane Michelfelder. In *Dialogue and Deconstruction*, pp. 93–101.

"*Destruktion* and Deconstruction." Trans. Geoff Waite and Richard Palmer. In *Dialogue and Deconstruction*, pp. 102–13.

"Religion and Religiosity in Socrates." *Proceedings of the Boston Area Colloquium in Ancient Philosophy*, 1 (1985), pp. 53–76.

"Natural Science and Hermeneutics: The Concept of Nature in Ancient Philosophy." *Proceedings of the Boston Area Colloquium in Ancient Philosophy*, 1 (1985), pp. 39–52.

"A New Epoch in the History of the World Begins Here and Now." In *The Philosophy of Immanual Kant*, Ed. Richard Kennington. Washington, D.C.: Catholic University of America Press, 1985. pp. 1–14.

"Philosophy and Literature." Trans. Anthony Steinbock. *Man and World*, 18 (1985), pp 241–59.

1986

The Relevance of the Beautiful and Other Essays. Trans. Nicholas Walker. Ed. Robert Bernasconi. Cambridge: Cambridge University Press, 1986.

"The History of Concepts and the Language of Philosophy." *International Studies in Philosophy*, 18 (Fall 1986), pp. 1–16.

The Idea of the Good in Platonic Aristotelian Philosophy. Trans. with an introduction and annotations by Christopher Smith. New Haven: Yale University Press, 1986. *Idee des Gutes zwischen Plato und Aristoteles*. Heidelberg: Winter, 1978.

1987

"Hermeneutics and Logocentrism." Trans. Richard Palmer and Diane Michelfelder. In *Dialogue and Deconstruction*, pp. 114–25.

"The Relevance of Greek Philosophy for Modern Thought." *South African Journal of Philosophy*, 6 (May 1987), pp. 39–42.

1988

"On the Circle of Understanding." In *Hermeneutics versus Science?: Essays by H.-G. Gadamer, E. K. Specht, W. Stegmuller*, Trans. and ed. John M. Connolly and Thomas Keutner. Notre Dame: University of Notre Dame Press, 1988. pp. 68–78.

"Mythopoetic Inversion in Rilke's *Duino Elegies*." In *Hermeneutics versus Science?* pp. 79–101.

1989

"Back from Syracuse?" *Critical Inquiry*, vol. 15, no. 2 (Winter 1989), pp. 427–31.

Selected Bibliography of Publications in English on Gadamer and Hermeneutics

Books

Adorno, Theodor and Horkheimer, Max. *The Dialectic of Enlightenment*. Trans. John Cumming. New York: Seabury, 1972.

Apel, Karl-Otto. *Towards a Transformation of Philosophy*. Trans. G. Adey and D. Frisby. London: Routledge and Kegan Paul, 1980.

Barthes, Roland. *Image-Music-Text*. Trans. Stephen Heath. New York: Hill and Wang, 1977.

———. *The Pleasure of the Text*. Trans. Richard Miller. New York: Hill and Wang, 1975.

Benhabib, Seyla. *Critique, Norm, and Utopia: A Study of the Foundations of Critical Theory*. New York: Columbia University Press, 1986.

Bernstein, Richard J. *Philosophical Profiles*. Philadelphia: University of Pennsylvania Press, 1986.

———. *Beyond Objectivism and Relativism: Science, Hermeneutics, and Praxis*. Philadelphia: University of Pennsylvania Press, 1983.

Bleicher, Josef. *Contemporary Hermeneutics: Hermeneutics as Method, Philosophy and Critique*. London: Routledge and Kegan Paul, 1980.

Caputo, John D. *Radical Hermeneutics*. Bloomington: Indiana University Press, 1987.

Derrida, Jacques. *The Archeology of the Frivolous: Reading Condillac*. Trans. J. P. Leavey Jr. Pittsburgh: Duquesne University Press, 1980.

———. *Dissemination*. Trans. B. Johnson. Chicago: The University of Chicago Press, 1981.

———. *Of Grammatology*. Trans. Gayatri Spivak. Baltimore: The Johns Hopkins University Press, 1974.

———. *Margins of Philosophy*. Trans. Alan Bass. Chicago: University of Chicago Press, 1982.

———. *Positions*. Trans. Alan Bass. Chicago: The University of Chicago Press, 1981.

———. *The Post Card: From Socrates to Freud and Beyond*. Trans. Alan Bass. Chicago: University of Chicago Press, 1987.

———. *Speech and Phenomena*. Trans. David Allison. Evanston: Northwestern University Press, 1973.

———. *Spurs/Eperons*. Trans. Barbara Harlow. Chicago: University of Chicago Press, 1979.

———. *Writing and Difference*. Trans. Alan Bass. Chicago: The University of Chicago Press, 1978.

Duhem, Pierre. *Aim and Structure of Physical Theory*. Princeton: Princeton University Press, 1954.

Eagleton, Terry. *Literary Theory: An Introduction*. Oxford: Basil Blackwell, 1983.

Echeverria, E. J. *Criticism and Commitment: Major Themes in Contemporary Post-Critical Philosophy*. Atlantic Highlands: Humanities Press, 1981.

Elshtain, Jean Bethke. *Public Man, Private Woman: Woman in Social and Political Thought*. Princeton: Princeton University Press, 1984.

Freud, Sigmund. *The Interpretation of Dreams*. Trans. and ed. James Strachey. New York: Avon, 1965.

Geertz, Clifford. *The Interpretation of Cultures*. New York: Basic Books, 1973.

Gilligan, Carol. *In a Different Voice: Psychological Theory and Women's Development*. Cambridge: Harvard University Press, 1982.

Habermas, Jürgen. *Communication and the Evolution of Society*. Trans. T. McCarthy. Boston: Beacon Press, 1979.

———. *Knowledge and Human Interests*. Trans. J. J. Shapiro. Boston: Beacon Press, 1971.

———. *Legitimation Crisis*. Boston: Beacon Press, 1984.

———. *The Philosophical Discourse of Modernity*. Trans. F. Lawrence. New York: Political Press, 1988.

———. *Technology and Science as Ideology*. Boston: Beacon Press, 1970.

———. *Theory of Communicative Action*. Boston: Beacon Press, 1984.

Heelan, Patrick. *Space-Perception and the Philosophy of Science*. Berkeley: University of California Press, 1983.

Hesse, Mary. *Revolutions and Reconstructions in the Philosophy of Science*. Bloomington: Indiana University Press, 1980.

Heidegger, Martin. *Being and Time*. Trans. John Macquarrie and Edward Robinson. New York: Harper and Row, 1962.

———. *Poetry, Language, Thought*. Trans. Albert Hofstadter. New York: Harper and Row, 1971.

———. *The Question Concerning Technology and Other Essays*. Trans. W. Lovitt. New York: Harper Colophon, 1977.

Hekman, Susan. *Hermeneutics and the Sociology of Knowledge*. Notre Dame: University of Notre Dame Press, 1986.

Hollinger, Robert, ed. *Hermeneutics and Praxis*. Notre Dame: University of Notre Dame Press, 1985.

Howard, Roy T. *Thee Faces of Hermeneutics: An Introduction to Current Theories of Understanding*. Berkeley: University of California Press, 1982.

Hoy, David Couzens. *The Critical Circle: Literature and History in Contemporary Hermeneutics*. Berkeley: University of California Press, 1978.

Husserl, Edmund. *The Crisis of European Sciences and Transcendental Phenomenology*. Trans. David Carr. Evanston: Northwestern University Press, 1970.

Johnson, Patricia Alterbernd. *A Hermeneutical Analysis of Human Speaking: An Examination and Extension of the Work on Language of Martin Heidegger, Paul Ricoeur, and Hans-Georg Gadamer*. Ph.D Thesis. University of Toronto, 1979.

Kockelmans, Joseph. *Heidegger and Science*. Pittsburgh: CARP and University Presses of America, 1985.

Llewelyn, John. *Beyond Metaphysics: The Hermeneutic Circle in Contemporary Continental Philosophy*. Atlantic Highlands, N.J.: Humanities Press, 1985.

Lloyd, Genevieve. *The Man of Reason: "Male" and "Female" in Western Philosophy*. Minneapolis: University of Minnesota Press, 1984.

Merleau-Ponty, Maurice. *The Phenomenology of Perception*. Trans. Colin Smith. London: Routledge and Kegan Paul, 1962.

———. *The Primacy of Perception*. Ed. James M. Edie. Evanston: Northwestern University Press, 1964.

———. *The Visible and the Invisible*. Trans. Alphonso Lingis. Evanston: Northwestern University Press, 1968.

Marcuse, Herbert. *One Dimensional Man*. Boston: Beacon Press, 1964.

Marx, Werner. *Heidegger and the Tradition*. Evanson: Northwestern University Press, 1971.

Michelfelder, Diane P. and Palmer, Richard E., *Dialogue and Deconstruction: The Gadamer-Derrida Debate*. Albany: SUNY Press, 1989.

Mueller-Vollmer, Kurt, ed. *The Hermeneutics Reader: Texts of the German Tradition from the Enlightenment to the Present*. New York: Continuum, 1985.

Nagy, Gregory. *The Best of the Acheans*. Baltimore: Johns Hopkins University Press, 1979.

Nicholson, Graeme. *Seeing and Reading*. Atlantic Highlands, N.J.: Humanities Press, 1984.

Okin, Susan Moller. *Women in Western Political Thought*. Princeton: Princeton University Press, 1979.

Palmer, Richard E. *Hermeneutics: Interpretation Theory in Schleiermacher, Dilthey, Heidegger, and Gadamer*. Evanston: Northwestern University Press, 1969.

Pilotta, Joseph J., ed., *Interpersonal Communication: Essays in Phenomenology and Hermeneutics*. Lanham: University Press of America, 1982.

Richardson, J. *Existential Epistemology: A Heideggerian Critique of the Cartesian Project*. Oxford: Clarendon Press, 1986.

Ricoeur, Paul. *Fallible Man*. Trans. Charles Kelby. Chicago: Henry Regnery, 1965.

———. *Freud and Philosophy: An Essay on Interpretation*. Trans. Denis Savage. New Haven: Yale University Press, 1970.

———. *Hermeneutics and the Human Sciences*. Trans. and ed. John B. Thompson. Cambridge: Cambridge University Press, 1981.

———. *Interpretation Theory: Discourse and the Surplus of Meaning*. Fort Worth: Texas Christian University Press, 1976.

———. *The Philosophy of Paul Ricoeur*. Eds. Charles Reagan and David Stewart. Boston: Beacon Press, 1978.

———. *The Rule of Metaphor*. Trans. Robert Czerny et al. Toronto: University of Toronto Press, 1977.

———. *The Symbolism of Evil*. Boston: Beacon Press, 1957.

———. *Time and Narrative*. Trans. Kathleen Mclaughlin and David Pellauer. Chicago: University of Chicago Press, 1984.

Rorty, Richard. *Consequences of Pragmatism*. Minneapolis: University of Minnesota Press, 1982.

Saussure, Ferdinand de. *Course in General Linguistics*. Trans. W. Baskin. New York: Philosophical Library, 1959.

Schmidt, Lawrence K. *The Epistemology of Hans-Georg Gadamer*. New York: Peter Lang, 1985.

Shapiro, Gary and Sica, Alan, eds. *Hermeneutics: Questions and Prospects*. Amherst: University of Massachusetts Press, 1984.

Silverman, Hugh J. *Inscriptions: Between Phenomenology and Structuralism.* New York: Routledge, 1987.

Silverman, Hugh J. and Ihde, Don, eds. *Hermeneutics and Deconstruction.* Albany: SUNY Press, 1985.

Singer, Milton. *Man's Glassy Essence: Explorations in Semiotic Anthropology.* Bloomington: Indiana University Press, 1984.

Thompson, John B. *Critical Hermeneutics: A Study in the Thought of Paul Ricoeur and Jurgen Habermas.* Cambridge: Cambridge University Press, 1979.

Toulmin, Stephen. *Human Understanding.* Oxford: Clarendon Press, 1972.

————. *Philosophy of Science.* New York: Harper, 1960.

Wachterhauser, Brice R. *Hermeneutics and Modern Philosophy.* Albany: SUNY Press, 1986.

Warnke, Georgia. *Gadamer: Hermeneutics, Tradition and Reason.* Stanford: Stanford University Press, 1987.

Wittgenstein, Ludwig. *Philosophical Investigations.* Trans. G. E. M. Anscombe. New York: Macmillan, 1953.

Weinsheimer, Joel. *Gadamer's Hermeneutics.* New Haven: Yale University Press, 1985.

Wigner, Eugene. *Reflections and Symmetries.* Bloomington: Indiana University Press, 1967.

Wolff, Janet. *Hermeneutics Philosophy and the Sociology of Art.* London: Routledge and Kegan Paul, 1975.

Articles

Ambrosio, Francis J. "Dawn and Dusk: Gadamer and Heidegger on Truth." *Man and World,* 19 (1986).

————. "Gadamer and the Ontology of Language: What remains unsaid." *The Journal of the British Society for Phenomenology,* 17 (May 1986), pp. 124–42.

————. "Gadamer: On Making Oneself at Home with Hegel." *Owl of Minerva,* 19 (Fall 1987), pp. 23–40.

————. "Gadamer, Plato and the Discipline of Dialogue." *International Philosophical Quarterly,* 27 (March 1987), pp. 17–32.

Bernasconi, Robert. "Bridging the Abyss: Heidegger and Gadamer." *Research in Phenomenology,* 16 (1986), pp. 1–24.

Bernstein, Richard. "From Hermeneutics to Praxis." *Review of Metaphysics,* 35 (June 1982), pp. 823–46.

————. "Heidegger on Humanism." *Praxis International,* 5 (July 1985), pp. 95–114.

Bertoldi, E. F. "Gadamer's Criticisms of Collingwood." *Idealistic Studies,* 14 (Spring 1984), pp. 213–28.

Black, Max. "Metaphor. "In *Philosophy Looks at the Arts: Contemporary Readings in Aesthetics.* Ed. Joseph Margolis. New York: Scribner's Press, 1962.

Bontekoe, Ron. "A Fusion of Horizons: Gadamer and Scleiermacher." *International Philosophical Quarterly,* 27 (March 1987), pp. 3–16.

Cockhorn, Klaus. "Hans-Georg Gadamer's *Truth and Method." Philosophy and Rhetoric,* 13 (Summer 1980), pp. 160–80.

Connolly, John M. "Gadamer and the Author's Authority: A Language-Game Approach." *The Journal of Aesthetics and Art Criticism,* 44 (Spring 1986), pp. 271–78.

Cook, Deborah. "Reflections on Gadamer's Notion of 'Sprachlichkeit.' " *Philosophy and Literature,* 10 (April 1986), pp. 84–92.

Davidson, Donald. "Radical Interpretation." In *Truth and Interpretation.* Oxford: Oxford University Press, 1984.

Derrida, Jacques. "White Mythology: Metaphor in the Text of Philosophy." *New Literary History,* no. 6 (1974), pp. 5–74.

Detsch, Richard. 'A Non-Subjectivist Concept of Play—Gadamer and Heidegger versus Rilke and Nietzsche,' *Philosophy Today,* 29, Summer 1985, pp. 156–172.

Dostal, Robert J. "The World Never Lost: The Hermeneutics of Trust." *Philosophy and Phenomenological Research,* 47 (March 1987), pp. 413–434.

Dunne, Joseph. "Aristotle After Gadamer: An Analysis of the Distinction Between the Concepts of Phronesis and Techne." *Irish Philosophical Journal,* 2 (Autumn 1985), pp. 105–23.

Garrett, Jan Edward. "Hans-Georg Gadamer on 'Fusion of Horizons.' " *Man and World,* 20 (1987), pp. 205–19.

Gilmour, John C. "Dewey and Gadamer on the Ontology of Art." *Man and World,* 20 (1987), pp. 205–19.

Giurlanda, Paul. "Habermas' Critique of Gadamer: Does it Stand Up?" *International Philosophical Quarterly,* 27 (March 1987), pp. 33–41.

Griswold, Charles. "Gadamer and the Interpretation of Plato." *Ancient Philosophy,* 1 (Spring 1981), pp. 171–78.

Habermas, Jurgen. "A Review of Gadamer's *Truth and Method."* In *Understanding and Social Inquiry.* Eds. Fred R. Dallmayr and Thomas A. McCarthy. Notre Dame: University of Notre Dame Press, 1977.

Habermas, J., and Gadamer, Hans-Georg. "The Habermas-Gadamer Debate." *New German Critique,* 18 (1979), pp. 44–75.

Hans, James S. "Hans-Georg Gadamer and Hermeneutic Phenomenology." *Philosophy Today,* 22 (Spring 1978), pp. 3–19.

Hekman, Susan. "Action as a Text: Gadamer's Hermeneutics and the Social Scientific Analysis of Action." *The Journal for the Theory of Social Behaviour,* 14 (October 1984), pp. 333–54.

Heelan, Patrick. "Experiment and Theory: Constitution and Reality." *The Journal of Philosophy,* vol. 85 (1988).

———. "A Heideggerian Mediation on Science and Art." In Joseph Kockelmans, ed. *Hermeneutic Phenomenology*. Pittsburgh: University Press and CARP, 1988.

———. "Natural Science as a Hermeneutic of Instrumentation." *The Philosophy of Science*, vol. 50 (1983).

———. "Perception as a Hermeneutical Act." *Review of Metaphysics*, vol. 37 (1983).

Hinman, Lawrence M. "Gadamer's Understanding of Hermeneutics." *Philosophy and Phenomenological Research*, 40 (June 1980), pp. 512–35.

Hirsch, E. D. Jr. "Truth and Method in Interpretation." *Review of Metaphysics*, 18 (1985), pp. 489–507.

Hjort, Anne Meete. "The Conditions of Dialogue: Approaches to the Habermas-Gadamer Debate." *Eidos*, 4 (June 1980), pp. 512–35.

Hogan, John. "Gadamer and the Hermeneutical Experience." *Philosophy Today*, 20 (Spring 1976), pp. 3–12.

Hollinger, Robert. "Practical Reason and Hermeneutics." *Philosophy and Rhetoric*, 18 (1985), pp. 481–500.

How, Alan. "Dialogue as Productive Limitation in Social Theory: The Habermas-Gadamer Debate." *Journal of the British Society for Phenomenology*, 11 (1980), pp. 131–43.

———. "A Case of Misreading: Habermas's Evolution of Gadamer's Hermeneutics." *The Journal of the British Society for Phenomenology*, 16 (May 1985), pp. 131–43.

Howard, Dick. "Enlightenment as Political." In *Critical and Dialectical Phenomenology*, pp. 76–87. Eds. Donn Welton and Hugh J. Silverman. Albany: SUNY Press, 1987.

Ihde, Don. "Interpreting Hermeneutics." *Man and World*, 13 (1980), pp. 325–44.

Kelly, Michael. "On Hermeneutics and Science: Why Hermeneutics is not Anti-Science." *Southern Journal of Philosophy*, 25 (Winter 1987), pp. 481–500.

Kirkland, Frank M. "Gadamer and Ricoeur: The Paradigm of the Text." *Graduate Faculty Philosophy Journal*, 6 (Winter 1977), pp. 358–85.

Kisiel, Theodore. "The Happening of Tradition: The Hermeneutics of Gadamer and Heidegger." *Man and World*, 2 (August 1969), pp. 358–85.

———. "On the Dimensions of a Phenomenology of Science in Husserl and the Young Doctor Heidegger." *Journal of the British Society for Phenomenology*, no. 4 (1973), pp. 217–34.

Knapke, Margaret Lee. "The Hermeneutical Focus of Heidegger and Gadamer: The Nullity of Understanding." *Kinesis*, 12 (Fall 1982), pp. 3–18.

Kockelmans, Joseph. "On the Hermeneutic Dimensions of Natural Science." *Etudes Phenomenologiques*, no. 3 (1986).

————. "On Myth and Its Relationship of Hermeneutics." *Cultural Hermeneutics*, 1 (1973), pp. 47–86.

Lawrence, Fred. "Gadamer and Lonergan: A Dialectical Comparison." *International Philosophical Quarterly*, 20 (1980), pp. 25–47.

Linge, David E. "Dilthey and Gadamer: Two Theories of Historical Understanding." *Journal of the American Academy of Religion*, 41 (1973), pp. 536–53.

MacKenzie, Ian. "Gadamer's Hermeneutics and the Uses of Forgery." *The Journal of Aesthetics and Art Criticism*, 45 (Fall 1986), pp. 41–48.

MacKinnon, Catherine. "Feminism, Marxism, Method, and the State." In *The Signs Reader: Women, Gender, and Scholarship*. Eds. Elizabeth Abel and Emily Abel. Chicago: University of Chicago Press, 1983.

Maddox, Randy L. "Contemporary Hermeneutic Philosophy and Theological Studies." *Religious Studies*, 21 (December 1985), pp. 517–29.

————. "Hermeneutic Circle-Viscious or Victorious?" *Philosophy Today*, 27 (Spring 1983), pp. 66–76.

Makkreel, Rudolf A. "Tradition and Orientation in Hermeneutics." *Research in Phenomenology*, 16 (1986), pp. 73–85.

Martin, Biddy and Mohanty, Chandra Talpade. "Feminist Politics: What's Home Got to Do with It?" In *Feminist Studies; Critical Studies*. Ed. Teresa de Laureitis. Bloomington: Indiana University Press, 1986.

Martland, T. R. "Quine's Half-Entities and Gadamer's Too." *Man and World*, 19 (1986), pp. 361–73. Also in *Literature as Philosophy/Philosophy as Literature*. Ed. Donald G. Marshall. Iowa City: University of Iowa Press, 1987.

Mendelson, Jack. "The Habermas Gadamer Debate." *New German Critique*, 18 (1979), pp. 44–73.

Misgeld, Dieter. "Critical Theory and Hermeneutics: The Debate Between Habermas and Gadamer." In *On Critical Theory*. Ed. John O'Neill. New York: Seabury Press, 1976.

————. "Discourse and Conversation: The Theory of Communicative Competence and Hermeneutics in the Light of the Debate Between Habermas and Gadamer." *Cultural Hermeneutics*, 4 (December 1977), pp. 321–44.

————. "On Gadamer's Hermeneutics." *Philosophy of the Social Sciences*. 9 (June 1979), pp. 221–39.

O'Collins, Gerald. "Hans-Georg Gadamer and Hans Kung: A Reflection." *Gregorianum*, 58 (1977), pp. 561–66.

Palmer, Richard. "The Scope of Hermeneutics and the Problem of Critique and the Crisis of Modernity." *Texte*, vol. 3 (1984), pp. 223–39.

Paslick, Robert H. "The Ontological Context of Gadamer's Fusion: Boehme, Heidegger, and Non-Duality." *Man and World*, 18 (1985), pp. 405–22.

Pavlovic, K. R. "Science and Autonomy." *Man and World*, no. 14 (1981), pp. 127–40.

Ricoeur, Paul. "Existence and Hermeneutics." In *The Conflict of Interpretations*. Ed. Don Ihde. Evanston: Northwestern University Press, 1974.

———. "The Function of Fiction." *Man and World*, 12 (1979), pp. 123–41.

———. "The Metaphorical Process as Cognition, Imagination and Feeling." In *Philosophical Perspectives on Metaphor*. Ed. Mark Johnson. Minneapolis: University of Minnesota Press, 1981.

Rodi, Frithjof. "Hermeneutics and the Meaning of Life." In *Hermeneutics and Deconstruction*. pp. 82–90. Ed. Hugh J. Silvermen. Albany: SUNY Press, 1985.

Rothberg, Donald Jay. "Gadamer, Rorty, Hermeneutics, and Truth: A Response to G. Warnke's Hermeneutics and the Social Sciences: A Gadamerian Critique of Rorty." *Inquiry*, 29 (Spring 1986), pp. 355–61.

Schuchman, Paul. "Aristotle's Phronesis and Gadamer's Hermeneutics." *Philosophy Today*, 23 (Spring 1979), pp. 41–50.

Serequeberhan, Tsenay. "Heidegger and Gadamer: Thinking as Meditative and as Effective-Historical Consciousness." *Man and World*, 20 (1987), pp. 41–64.

Shapiro, Gary. "Gadamer, Habermas, and the Death of Art." *British Journal of Aesthetics*, 26 (Winter 1986), pp. 39–47.

Siemek, Marek J. "Marxism and the Hermeneutics Tradition." In *Phenomenology and Marxism*. Ed. Bernhard Waldenfels. London: Routledge and Kegan Paul, 1985.

Silverman, Hugh J. "Phenomenology: From Hermeneutics to Deconstruction." *Research in Phenomenology*, 14 (1984), pp. 19–34.

———. "Hermeneutics and Interrogation." *Research in Phenomenology*, 16 (1986), pp. 87–94.

———. "Hermeneutics and Deconstruction." *Journal of Philosophy* (1986), pp. 14–15.

Simpson, Lorenzo. "Science, Language and Experience: Reflections on the Nature of Self-Understanding." *Man and World*, 16 (1983), pp. 25–42.

Smith, Barry D. "Distanciation and Textual Interpretation." *Laval Theologique et Philosophique*, 43 (June 1987), pp. 205–16.

Smith, Christopher P. "Gadamer on Language and Method, in Hegel's Dialectic." *Graduate Faculty Philosophy Journal*, 5 (Fall 1975), pp. 53–72.

Smith, Gary. "Gadamer's Hermeneutics and Ordinary Language Philosophy." *The Thomist*, 43 (April 1979), pp. 296–321.

Sullivan, Robert. "The Rationality Debate and Gadamer's Hermeneutics: Reflections on *Beyond Objectivism and Relativism*." *Philosophy and Social Criticism*, 11 (Summer 1985), pp. 85–100.

Taylor, Charles. "Interpretation and the Sciences of Man." *The Review of Metaphysics*, 25 (1971), pp. 3–51.

Valdes, Mario. "Paul Ricoeur's Hermeneutics as a Basis for Literary Criticism." *Revue de l'Université d'Ottawa/Ottawa Quarterly*, vol. 55, no. 4 (October–December 1985).

Velkley, Richard. "Gadamer and Kant: The Critique of Modern Aesthetic Consciousness in *Truth and Method*." *Interpretation*, 9 (September 1981), pp. 353–64.

Wallulis, Jerald. "Philosophical Hermeneutics and the Conflict of Ontologies." *International Philosophical Quarterly*, 24 (September 1984), pp. 283–302.

Walsh, Robert D. "When Love of Knowing Becomes Actual Knowing: Heidegger and Gadamer on Hegel's *Die Sache Selbst*." *Owl of Minerva*, 17 (Spring 1986).

Warnke, Georgia. "Hermeneutics and the Social Sciences: A Gadamerian Critique of Rorty." *Inquiry*, 28 (September 1985), pp. 339–58.

Weinsheimer, Joel. "History and the Future of Meaning." *Philosophy and Literature*, 9 (October 1985), pp. 139–51.

Zucker, Francis. "Phenomenological Evidence and the 'Idea' of Physics." In *Phenomenology Dialogues and Bridges*. Eds. Ronald Bruzina and Bruce Wilshire. Albany: SUNY Press, 1982.

NOTES ON CONTRIBUTORS

GARY E. AYLESWORTH

Gary E. Aylesworth is Assistant Professor of Philosophy at Eastern Illinois University. He taught previously at Siena College and the State University of New York at Stony Brook. He is co-editor of *The Textual Sublime: Deconstruction and its Differences* (1990) and is completing a translation of Heidegger's *Fundamental Concepts*.

DEBORAH COOK

Deborah Cook is Assistant Professor at the University of Windsor (Ontario). She taught previously at McMaster University and the University of Victoria in Canada. She has published a number of articles in aesthetics and the philosophy-literature interface, and particularly on Merleau-Ponty, Gadamer, Jauss, and Foucault.

VINCENT DESCOMBES

Vincent Descombes is Woodruff Professor of French at Emory University. He taught previously at the Johns Hopkins University and the University of Paris-I. He has published *Modern French Philosophy* (1980), *Objects of All Sorts: A Philosophical Grammar* (1983), *Proust: philosophie du roman* (1987) and *Philosophie par gros temps* (1989).

R. NICHOLAS DAVEY

R. Nicholas Davey is Senior Lecturer in Philosophy and Aesthetics and Course Director in the South Glamorgan Institute of Higher

Education, Cardiff (Wales). He taught previously at the City University (London) and the University of Manchester. He has published a range of articles on Aesthetics, Hermeneutics, Nietzsche, Baumgarten, Habermas, and Gadamer.

WAYNE J. FROMAN

Wayne J. Froman is Associate Professor of Philosophy at George Mason University. He is author of *Merleau-Ponty: Language and the Act of Speech* as well as articles on Heidegger, Merleau-Ponty, and Derrida.

PATRICK A. HEELAN

Patrick A. Heelan is Professor of Philosophy at the State University of New York at Stony Brook. He studied physics at University College, Dublin, The Dublin Institute for Advanced Studies, St. Louis University, and Princeton University, and he studied philosophy at the Catholic University of Louvain, Belgium. He is author of *Quantum Mechanics and Objectivity: The Physical Philosophy of Werner Heisenberg* (1965), and *Space-Perception and the Philosophy of Science* (1983), and numerous articles on the hermeneutical philosophy of physics.

JOSEPH J. KOCKELMANS

Joseph J. Kockelmans has been Professor of Philosophy at the Penn State University since 1968. Recently he was elected President of the American Philosophical Association, Eastern Division. He taught previously at the University of Pittsburgh, the New School for Social Research, and the Agricultural University at Wageningen, Netherlands. Among his many books, the most recent include *The World in Science and Philosophy* (1969); *On the Truth of Being* (1984); *Heidegger and Science* (1985); *Phenomenological Psychology: The Dutch School* (ed.), (1987).

LEONARD LAWLOR

Leonard Lawlor is Assistant Professor of Philosophy at Memphis State University. He taught previously at the State University of New York at Binghamton. He has published articles in *Philosophy Today*, *Research in Phenomenology*, and *Philosophy and Social Criticism*. His book on the Difference between Thought of Ricoeur and Derrida is planned for publication in 1992 with SUNY Press.

GARY B. MADISON

Gary B. Madison is Professor of Philosophy at McMaster University and in the Graduate Faculty at the University of Toronto. He is the author of *The Phenomenology of Merleau-Ponty* (Ohio, 1979), *Understanding: A Phenomenological-Pragmatic Analysis* (Greenwood, 1982), *The Logic of Liberty* (Greenwood, 1986), and *The Hermeneutics of Modernity: Figures and Themes* (Indiana, 1988). Madison is a founding member and former coordinator of The Canadian Society for Hermeneutics and Postmodern Thought.

DIETER MISGELD

Dieter Misgeld holds a doctorate from the University of Heidelberg, where he studied with Hans-Georg Gadamer. He now teaches at the University of Toronto and has co-edited a volume on *Modern German Sociology* (Columbia University Press) and has published a number of essays in the areas of hermeneutics and critical theory.

GRAEME NICHOLSON

Graeme Nicholson is Professor of Philosophy at Trinity College in the University of Toronto. He has written *Seeing and Reading* (Humanities Press, 1984) and *Illustrations of Being* (Humanities Press, forthcoming).

JAMES RISSER

James Risser is Associate Professor and Chair of the Department of Philosophy at Seattle University. He taught previously at Villanova University and has published articles on Nietzsche, Gadamer and Derrida, and Hermeneutics. He is completing a book on Gadamer's philosophical hermeneutics.

ROBIN SCHOTT

Robin Schott is Assistant Professor of Philosophy at the University of Louisville. She is author of *Cognition and Eros: A Critique of the Kantian Paradigm* (1988) and has contributed essays to various volumes and journals on feminist theory, social philosophy, and Kant.

P. CHRISTOPHER SMITH

P. Christopher Smith has taught at the University of Lowell since 1966, where he is presently Professor of Philosophy. In addition to numerous articles on Plato, Hegel, Rilke, Heidegger, and Gadamer, he has published annotated translations of three books by Gadamer: *Hegel's Dialectic, Dialogue and Dialectic,* and *The Idea of the Good in Platonic-Aristotelian Philosophy.* His book *Hermeneutics and Human Finitude: Towards a Theory of Ethical Understanding* is due to appear shortly.

JOEL WEINSHEIMER

Joel Weinsheimer is Professor of English at the University of Minnesota. He is the author of *Gadamer's Hermeneutics: A Reading of Truth and Method* and has recently completed a new book entitled *Philosophical Hermeneutics and Literary Theory.*

About the Editor
HUGH J. SILVERMAN

Hugh J. Silverman is Professor of Philosophy and Comparative Literature at the State University of New York at Stony Brook. He has held visiting teaching posts at the Universities of Warwick and Leeds (England), at the University of Nice (France), the University of Turin (Italy) and at Stanford University, Duquesne University, and New York University in the United States. He served as Executive Co-Director of the Society for Phenomenology and Existential Philosophy for six years (1980–86) and is currently Executive Director of the International Association for Philosophy and Literature. Author of *Inscriptions: Between Phenomenology and Structuralism* (Routledge, 1987) and more than sixty articles in continental philosophy, philosophical psychology, aesthetics, and literary/cultural theory, he has lectured widely in continental Europe, Britain, and North America. He is also editor of *Piaget, Philosophy and the Human Sciences* (Humanities/Harvester, 1980) and *Writing the Politics of Difference* (SUNY Press, 1991), coeditor of *Jean-Paul Sartre: Contemporary Approaches to his Philosophy* (Duquesne/Harvester, 1980), *Continental Philosophy in America* (Duquesne, 1983), *Descriptions* (SUNY Press, 1985), *Hermeneutics and Deconstruction* (SUNY Press, 1985), *Critical and Dialectical Phenomenology* (SUNY Press, 1987), *The Horizons of Continental Philosophy: Essays of Husserl, Heidegger, and Merleau-Ponty* (Nijhoff/Kluwer, 1988), *Postmodernism and Continental Philosophy* (SUNY Press, 1988), *The Textual Sublime: Deconstruction and its Differences* (SUNY Press, 1990), and *Merleau-Ponty: Texts and Dialogues* (Humanities Press, 1991) as well as the first three volumes of *Continental Philosophy*, namely *Philosophy and Non-Philosophy since Merleau-Ponty* (Routledge, 1988), *Derrida and Deconstruction* (Routledge, 1989), and *Postmodernism—Philosophy and the Arts* (Routledge, 1990).